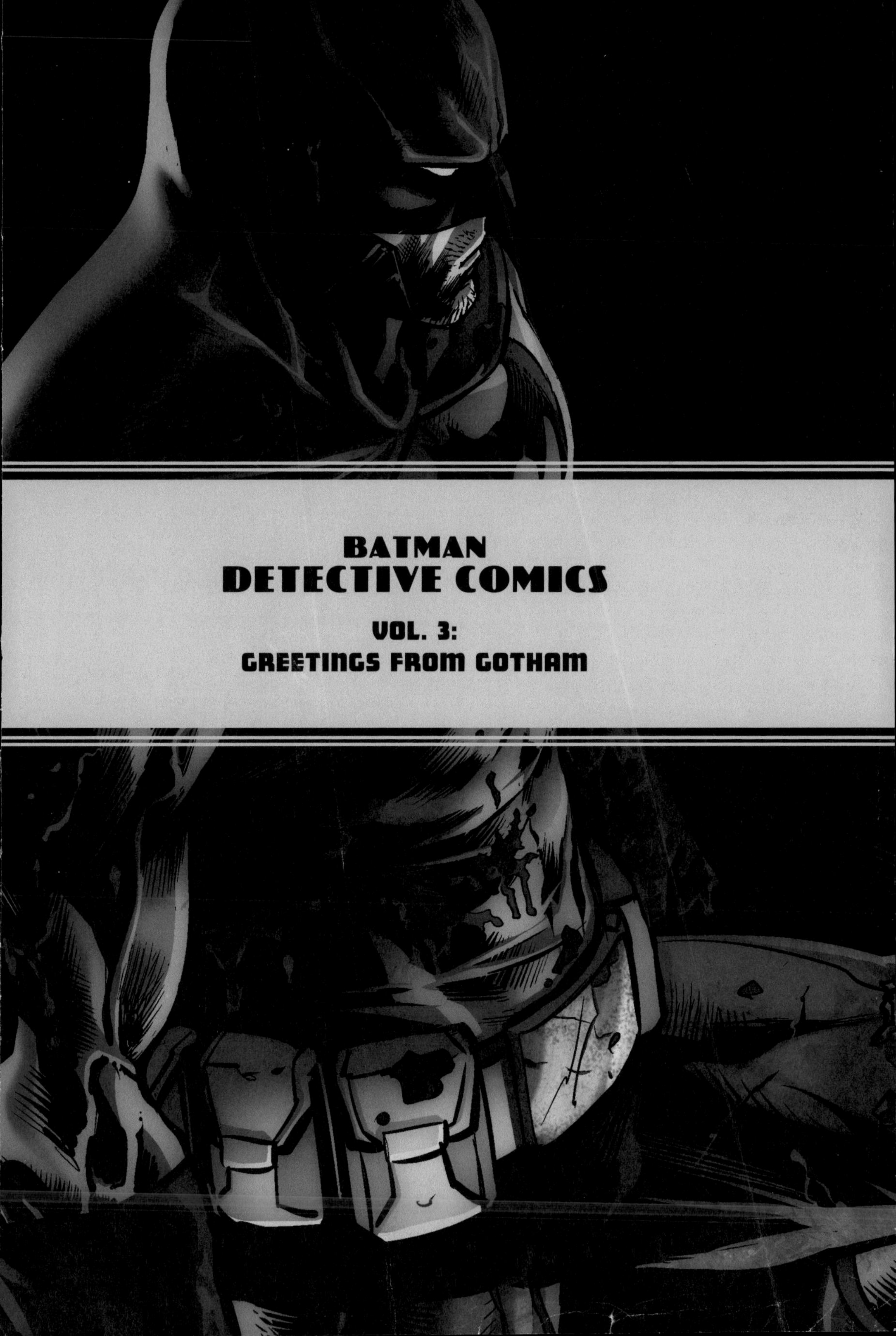

BATMAN
DETECTIVE COMICS

VOL. 3:
GREETINGS FROM GOTHAM

BATMAN
DETECTIVE COMICS

VOL. 3:
GREETINGS
FROM GOTHAM

PETER J. TOMASI
WRITER

DAVID BARON
LUIS GUERRERO
COLORISTS

ROB LEIGH
LETTERER

CHRISTIAN DUCE
KYLE HOTZ
DOUG MAHNKE
JAIME MENDOZA
ARTISTS

DOUG MAHNKE,
JAIME MENDOZA,
and DAVID BARON
COLLECTION COVER ARTISTS

BATMAN CREATED BY **BOB KANE** WITH **BILL FINGER**

JAMIE S. RICH Group Editor – Original Series
MOLLY MAHAN Editor – Original Series
DAVE WIELGOSZ Assistant Editor – Original Series
JEB WOODARD Group Editor – Collected Editions
ERIKA ROTHBERG Editor – Collected Edition
STEVE COOK Design Director – Books
LOUIS PRANDI Publication Design
CHRISTY SAWYER Publication Production

BOB HARRAS Senior VP – Editor-in-Chief, DC Comics

DAN DiDIO Publisher
JIM LEE Publisher & Chief Creative Officer
BOBBIE CHASE VP – New Publishing Initiatives
DON FALLETTI VP – Manufacturing Operations & Workflow Management
LAWRENCE GANEM VP – Talent Services
ALISON GILL Senior VP – Manufacturing & Operations
HANK KANALZ Senior VP – Publishing Strategy & Support Services
DAN MIRON VP – Publishing Operations
NICK J. NAPOLITANO VP – Manufacturing Administration & Design
NANCY SPEARS VP – Sales
JONAH WEILAND VP – Marketing & Creative Services
MICHELE R. WELLS VP & Executive Editor, Young Reader

BATMAN: DETECTIVE COMICS VOL. 3: GREETINGS FROM GOTHAM

DC Comics, 2900 West Alameda Ave., Burbank, CA 91505
Printed by LSC Communications, Kendallville, IN, USA. 3/27/20. First Printing.
ISBN: 978-1-4012-8861-7

Library of Congress Cataloging-in-Publication Data is available.

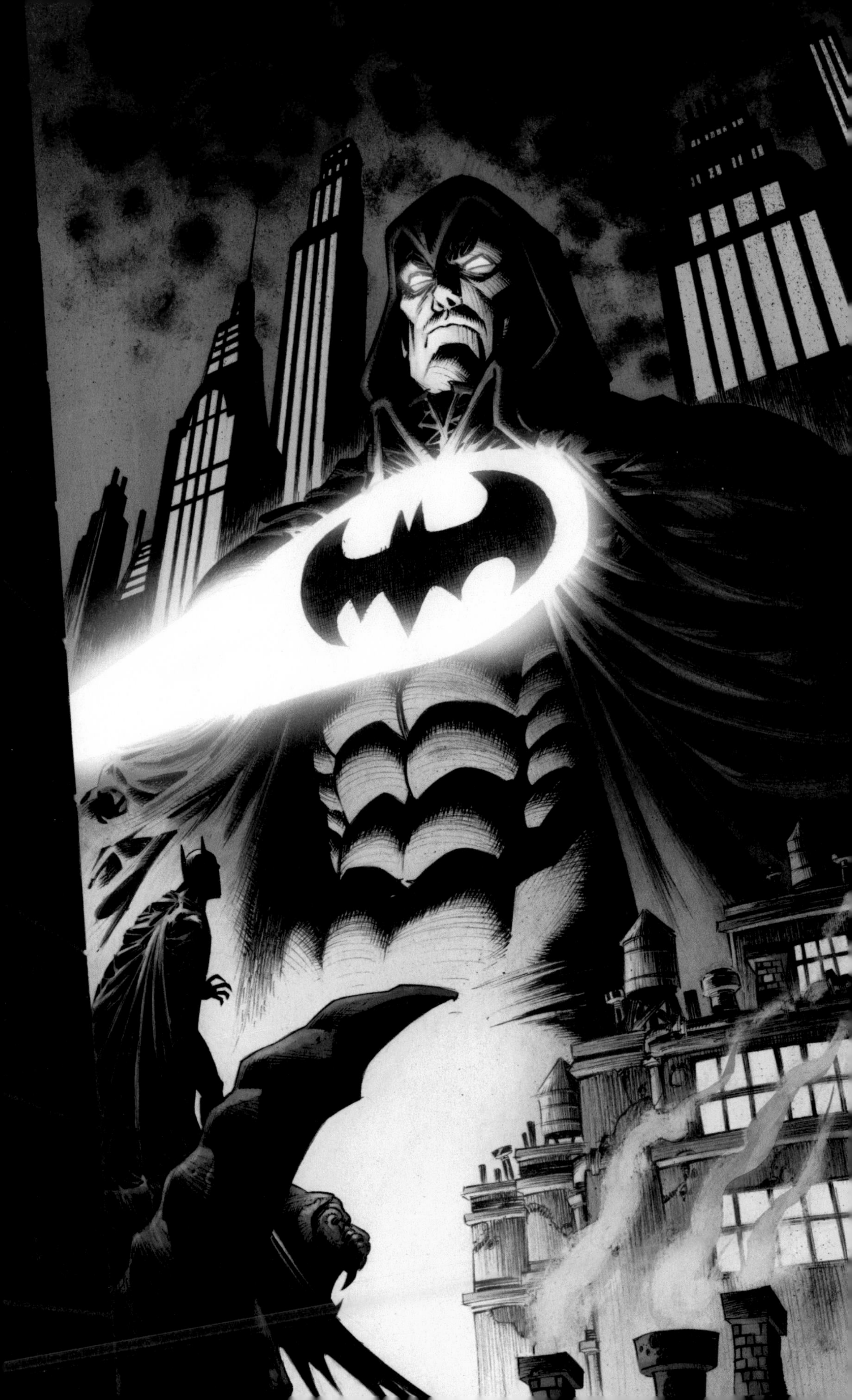

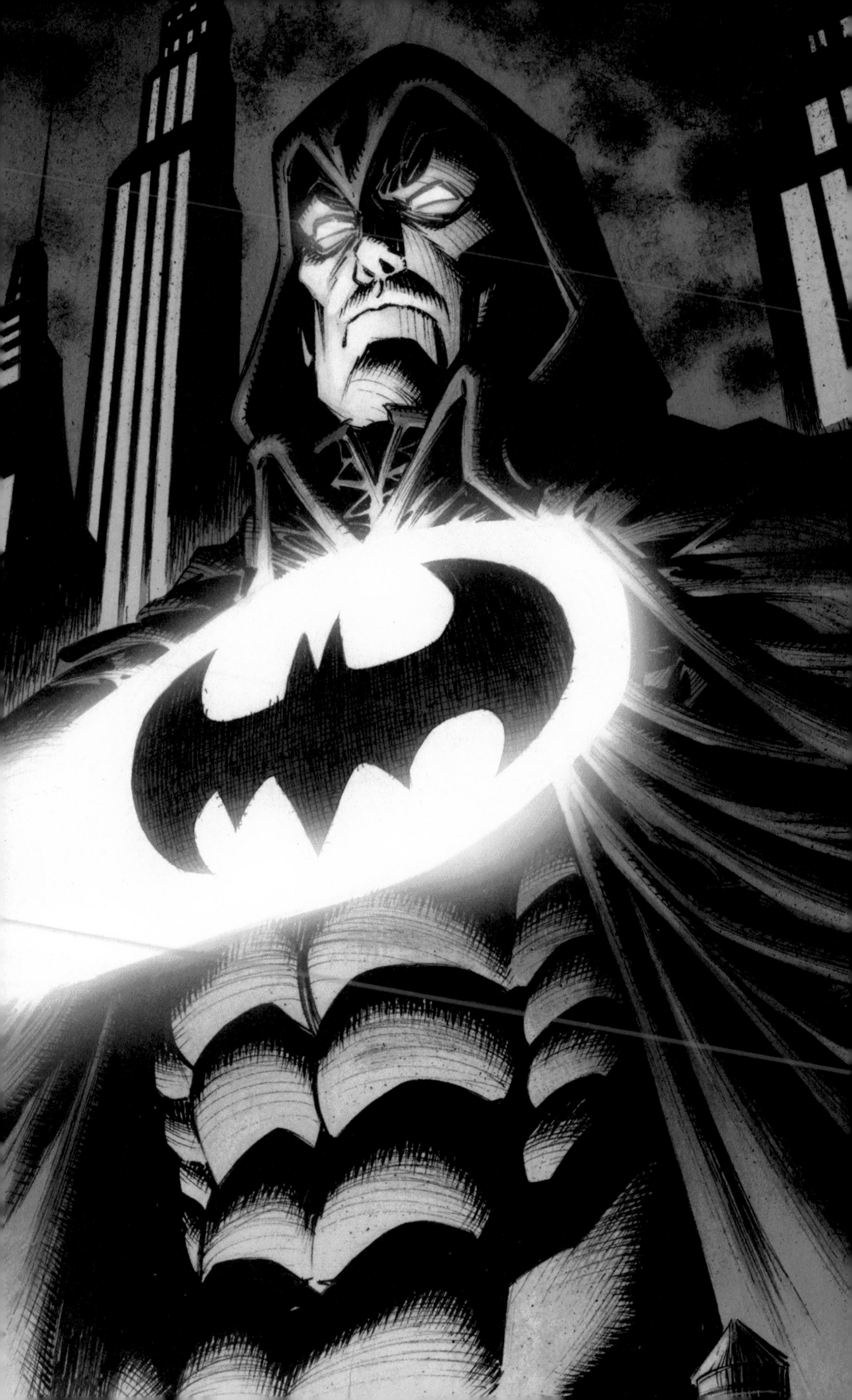

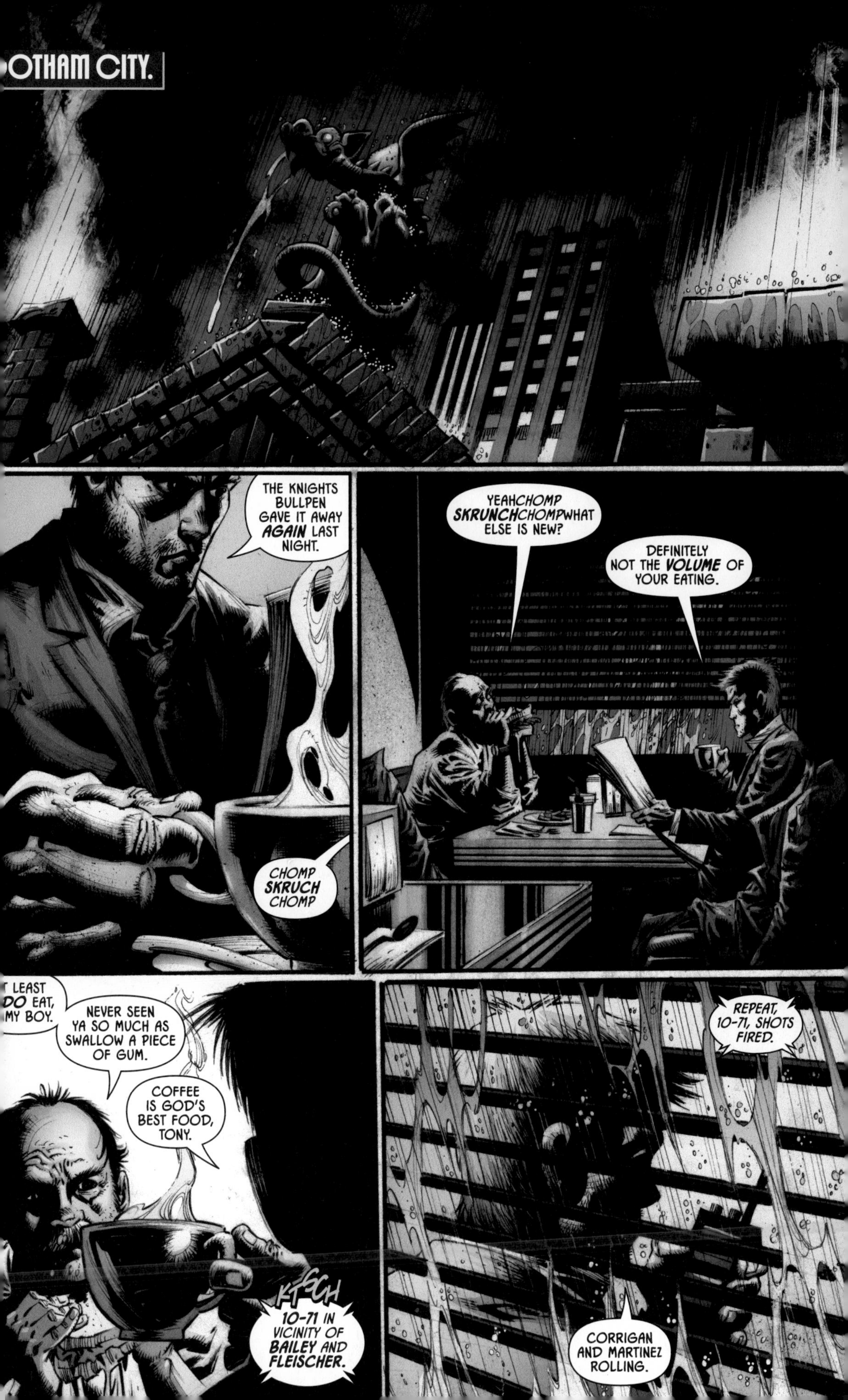
OTHAM CITY.
THE KNIGHTS BULLPEN GAVE IT AWAY AGAIN LAST NIGHT.
CHOMP SKRUCH CHOMP
YEAHCHOMP SKRUNCHCHOMPWHAT ELSE IS NEW?
DEFINITELY NOT THE VOLUME OF YOUR EATING.
T LEAST DO EAT, MY BOY.
NEVER SEEN YA SO MUCH AS SWALLOW A PIECE OF GUM.
COFFEE IS GOD'S BEST FOOD, TONY.
KTSCH
10-71 IN VICINITY OF BAILEY AND FLEISCHER.
REPEAT, 10-71, SHOTS FIRED.
CORRIGAN AND MARTINEZ ROLLING.

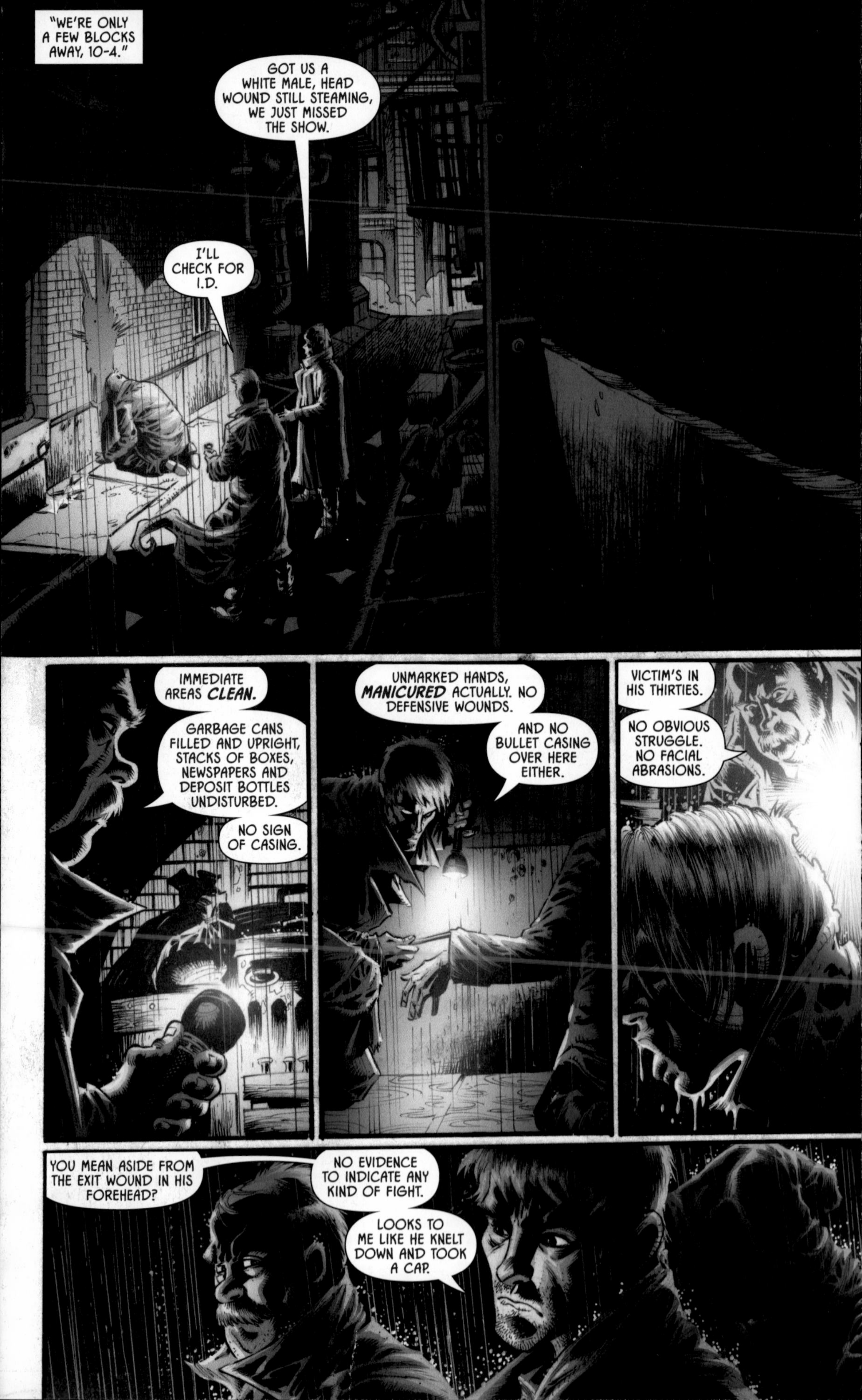
"WE'RE ONLY A FEW BLOCKS AWAY, 10-4."
GOT US A WHITE MALE, HEAD WOUND STILL STEAMING, WE JUST MISSED THE SHOW.
I'LL CHECK FOR I.D.
IMMEDIATE AREAS CLEAN.
GARBAGE CANS FILLED AND UPRIGHT, STACKS OF BOXES, NEWSPAPERS AND DEPOSIT BOTTLES UNDISTURBED.
NO SIGN OF CASING.
UNMARKED HANDS, MANICURED ACTUALLY. NO DEFENSIVE WOUNDS.
AND NO BULLET CASING OVER HERE EITHER.
VICTIM'S IN HIS THIRTIES.
NO OBVIOUS STRUGGLE. NO FACIAL ABRASIONS.
NO EVIDENCE TO INDICATE ANY KIND OF FIGHT.
YOU MEAN ASIDE FROM THE EXIT WOUND IN HIS FOREHEAD?
LOOKS TO ME LIKE HE KNELT DOWN AND TOOK A CAP.

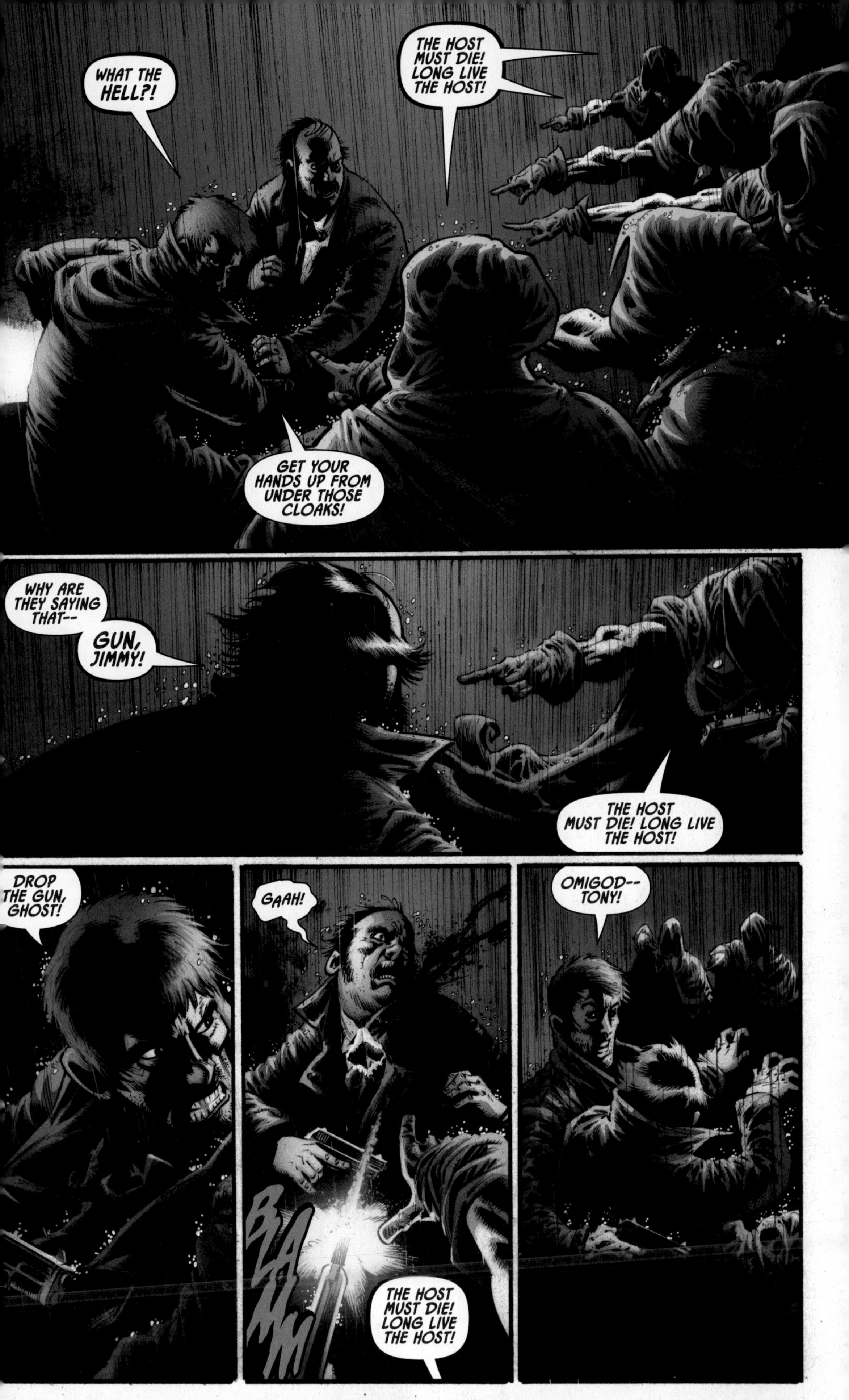
WHAT THE HELL?!
THE HOST MUST DIE! LONG LIVE THE HOST!
GET YOUR HANDS UP FROM UNDER THOSE CLOAKS!
WHY ARE THEY SAYING THAT--
GUN, JIMMY!
THE HOST MUST DIE! LONG LIVE THE HOST!
DROP THE GUN, GHOST!
GAAH!
BLAMM
THE HOST MUST DIE! LONG LIVE THE HOST!
OMIGOD-- TONY!

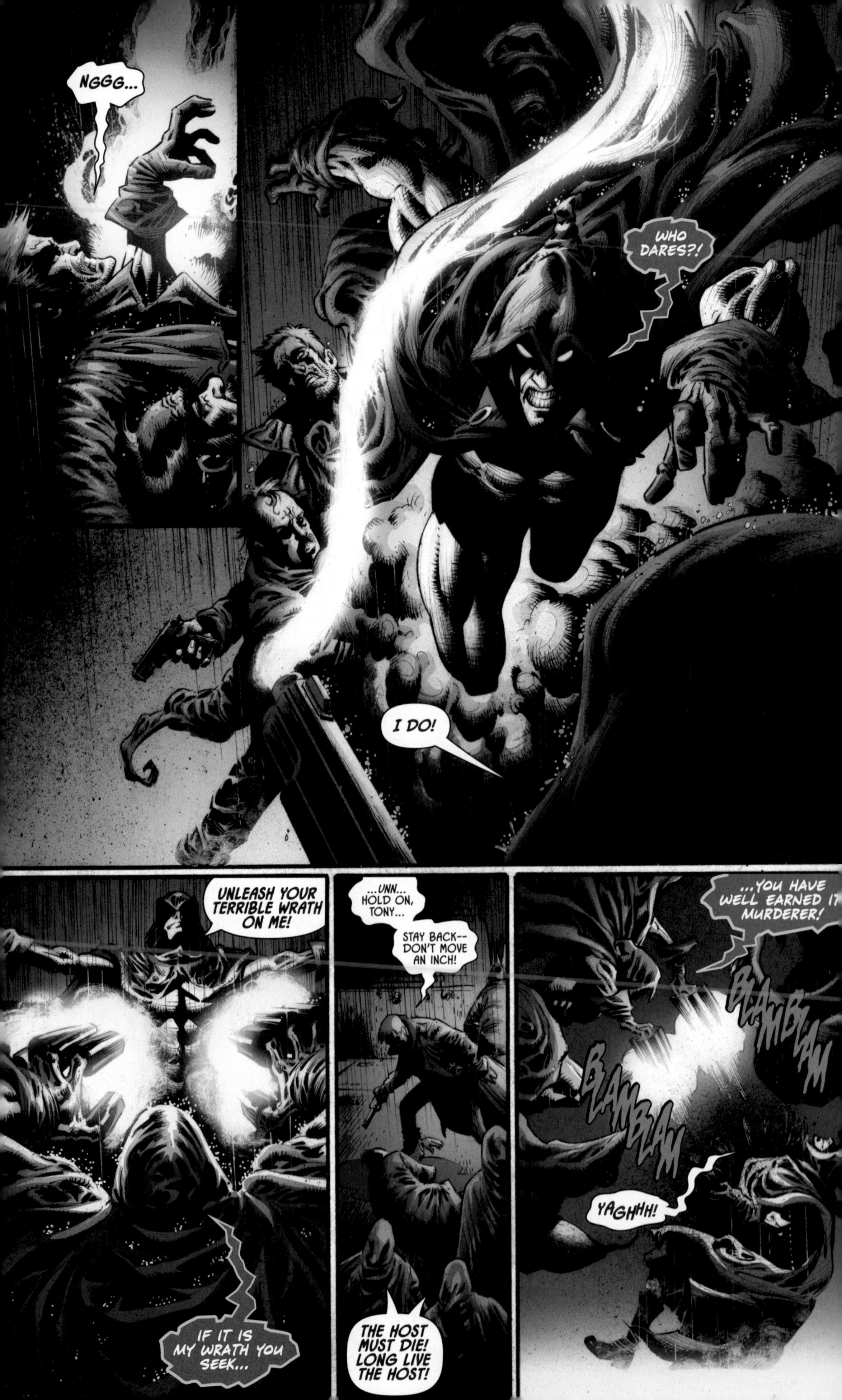
NGGG...
WHO DARES?!
I DO!
UNLEASH YOUR TERRIBLE WRATH ON ME!
IF IT IS MY WRATH YOU SEEK...
...UNN... HOLD ON, TONY...
STAY BACK-- DON'T MOVE AN INCH!
THE HOST MUST DIE! LONG LIVE THE HOST!
...YOU HAVE WELL EARNED IT, MURDERER!
BLAMBLAM
BLAMBLAM
YAGHHH!

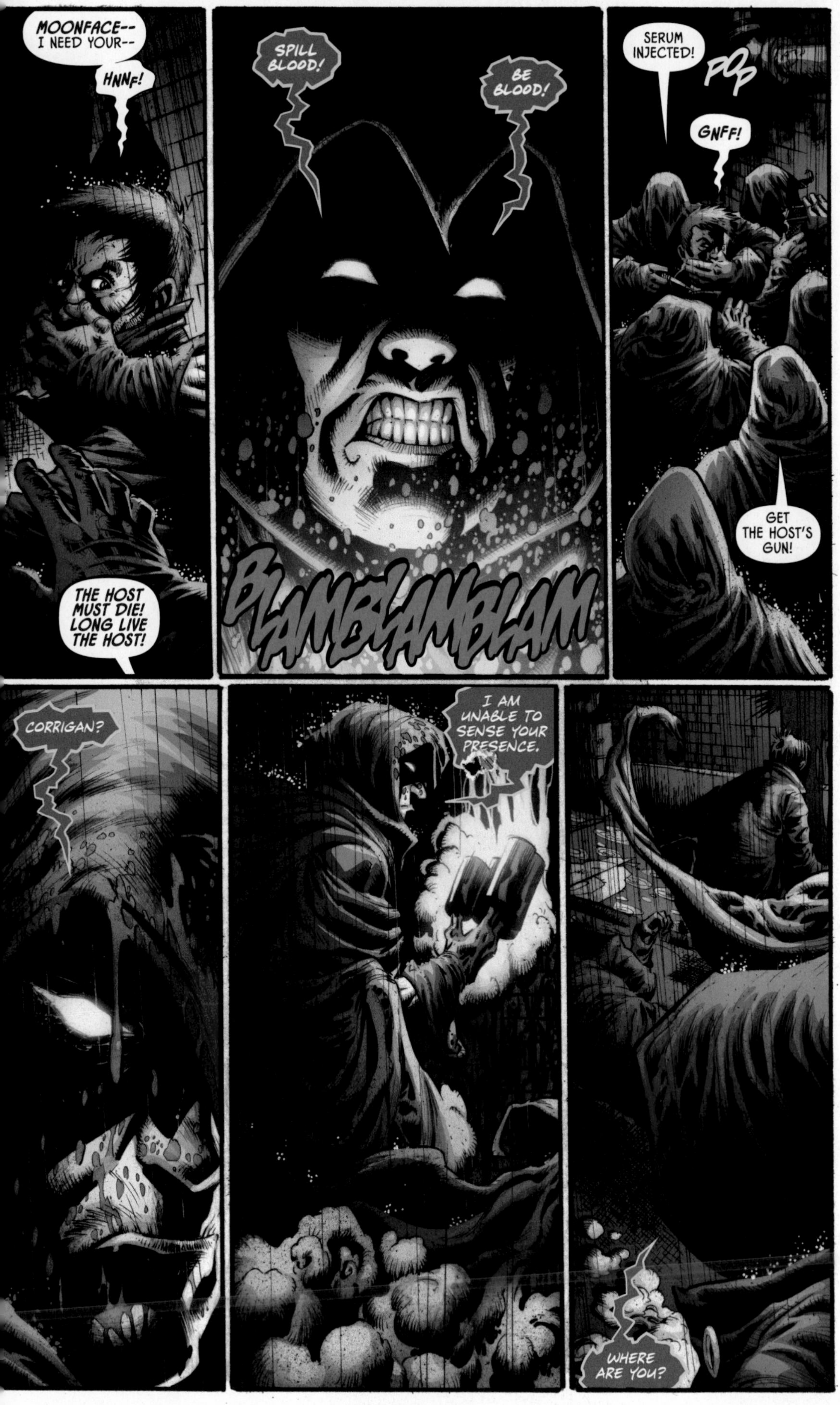
MOONFACE-- I NEED YOUR--
HNNF!
THE HOST MUST DIE! LONG LIVE THE HOST!
SPILL BLOOD!
BE BLOOD!
BLAMBLAMBLAM
SERUM INJECTED!
POP
GNFF!
GET THE HOST'S GUN!
CORRIGAN?
I AM UNABLE TO SENSE YOUR PRESENCE.
WHERE ARE YOU?

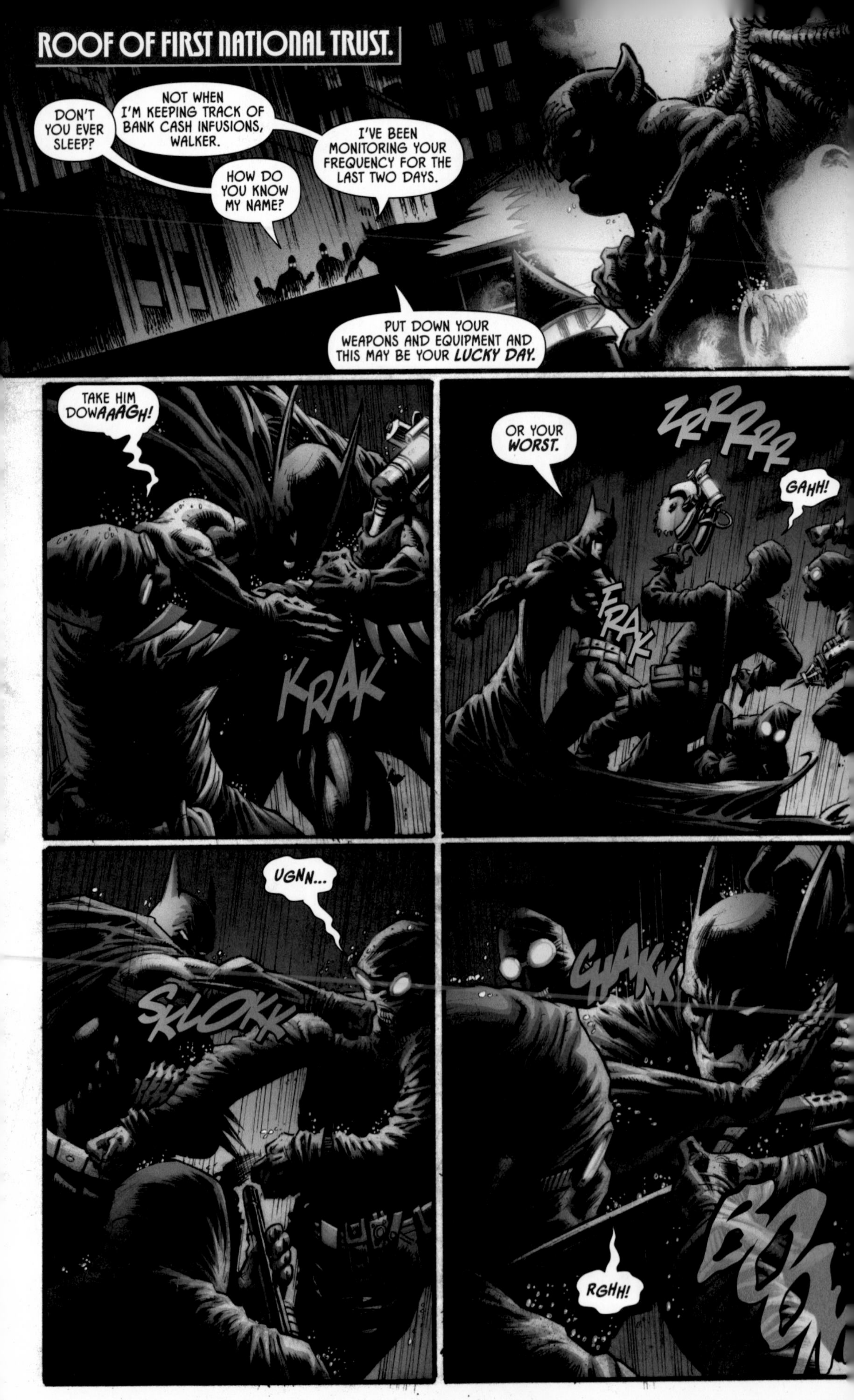
ROOF OF FIRST NATIONAL TRUST.
DON'T YOU EVER SLEEP?
NOT WHEN I'M KEEPING TRACK OF BANK CASH INFUSIONS, WALKER.
HOW DO YOU KNOW MY NAME?
I'VE BEEN MONITORING YOUR FREQUENCY FOR THE LAST TWO DAYS.
PUT DOWN YOUR WEAPONS AND EQUIPMENT AND THIS MAY BE YOUR LUCKY DAY.
TAKE HIM DOWAAAGH!
KRAK
OR YOUR WORST.
ZRRRRRR
GAHH!
FRAK
UGNN...
SKLOKK
CHAKK
RGHH!

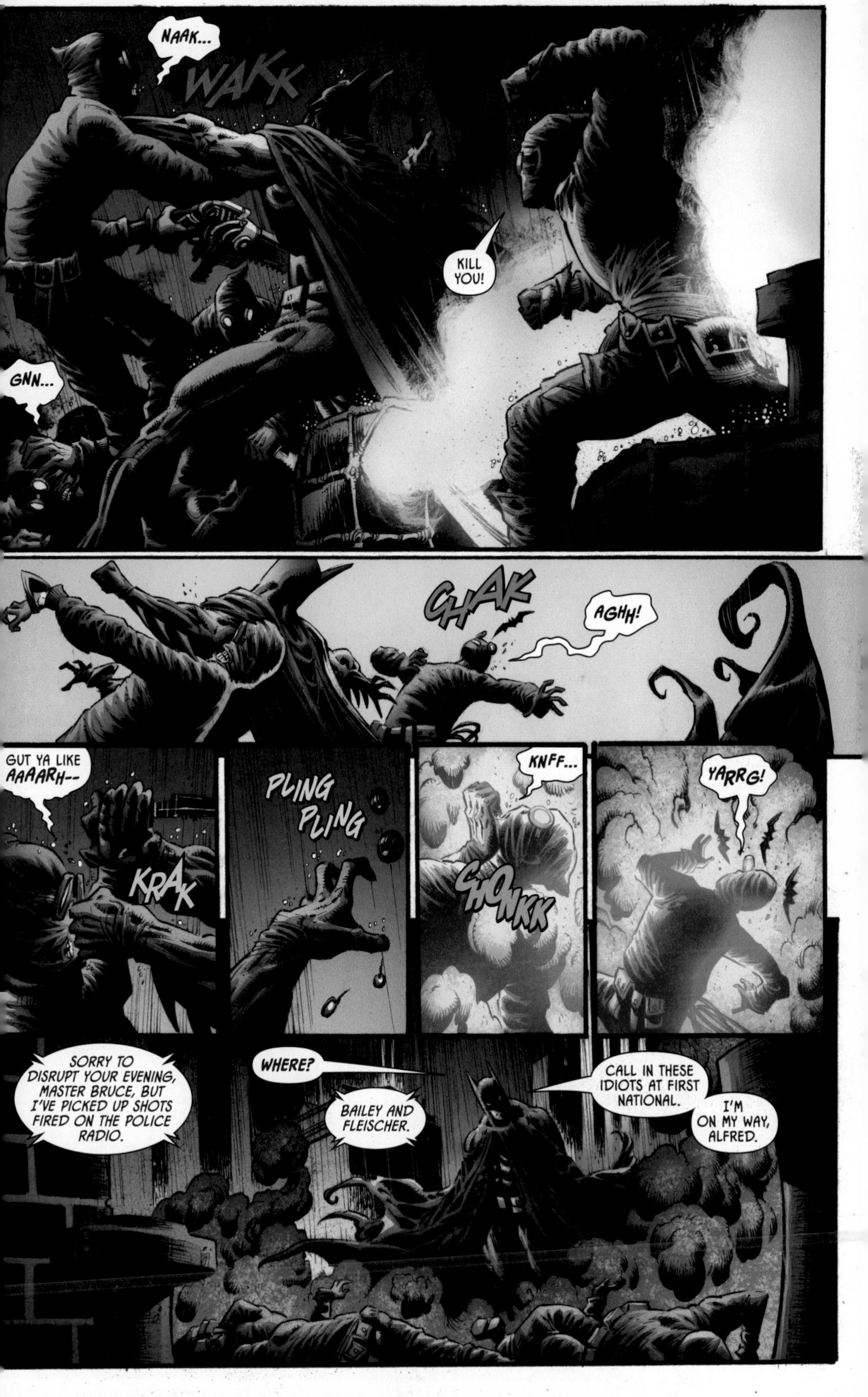
NAAK...
WAKK
KILL YOU!
GNN...
CHAK
AGHH!
GUT YA LIKE AAAARH--
KRAK
PLING PLING
KNFF...
CHONKK
YARRG!
SORRY TO DISRUPT YOUR EVENING, MASTER BRUCE, BUT I'VE PICKED UP SHOTS FIRED ON THE POLICE RADIO.
WHERE?
BAILEY AND FLEISCHER.
CALL IN THESE IDIOTS AT FIRST NATIONAL.
I'M ON MY WAY, ALFRED.

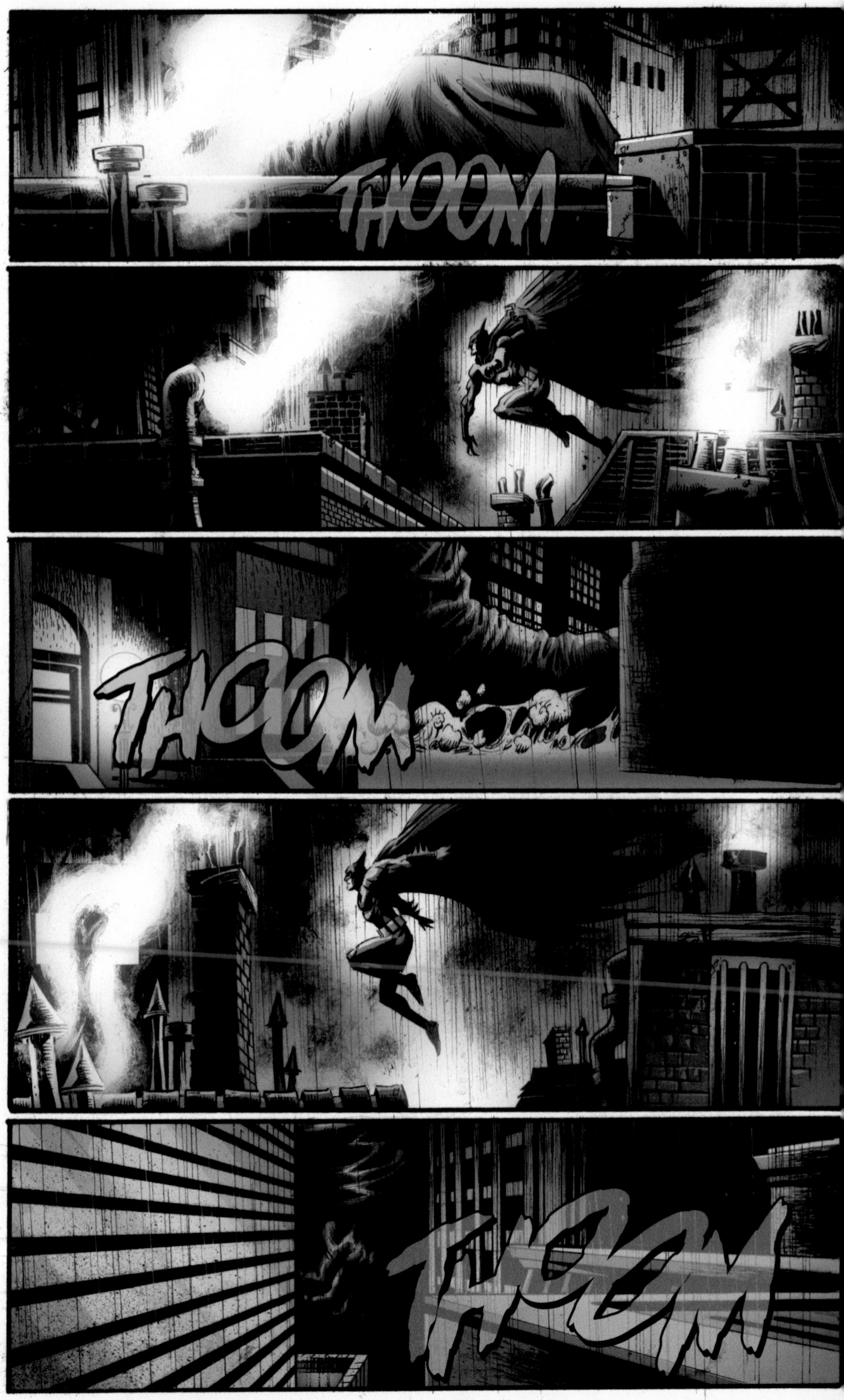
THOOM
THOOM
THOOM

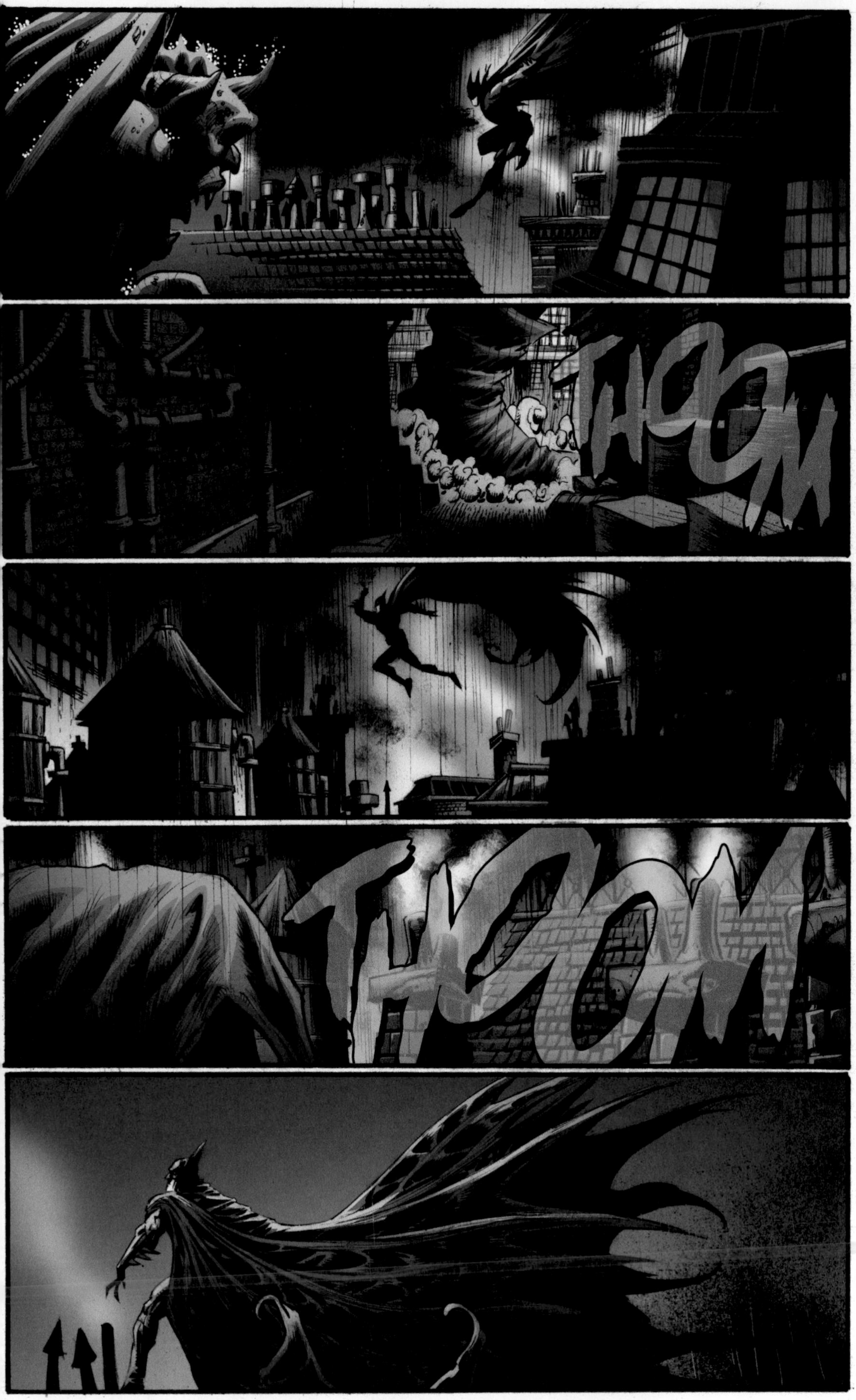
THOOM
THOOM

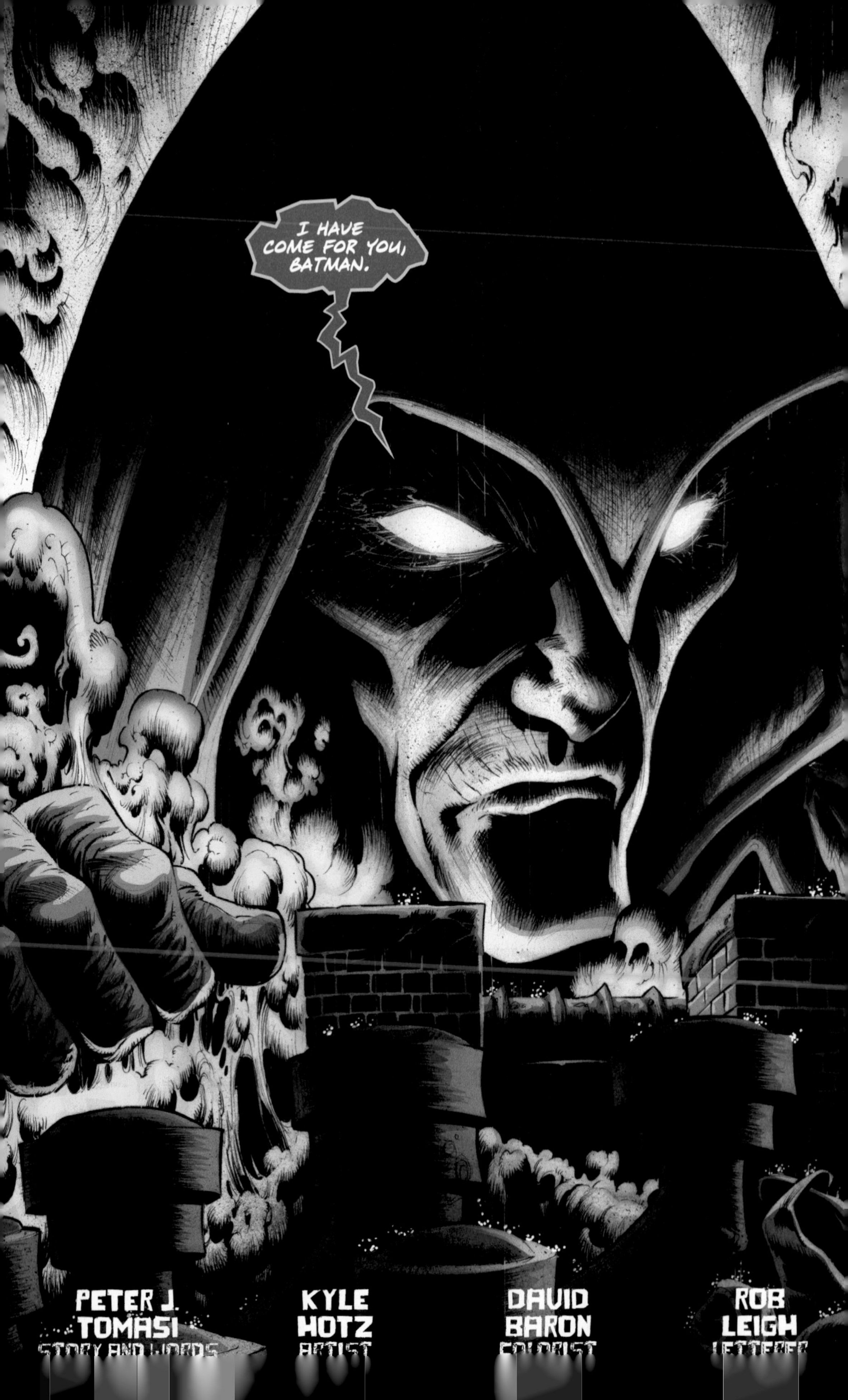
I HAVE COME FOR YOU, BATMAN.
PETER J. TOMASI
KYLE HOTZ
DAVID BARON
ROB LEIGH

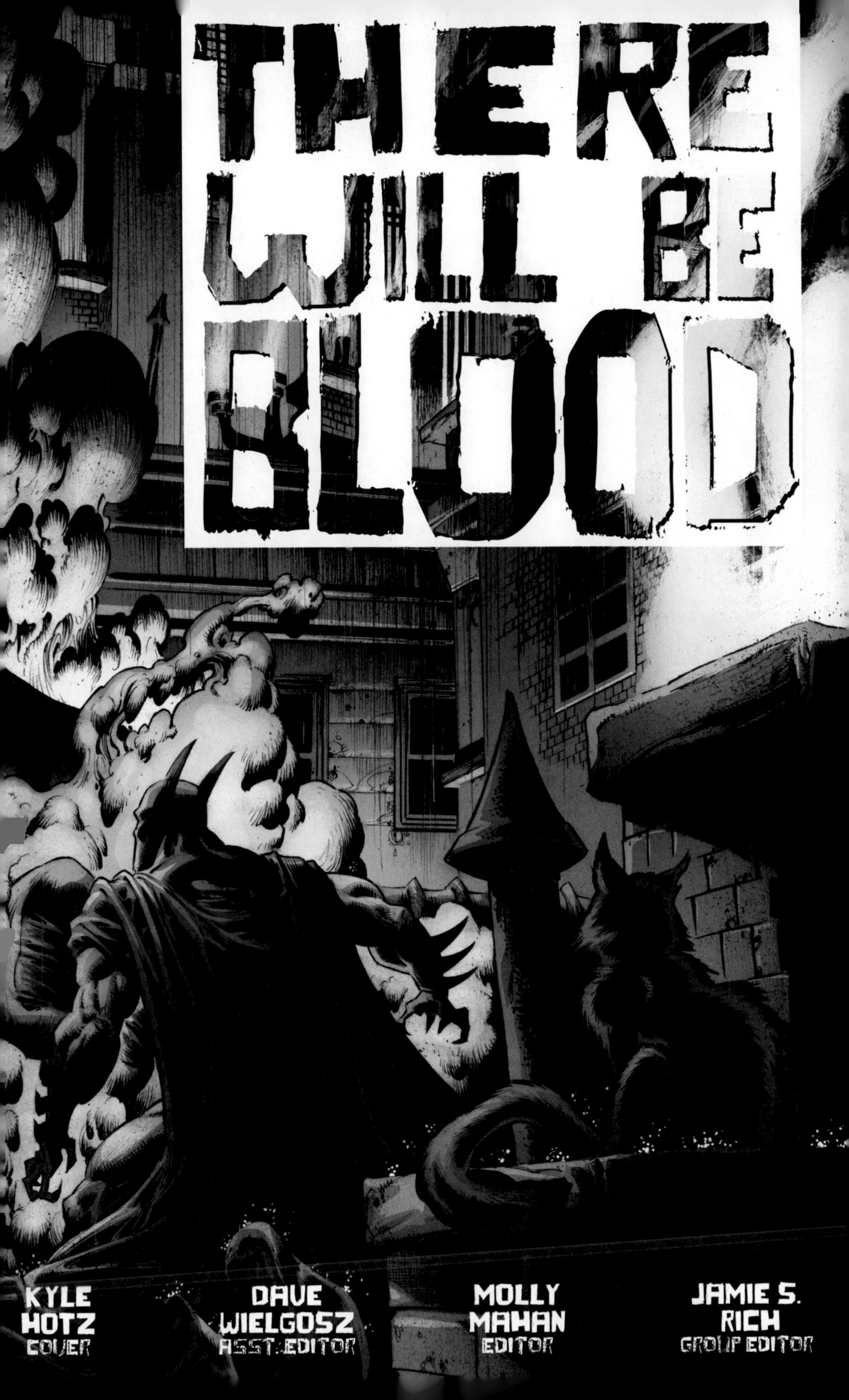
THERE WILL BE BLOOD
KYLE HOTZ COVER
DAVE WIELGOSZ ASST. EDITOR
MOLLY MAHAN EDITOR
JAMIE S. RICH GROUP EDITOR

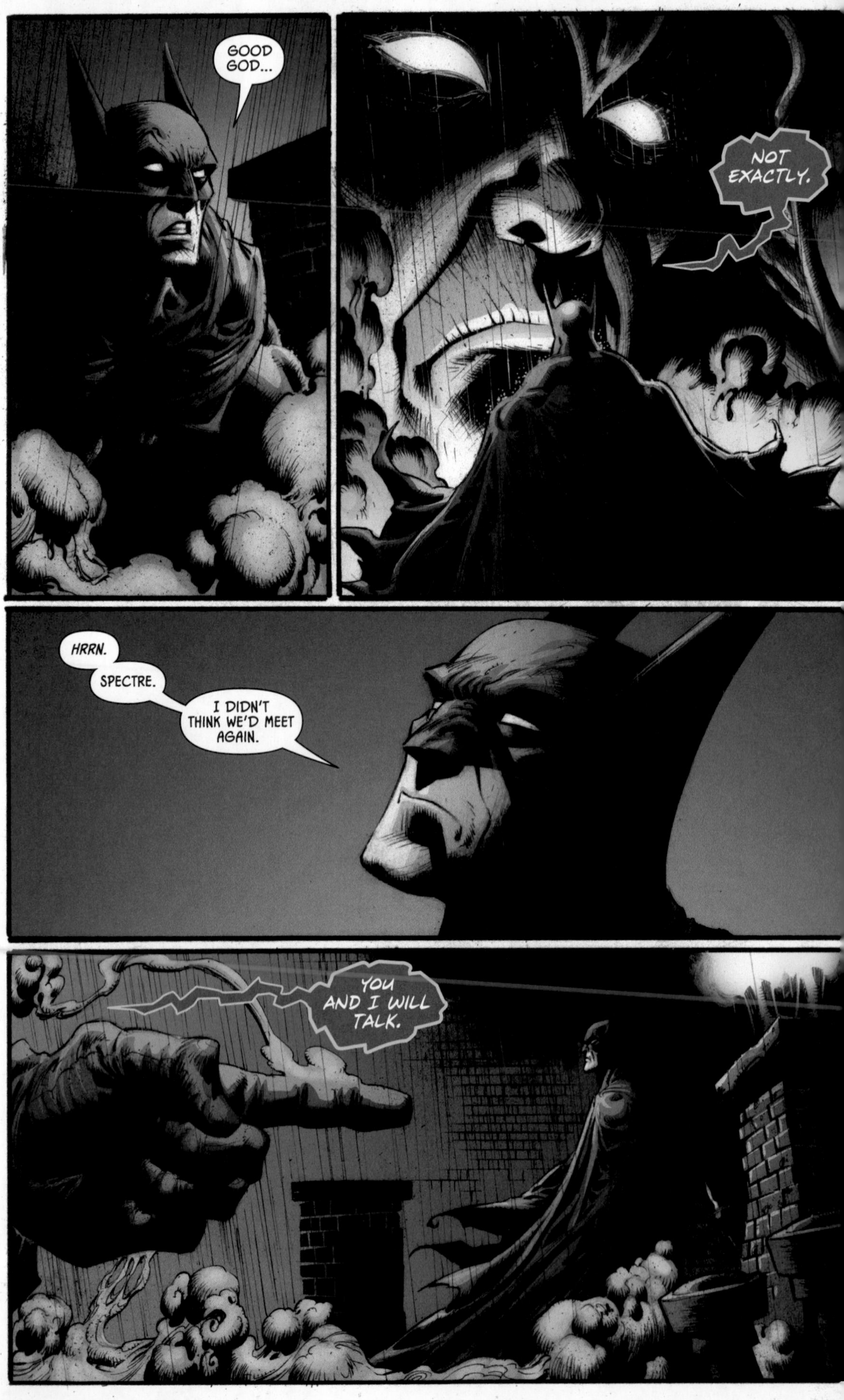
GOOD GOD...
NOT EXACTLY.
HRRN.
SPECTRE.
I DIDN'T THINK WE'D MEET AGAIN.
YOU AND I WILL TALK.

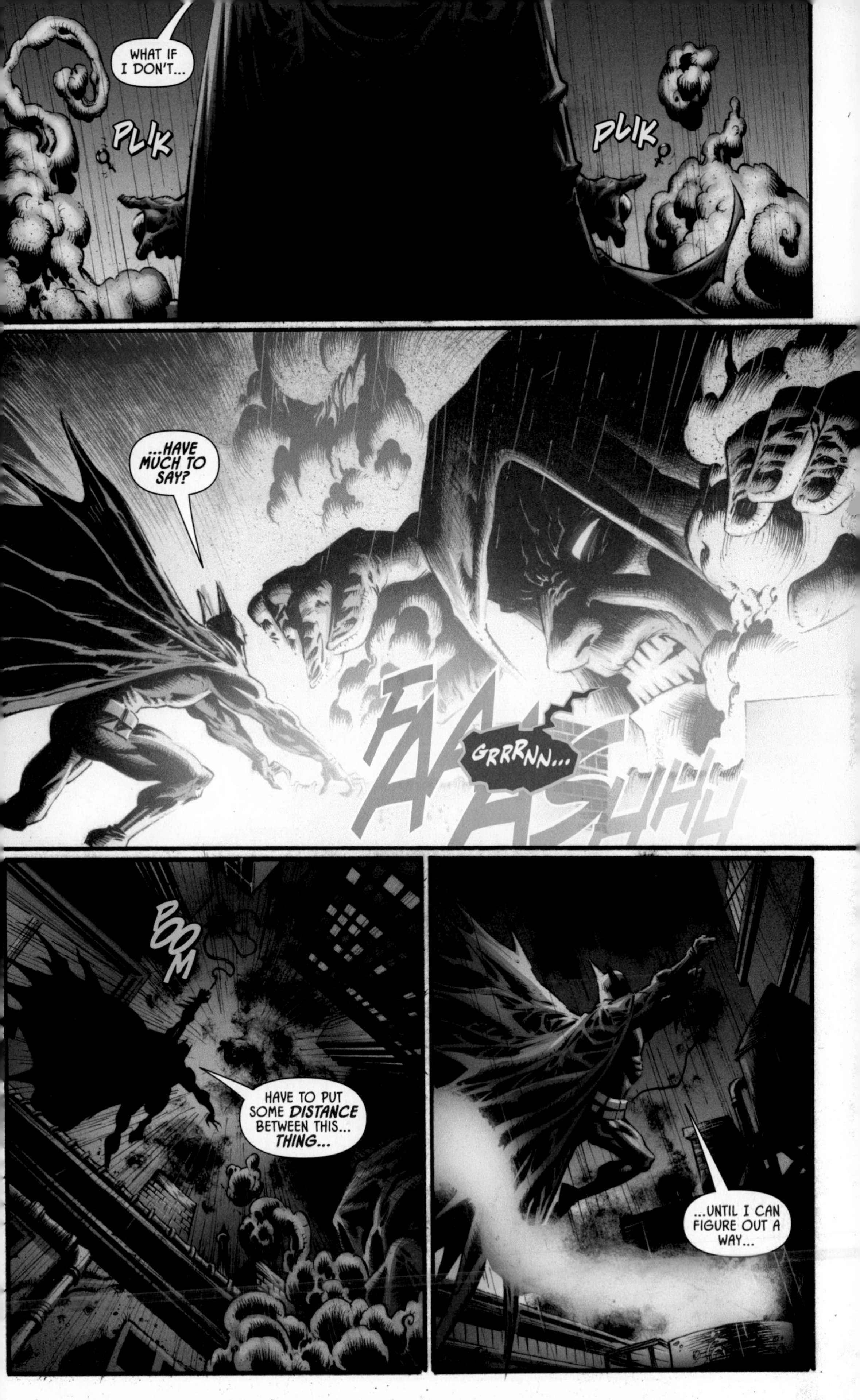
WHAT IF I DON'T...
PLIK
PLIK
...HAVE MUCH TO SAY?
GRRRNN...
BOOM
HAVE TO PUT SOME DISTANCE BETWEEN THIS... THING...
...UNTIL I CAN FIGURE OUT A WAY...

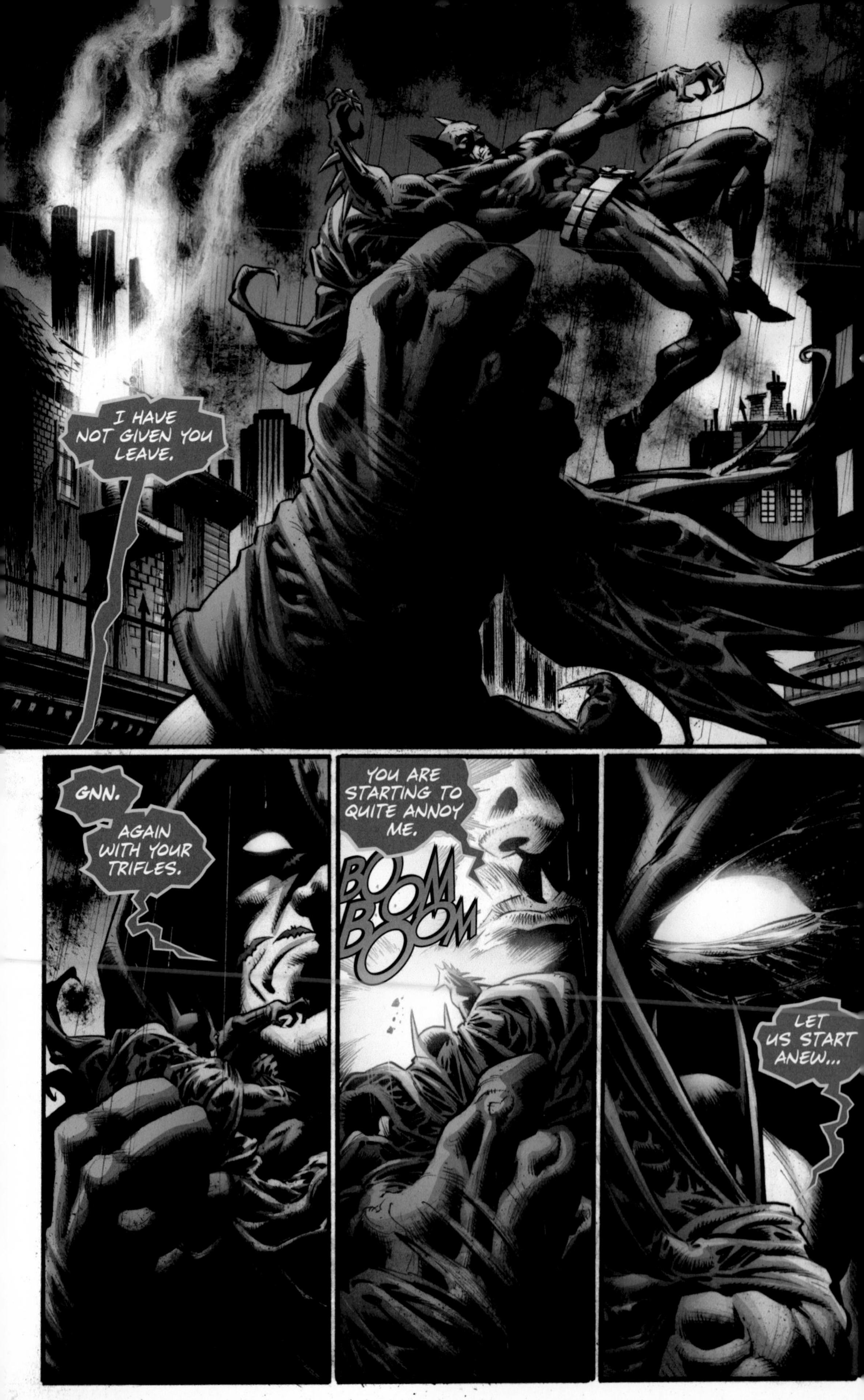
I HAVE NOT GIVEN YOU LEAVE.
GNN.
AGAIN WITH YOUR TRIFLES.
YOU ARE STARTING TO QUITE ANNOY ME.
BOOM BOOM BOOM
LET US START ANEW...

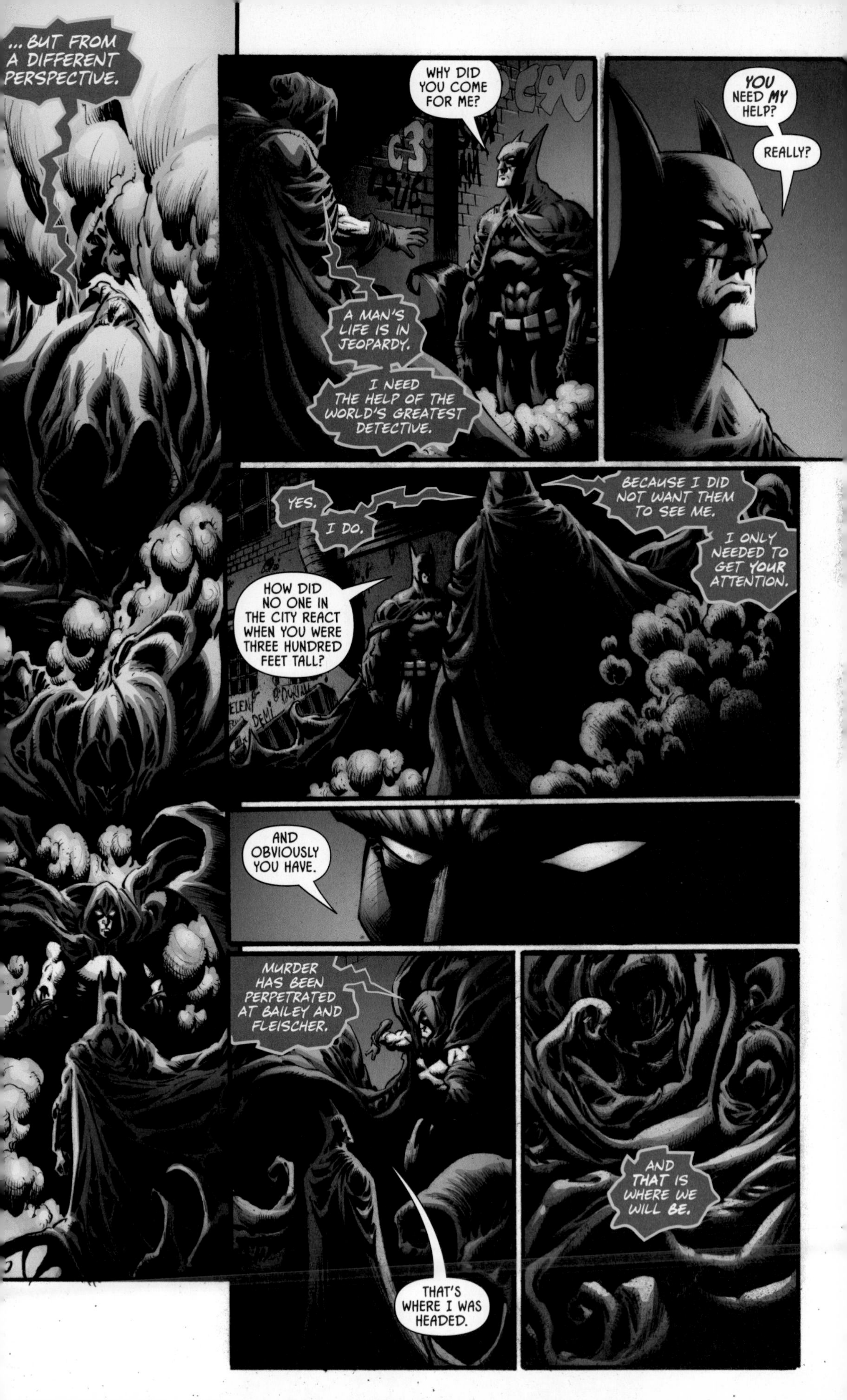
...BUT FROM A DIFFERENT PERSPECTIVE.
WHY DID YOU COME FOR ME?
A MAN'S LIFE IS IN JEOPARDY.
I NEED THE HELP OF THE WORLD'S GREATEST DETECTIVE.
YOU NEED MY HELP?
REALLY?
YES.
I DO.
HOW DID NO ONE IN THE CITY REACT WHEN YOU WERE THREE HUNDRED FEET TALL?
BECAUSE I DID NOT WANT THEM TO SEE ME.
I ONLY NEEDED TO GET YOUR ATTENTION.
AND OBVIOUSLY YOU HAVE.
MURDER HAS BEEN PERPETRATED AT BAILEY AND FLEISCHER.
THAT'S WHERE I WAS HEADED.
AND THAT IS WHERE WE WILL BE.

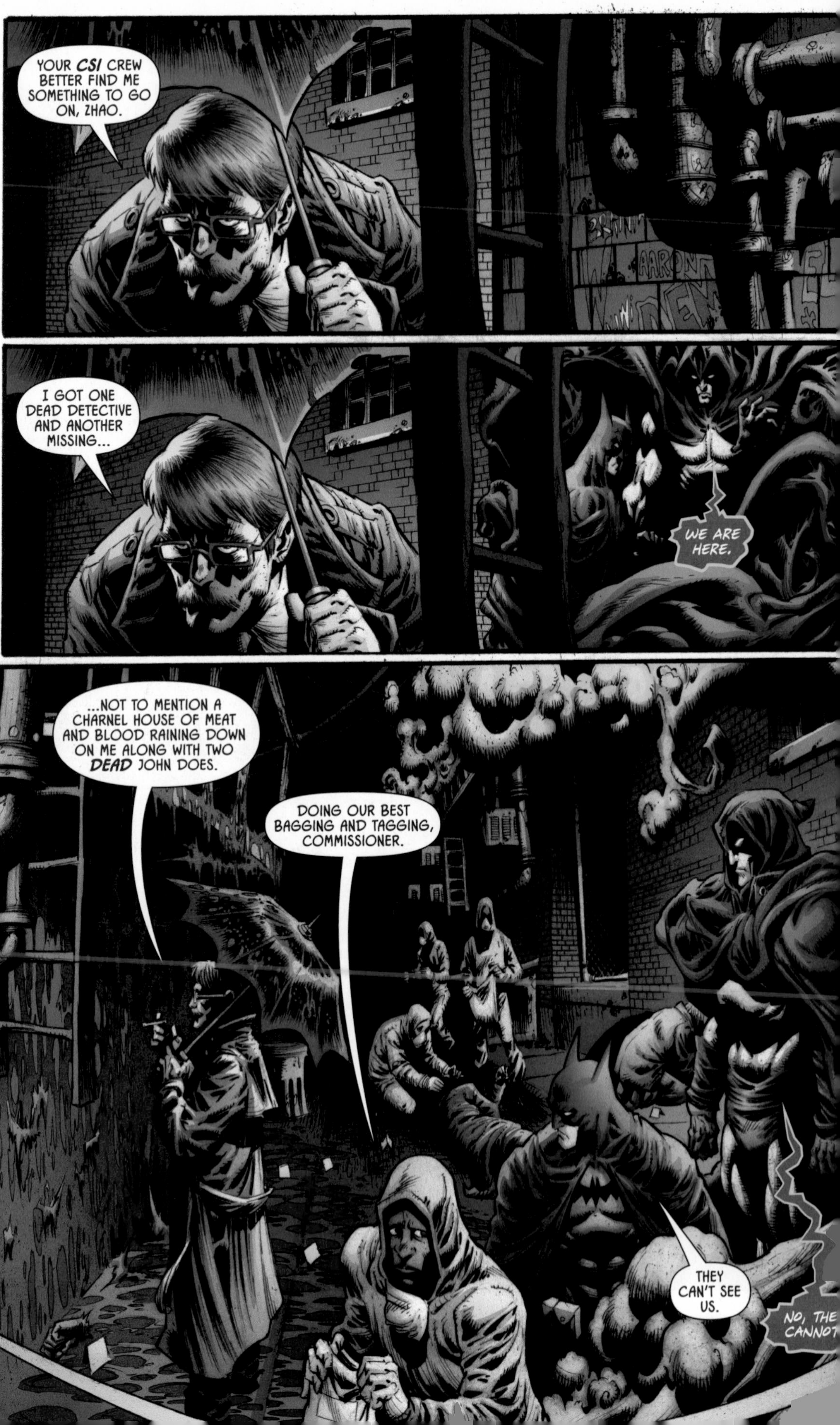

YOUR CSI CREW BETTER FIND ME SOMETHING TO GO ON, ZHAO.
I GOT ONE DEAD DETECTIVE AND ANOTHER MISSING...
WE ARE HERE.
...NOT TO MENTION A CHARNEL HOUSE OF MEAT AND BLOOD RAINING DOWN ON ME ALONG WITH TWO DEAD JOHN DOES.
DOING OUR BEST BAGGING AND TAGGING, COMMISSIONER.
THEY CAN'T SEE US.
NO, THE CANNOT

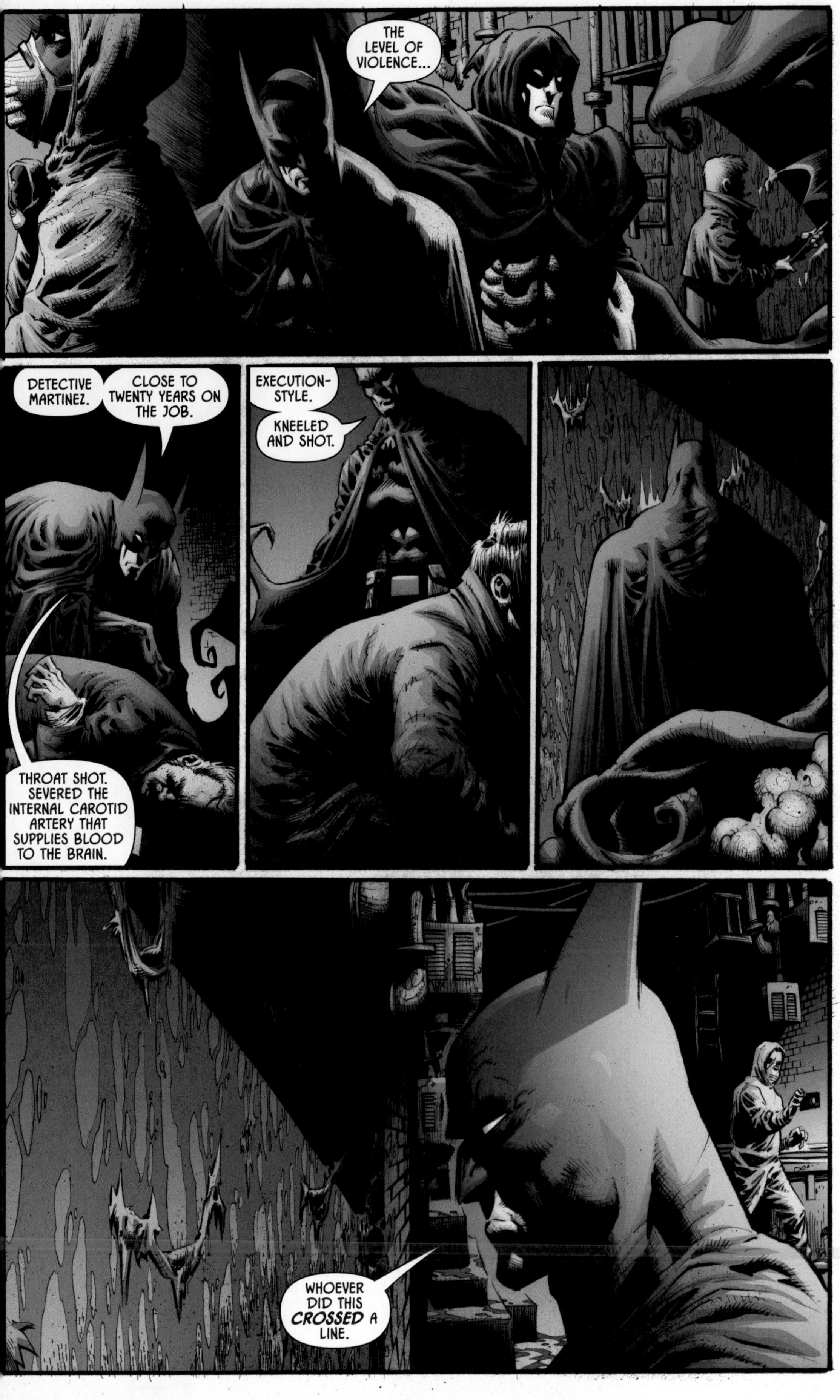
THE LEVEL OF VIOLENCE...
DETECTIVE MARTINEZ.
CLOSE TO TWENTY YEARS ON THE JOB.
THROAT SHOT. SEVERED THE INTERNAL CAROTID ARTERY THAT SUPPLIES BLOOD TO THE BRAIN.
EXECUTION-STYLE.
KNEELED AND SHOT.
WHOEVER DID THIS CROSSED A LINE.

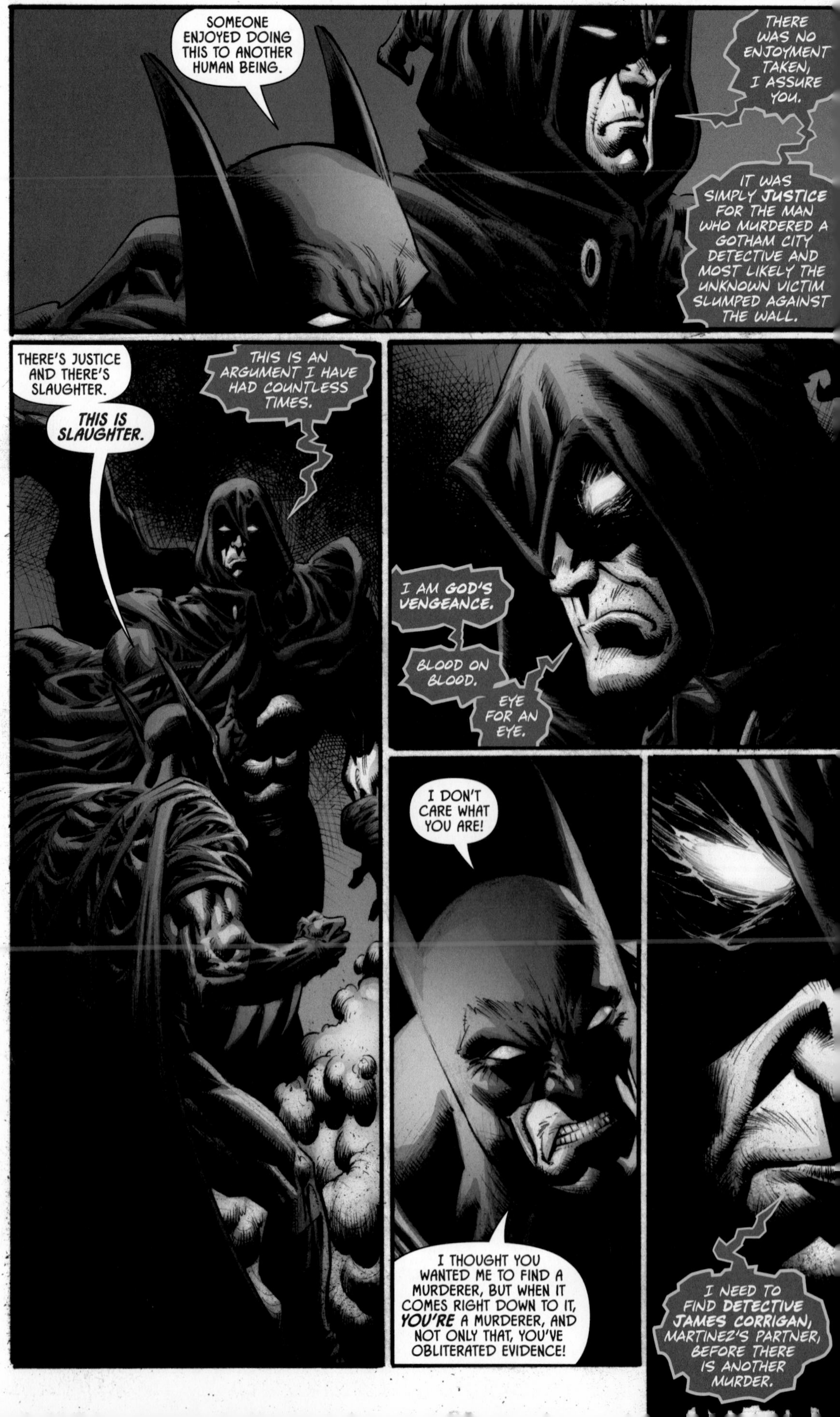
SOMEONE ENJOYED DOING THIS TO ANOTHER HUMAN BEING.
THERE WAS NO ENJOYMENT TAKEN, I ASSURE YOU.
IT WAS SIMPLY JUSTICE FOR THE MAN WHO MURDERED A GOTHAM CITY DETECTIVE AND MOST LIKELY THE UNKNOWN VICTIM SLUMPED AGAINST THE WALL.
THERE'S JUSTICE AND THERE'S SLAUGHTER.
THIS IS SLAUGHTER.
THIS IS AN ARGUMENT I HAVE HAD COUNTLESS TIMES.
I AM GOD'S VENGEANCE.
BLOOD ON BLOOD.
EYE FOR AN EYE.
I DON'T CARE WHAT YOU ARE!
I THOUGHT YOU WANTED ME TO FIND A MURDERER, BUT WHEN IT COMES RIGHT DOWN TO IT, YOU'RE A MURDERER, AND NOT ONLY THAT, YOU'VE OBLITERATED EVIDENCE!
I NEED TO FIND DETECTIVE JAMES CORRIGAN, MARTINEZ'S PARTNER, BEFORE THERE IS ANOTHER MURDER.

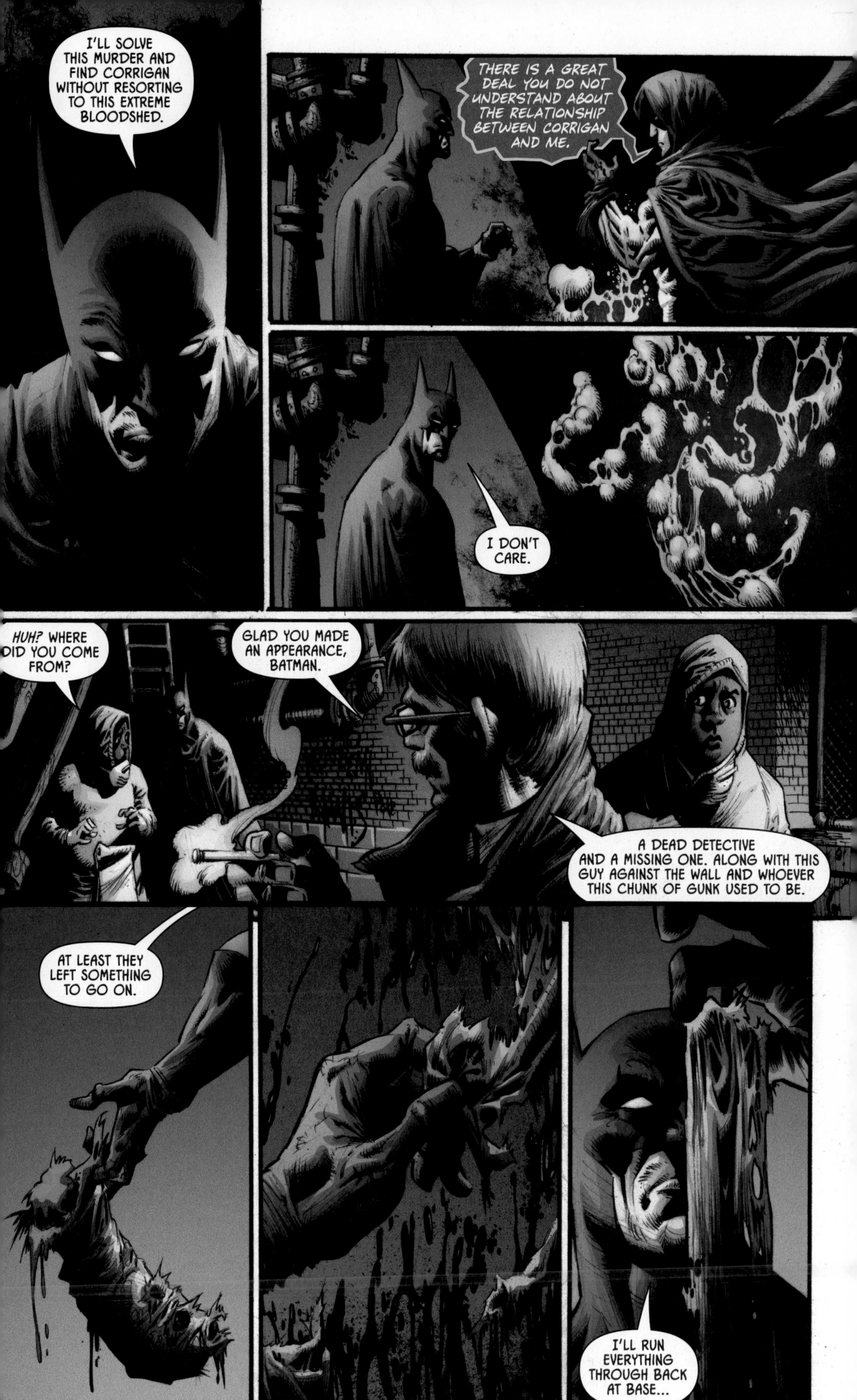
I'LL SOLVE THIS MURDER AND FIND CORRIGAN WITHOUT RESORTING TO THIS EXTREME BLOODSHED.
THERE IS A GREAT DEAL YOU DO NOT UNDERSTAND ABOUT THE RELATIONSHIP BETWEEN CORRIGAN AND ME.
I DON'T CARE.
HUH? WHERE DID YOU COME FROM?
GLAD YOU MADE AN APPEARANCE, BATMAN.
A DEAD DETECTIVE AND A MISSING ONE. ALONG WITH THIS GUY AGAINST THE WALL AND WHOEVER THIS CHUNK OF GUNK USED TO BE.
AT LEAST THEY LEFT SOMETHING TO GO ON.
I'LL RUN EVERYTHING THROUGH BACK AT BASE...

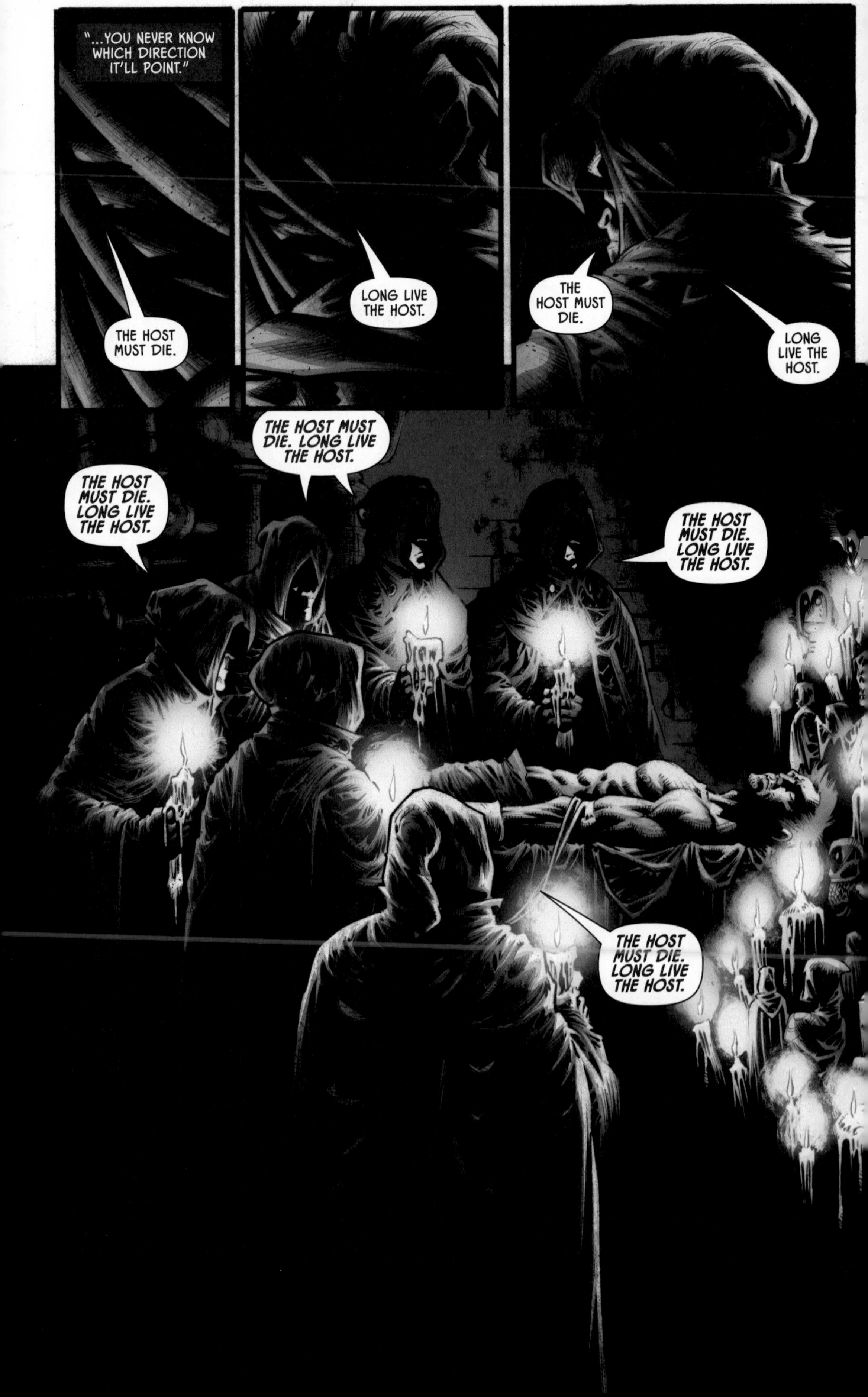
"...YOU NEVER KNOW WHICH DIRECTION IT'LL POINT."
THE HOST MUST DIE.
LONG LIVE THE HOST.
THE HOST MUST DIE.
LONG LIVE THE HOST.
THE HOST MUST DIE. LONG LIVE THE HOST.
THE HOST MUST DIE. LONG LIVE THE HOST.
THE HOST MUST DIE. LONG LIVE THE HOST.
THE HOST MUST DIE. LONG LIVE THE HOST.

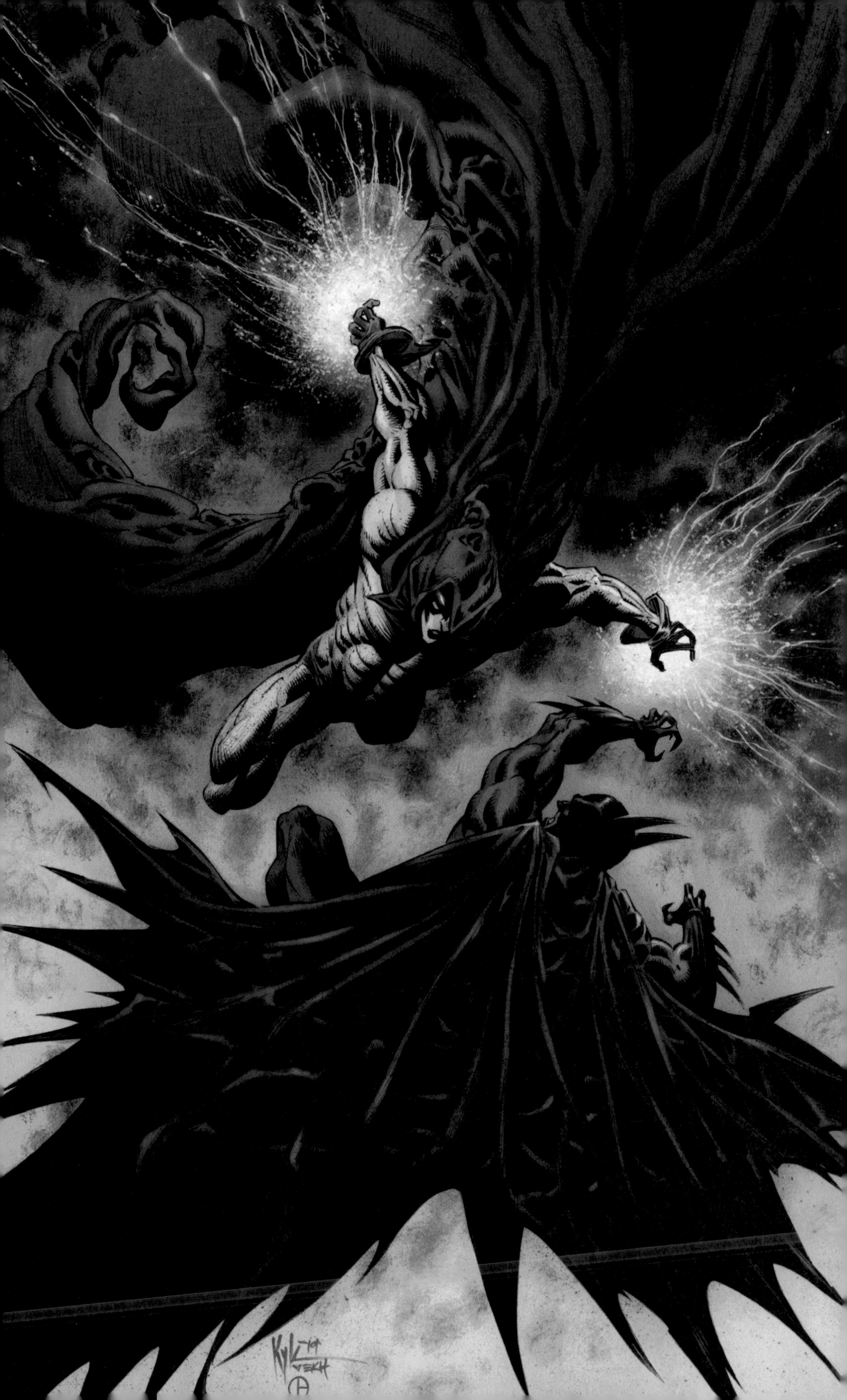

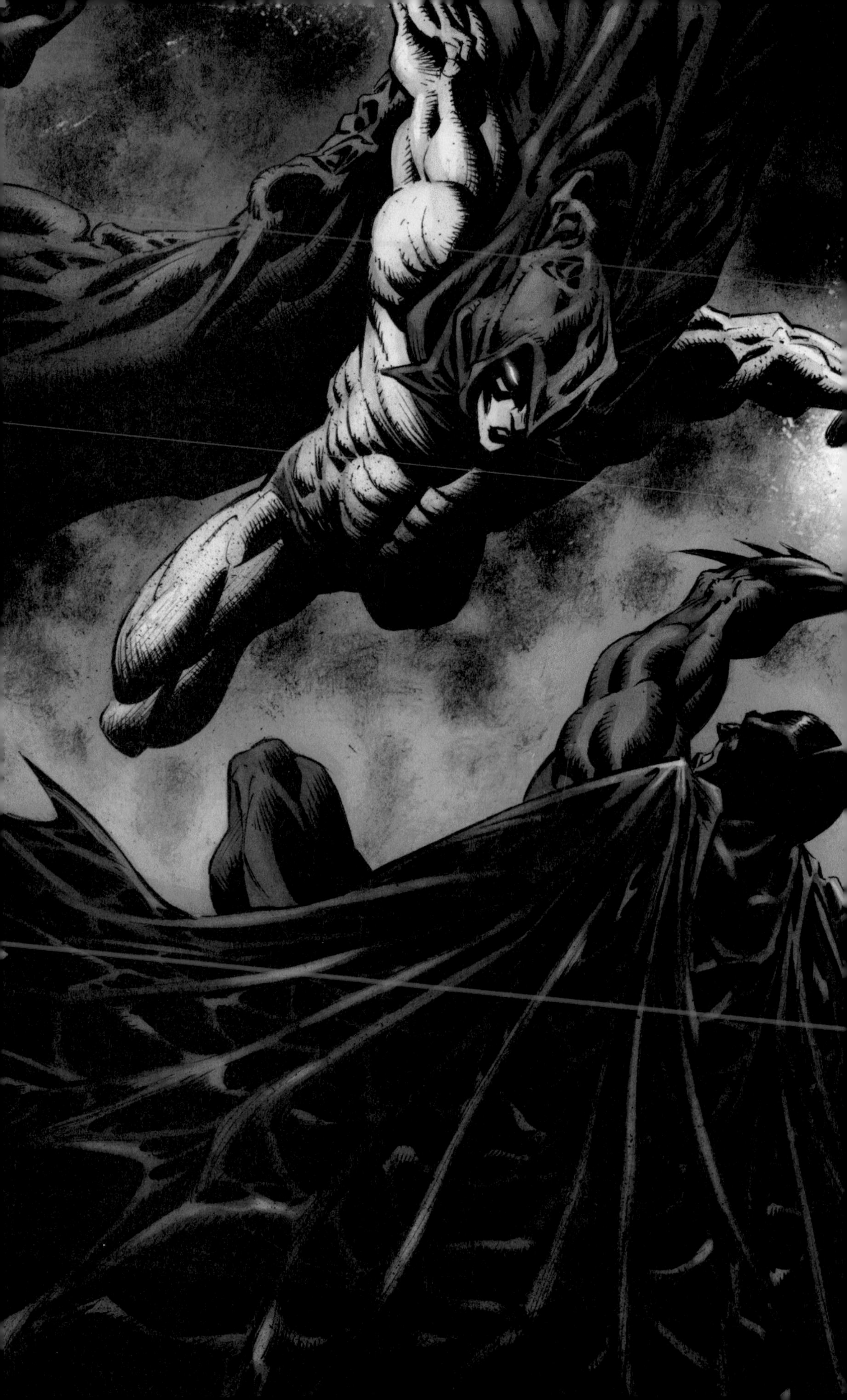

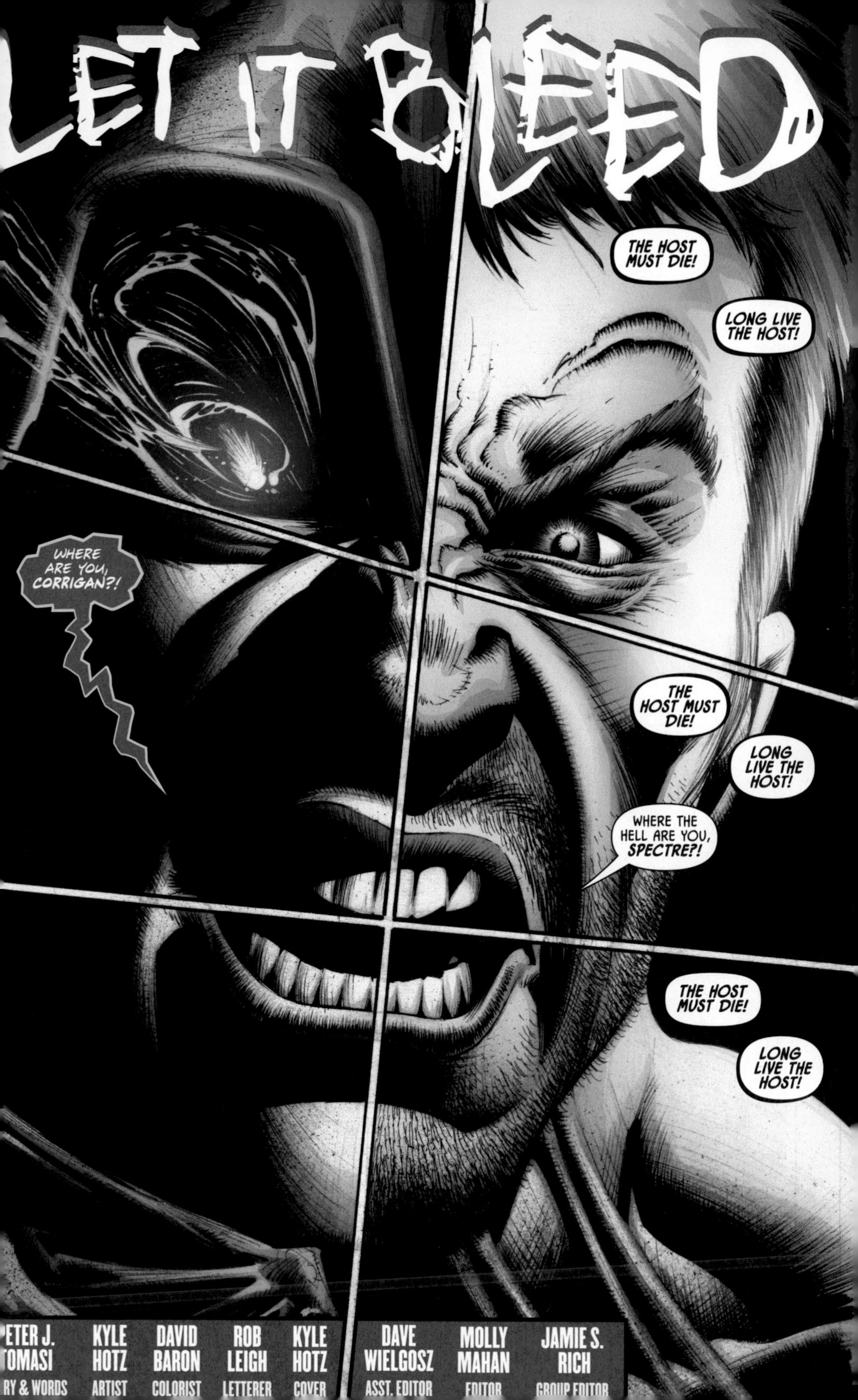
LET IT BLEED
THE HOST MUST DIE!
LONG LIVE THE HOST!
WHERE ARE YOU, CORRIGAN?!
THE HOST MUST DIE!
LONG LIVE THE HOST!
WHERE THE HELL ARE YOU, SPECTRE?!
THE HOST MUST DIE!
LONG LIVE THE HOST!
ETER J. TOMASI RY & WORDS
KYLE HOTZ ARTIST
DAVID BARON COLORIST
ROB LEIGH LETTERER
KYLE HOTZ COVER
DAVE WIELGOSZ ASST. EDITOR
MOLLY MAHAN EDITOR
JAMIE S. RICH GROUP EDITOR

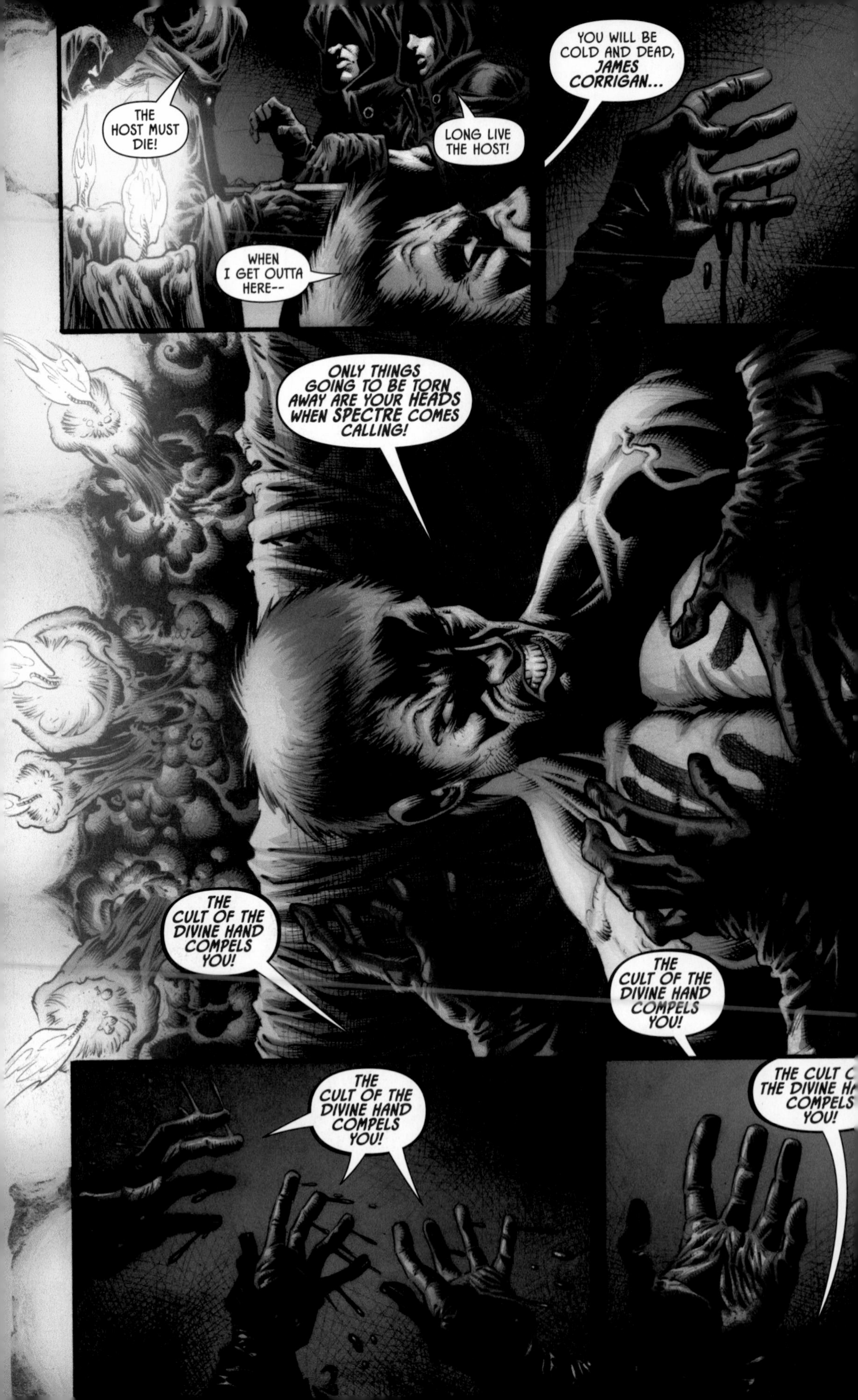
THE HOST MUST DIE!
LONG LIVE THE HOST!
WHEN I GET OUTTA HERE--
YOU WILL BE COLD AND DEAD, JAMES CORRIGAN...
ONLY THINGS GOING TO BE TORN AWAY ARE YOUR HEADS WHEN SPECTRE COMES CALLING!
THE CULT OF THE DIVINE HAND COMPELS YOU!
THE CULT OF THE DIVINE HAND COMPELS YOU!
THE CULT OF THE DIVINE HAND COMPELS YOU!
COMPELS YOU!

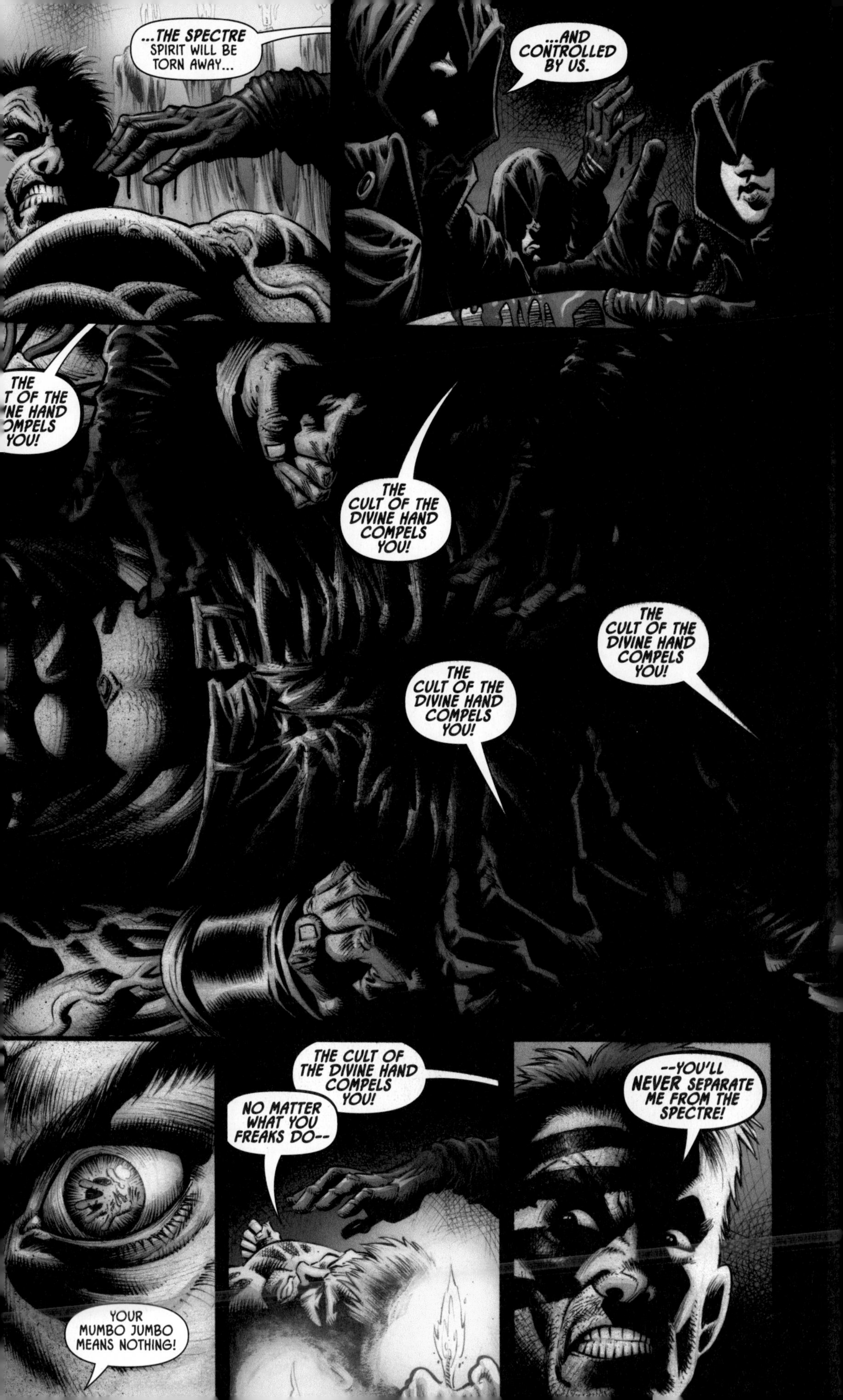
...THE SPECTRE SPIRIT WILL BE TORN AWAY...
...AND CONTROLLED BY US.
THE CULT OF THE DIVINE HAND COMPELS YOU!
THE CULT OF THE DIVINE HAND COMPELS YOU!
THE CULT OF THE DIVINE HAND COMPELS YOU!
THE CULT OF THE DIVINE HAND COMPELS YOU!
YOUR MUMBO JUMBO MEANS NOTHING!
THE CULT OF THE DIVINE HAND COMPELS YOU!
NO MATTER WHAT YOU FREAKS DO--
--YOU'LL NEVER SEPARATE ME FROM THE SPECTRE!

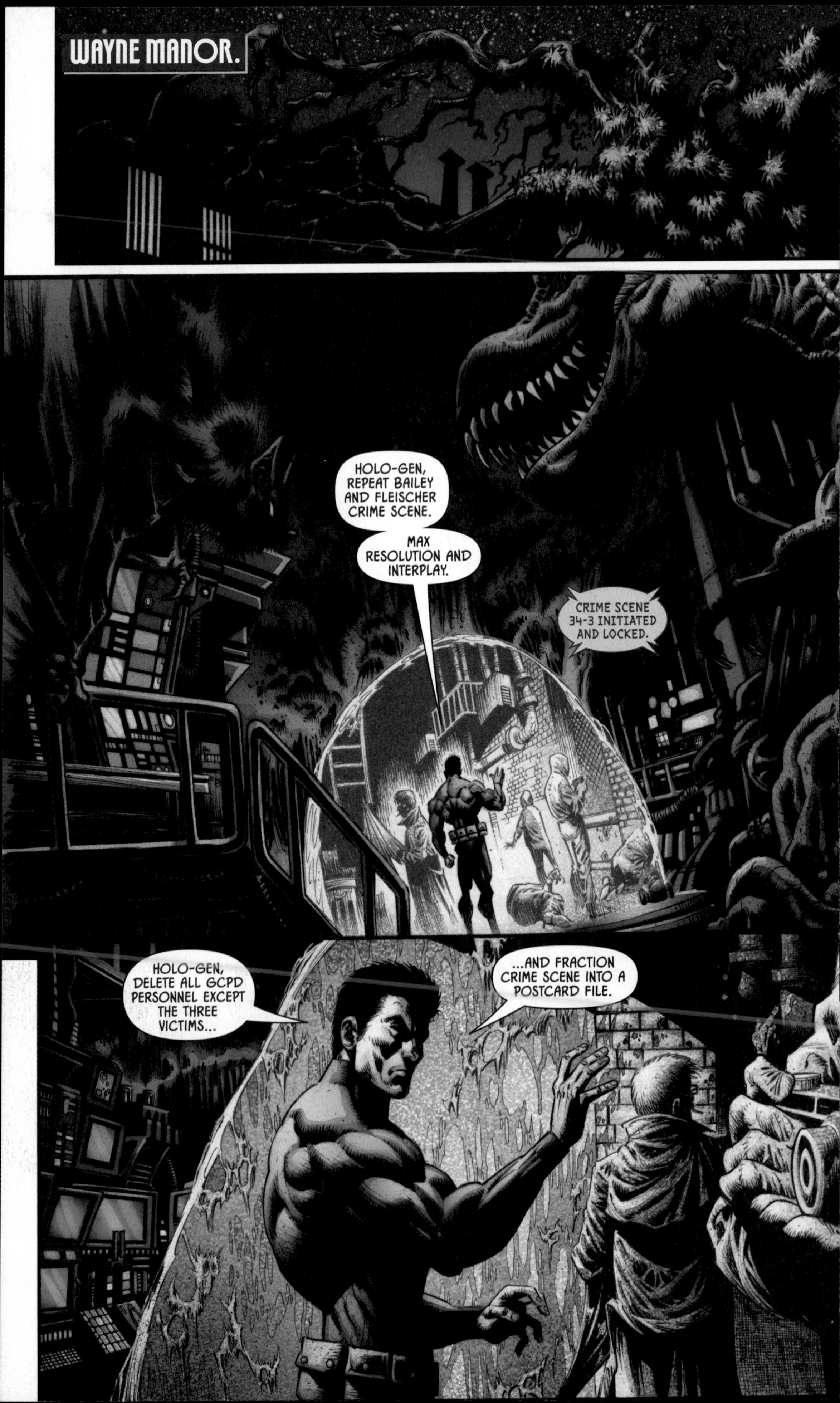
WAYNE MANOR.
HOLO-GEN, REPEAT BAILEY AND FLEISCHER CRIME SCENE.
MAX RESOLUTION AND INTERPLAY.
CRIME SCENE 34-3 INITIATED AND LOCKED.
HOLO-GEN, DELETE ALL GCPD PERSONNEL EXCEPT THE THREE VICTIMS...
...AND FRACTION CRIME SCENE INTO A POSTCARD FILE.

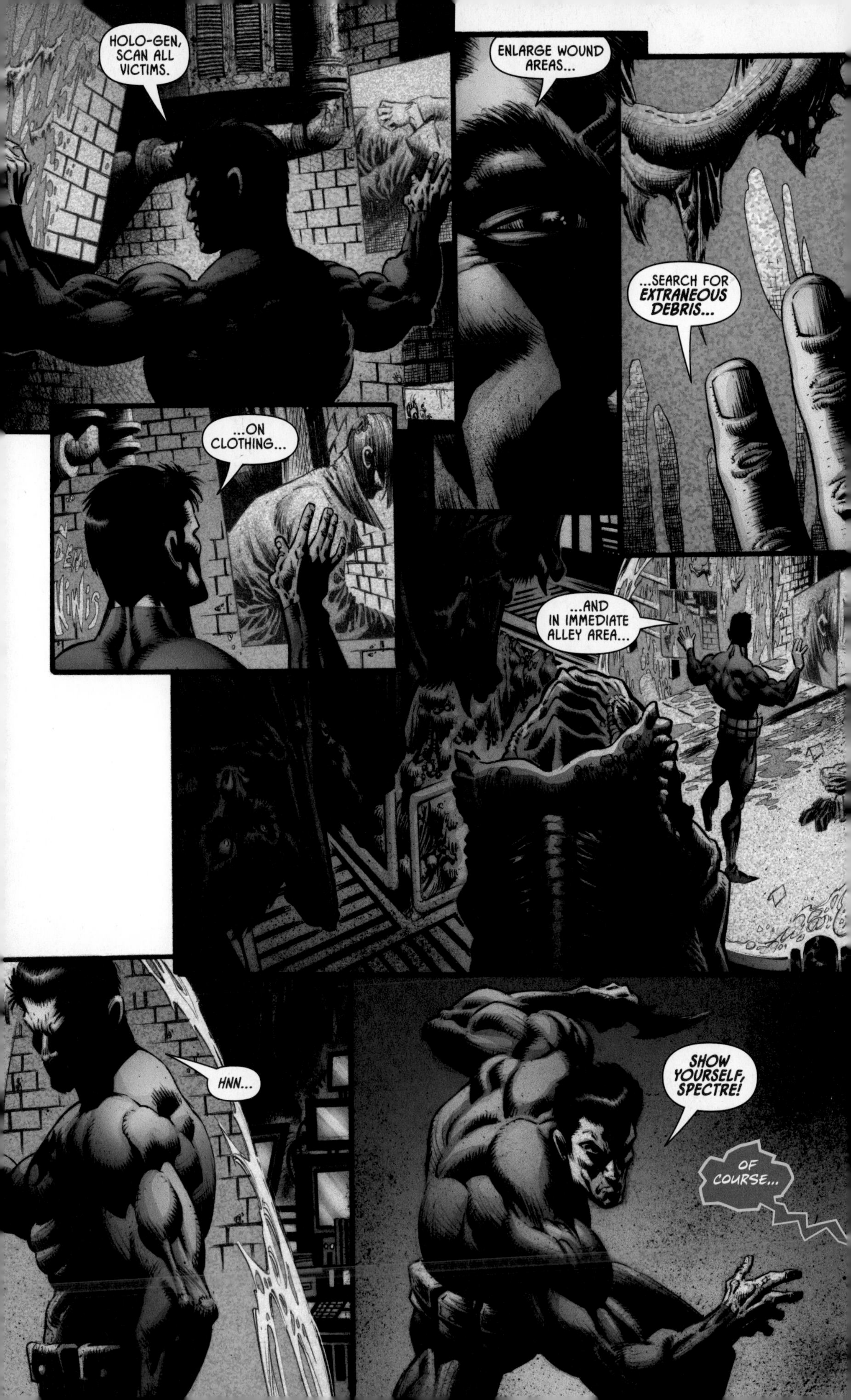
HOLO-GEN, SCAN ALL VICTIMS.
ENLARGE WOUND AREAS...
...SEARCH FOR EXTRANEOUS DEBRIS...
...ON CLOTHING...
...AND IN IMMEDIATE ALLEY AREA...
HNN...
SHOW YOURSELF, SPECTRE!
OF COURSE...

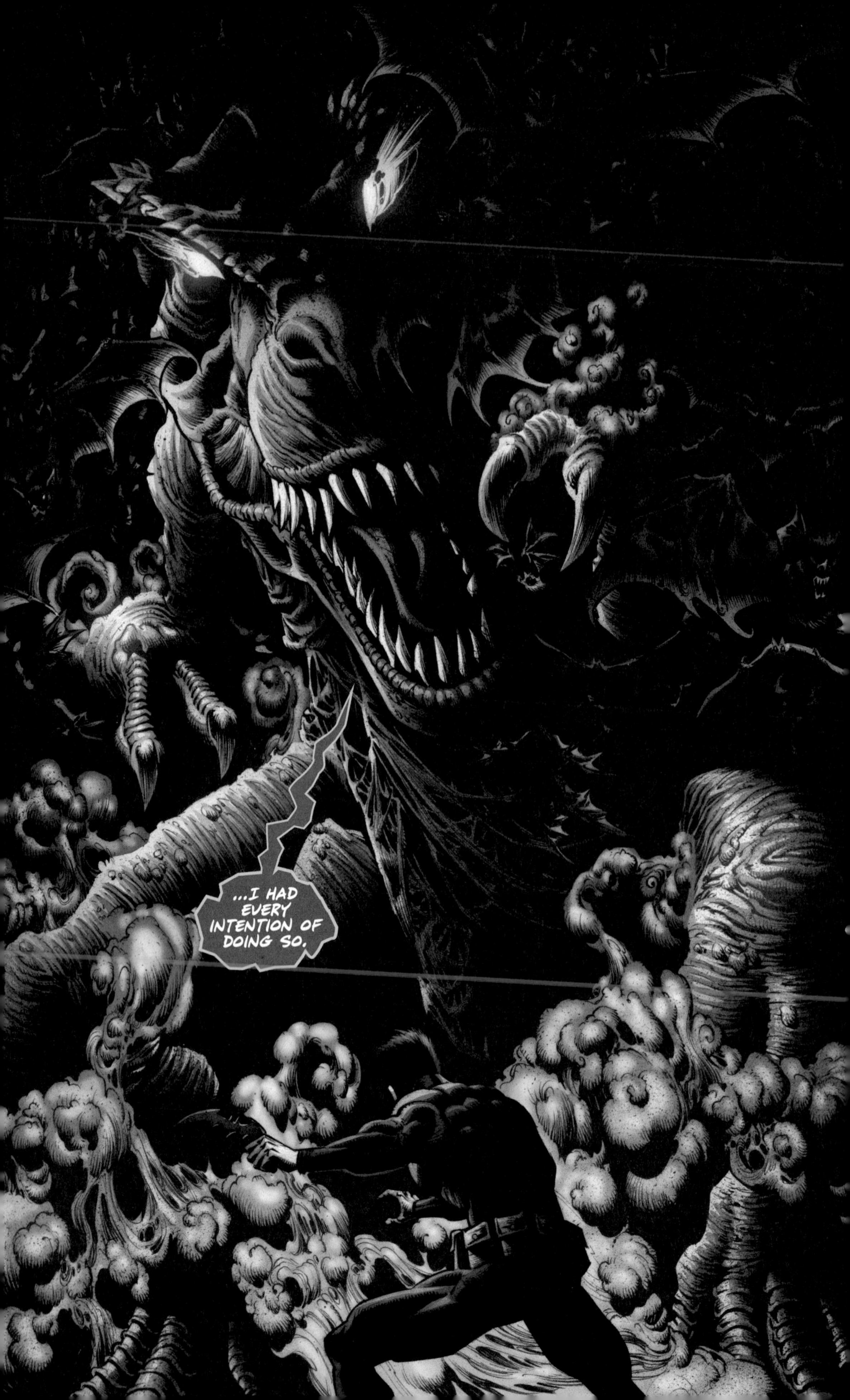
...I HAD EVERY INTENTION OF DOING SO.

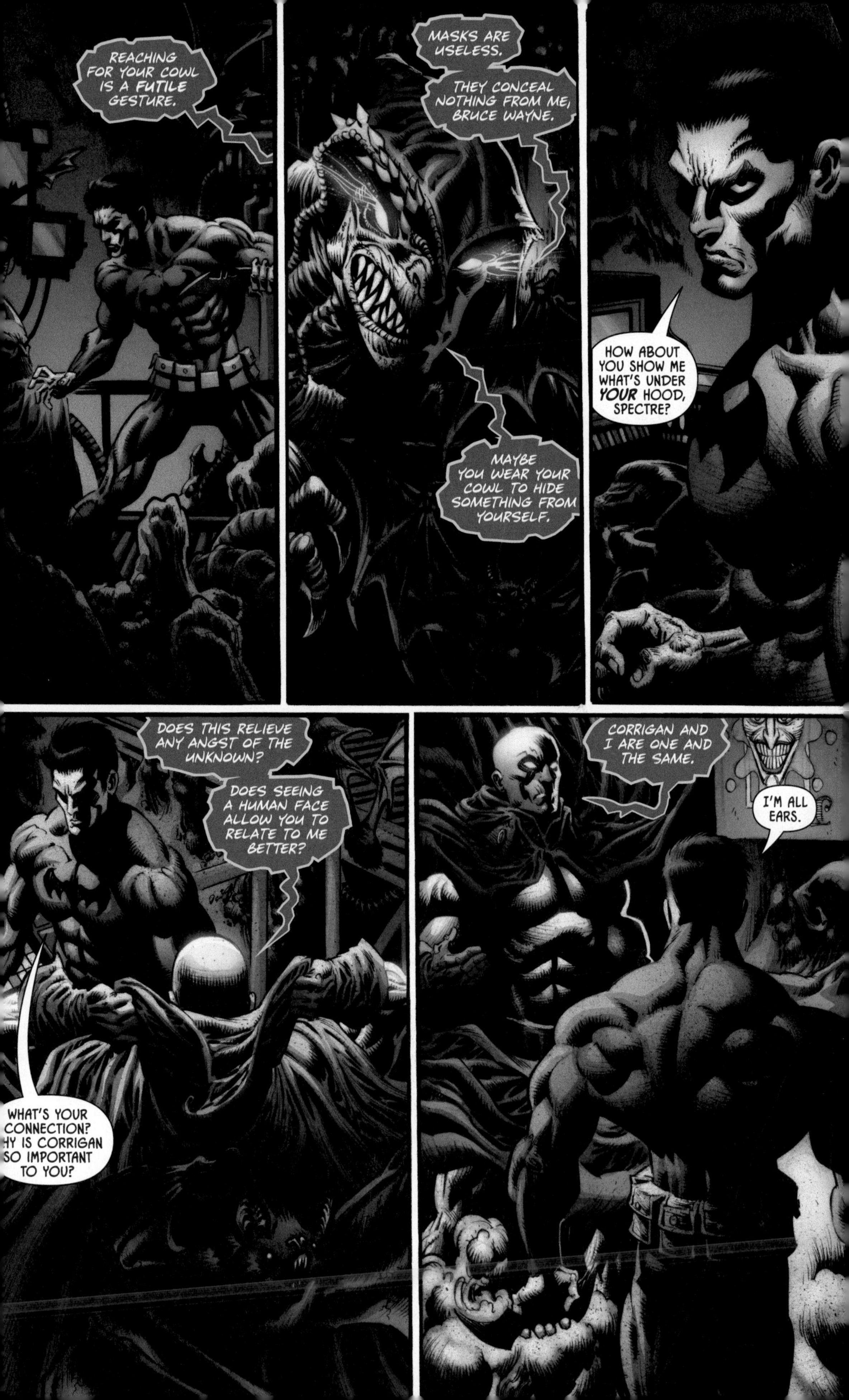
REACHING FOR YOUR COWL IS A FUTILE GESTURE.
MASKS ARE USELESS.
THEY CONCEAL NOTHING FROM ME, BRUCE WAYNE.
MAYBE YOU WEAR YOUR COWL TO HIDE SOMETHING FROM YOURSELF.
HOW ABOUT YOU SHOW ME WHAT'S UNDER YOUR HOOD, SPECTRE?
DOES THIS RELIEVE ANY ANGST OF THE UNKNOWN?
DOES SEEING A HUMAN FACE ALLOW YOU TO RELATE TO ME BETTER?
WHAT'S YOUR CONNECTION? HY IS CORRIGAN SO IMPORTANT TO YOU?
CORRIGAN AND I ARE ONE AND THE SAME.
I'M ALL EARS.

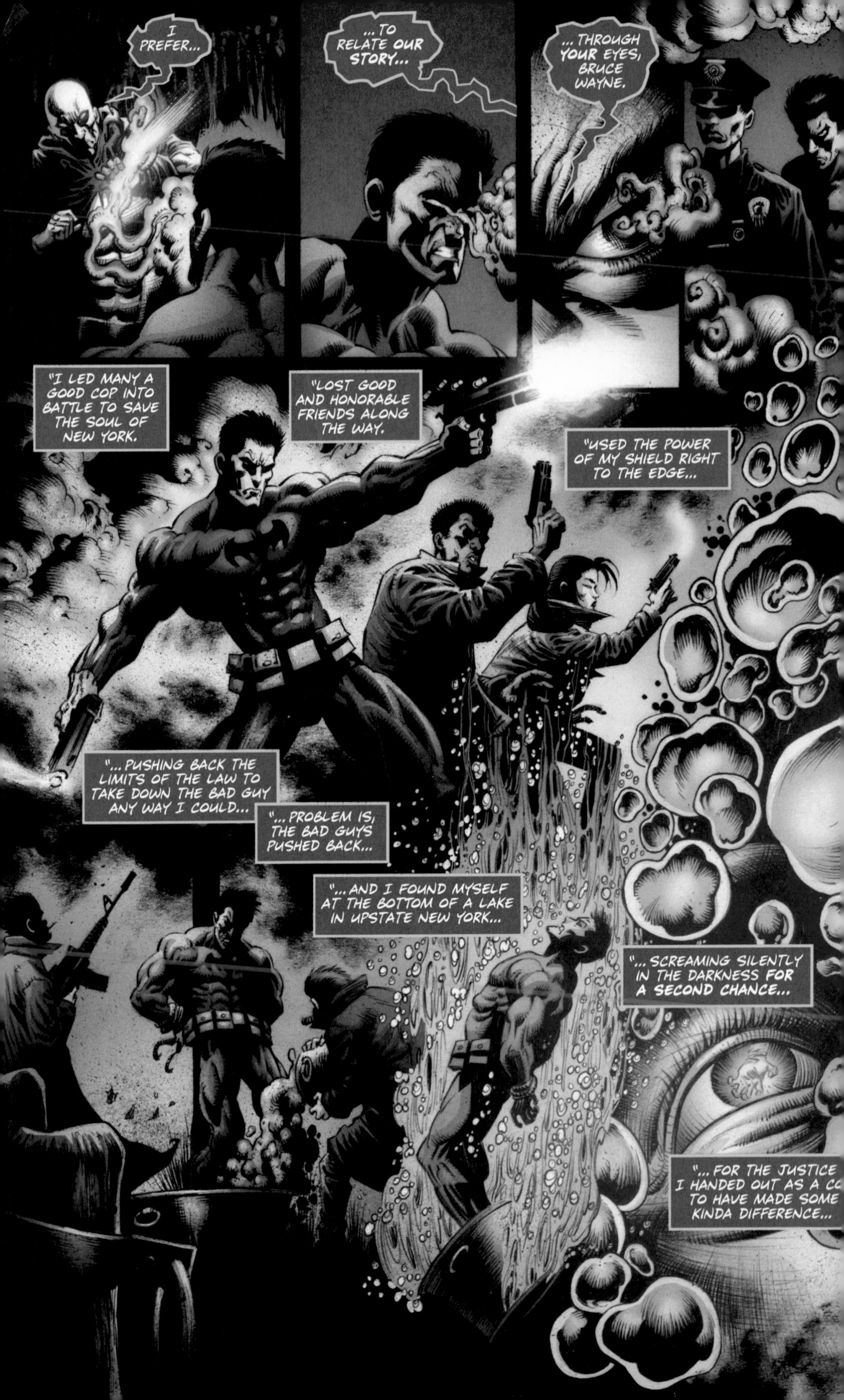
I PREFER...
...TO RELATE OUR STORY...
...THROUGH YOUR EYES, BRUCE WAYNE.
"I LED MANY A GOOD COP INTO BATTLE TO SAVE THE SOUL OF NEW YORK.
"LOST GOOD AND HONORABLE FRIENDS ALONG THE WAY.
"USED THE POWER OF MY SHIELD RIGHT TO THE EDGE...
"...PUSHING BACK THE LIMITS OF THE LAW TO TAKE DOWN THE BAD GUY ANY WAY I COULD...
"...PROBLEM IS, THE BAD GUYS PUSHED BACK...
"...AND I FOUND MYSELF AT THE BOTTOM OF A LAKE IN UPSTATE NEW YORK...
"...SCREAMING SILENTLY IN THE DARKNESS FOR A SECOND CHANCE...
"...FOR THE JUSTICE I HANDED OUT AS A CO
TO HAVE MADE SOME KINDA DIFFERENCE...

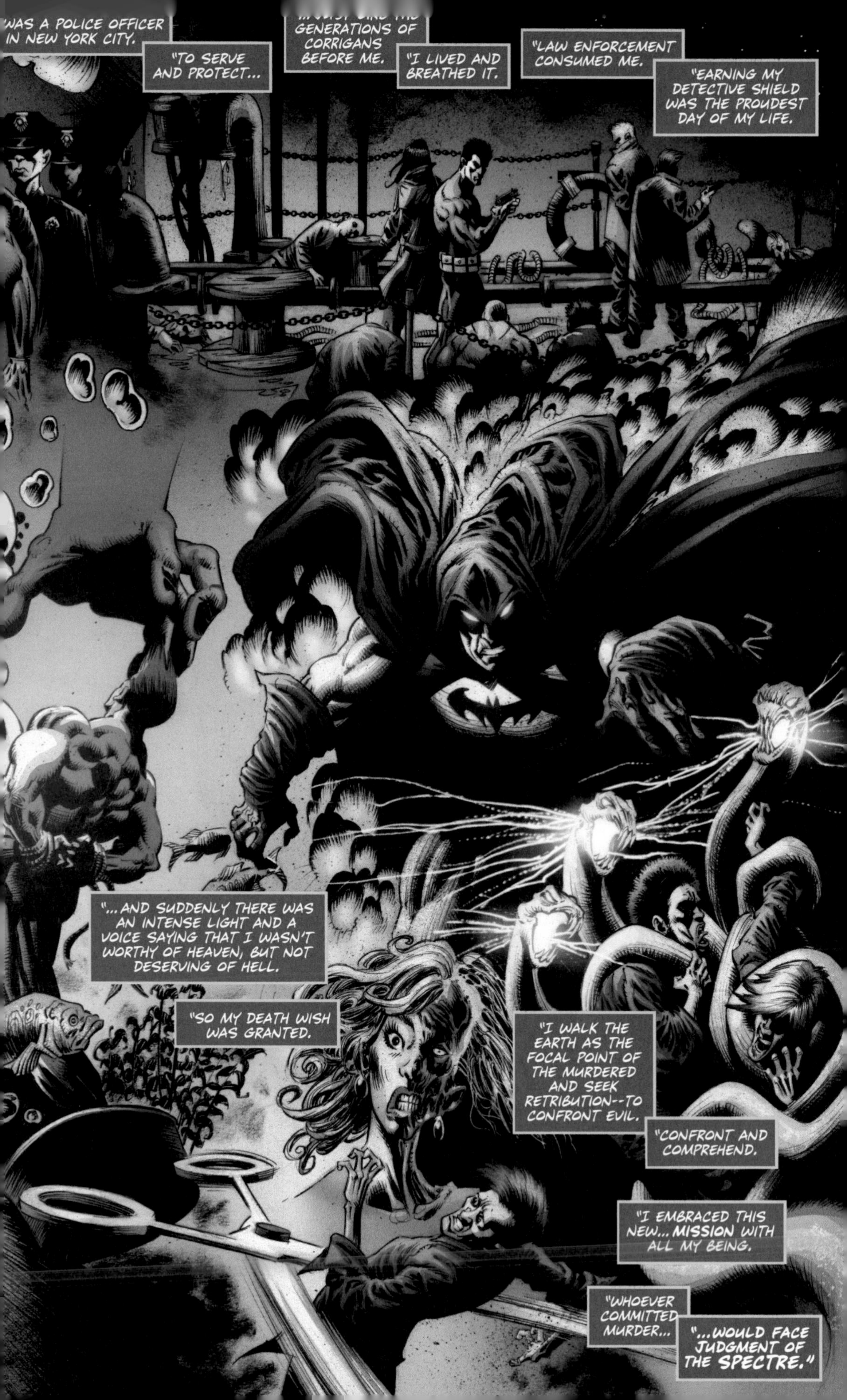

WAS A POLICE OFFICER IN NEW YORK CITY.
"TO SERVE AND PROTECT...
GENERATIONS OF CORRIGANS BEFORE ME.
"I LIVED AND BREATHED IT.
"LAW ENFORCEMENT CONSUMED ME.
"EARNING MY DETECTIVE SHIELD WAS THE PROUDEST DAY OF MY LIFE.
"...AND SUDDENLY THERE WAS AN INTENSE LIGHT AND A VOICE SAYING THAT I WASN'T WORTHY OF HEAVEN, BUT NOT DESERVING OF HELL.
"SO MY DEATH WISH WAS GRANTED.
"I WALK THE EARTH AS THE FOCAL POINT OF THE MURDERED AND SEEK RETRIBUTION--TO CONFRONT EVIL.
"CONFRONT AND COMPREHEND.
"I EMBRACED THIS NEW... MISSION WITH ALL MY BEING.
"WHOEVER COMMITTED MURDER...
"...WOULD FACE JUDGMENT OF THE SPECTRE."

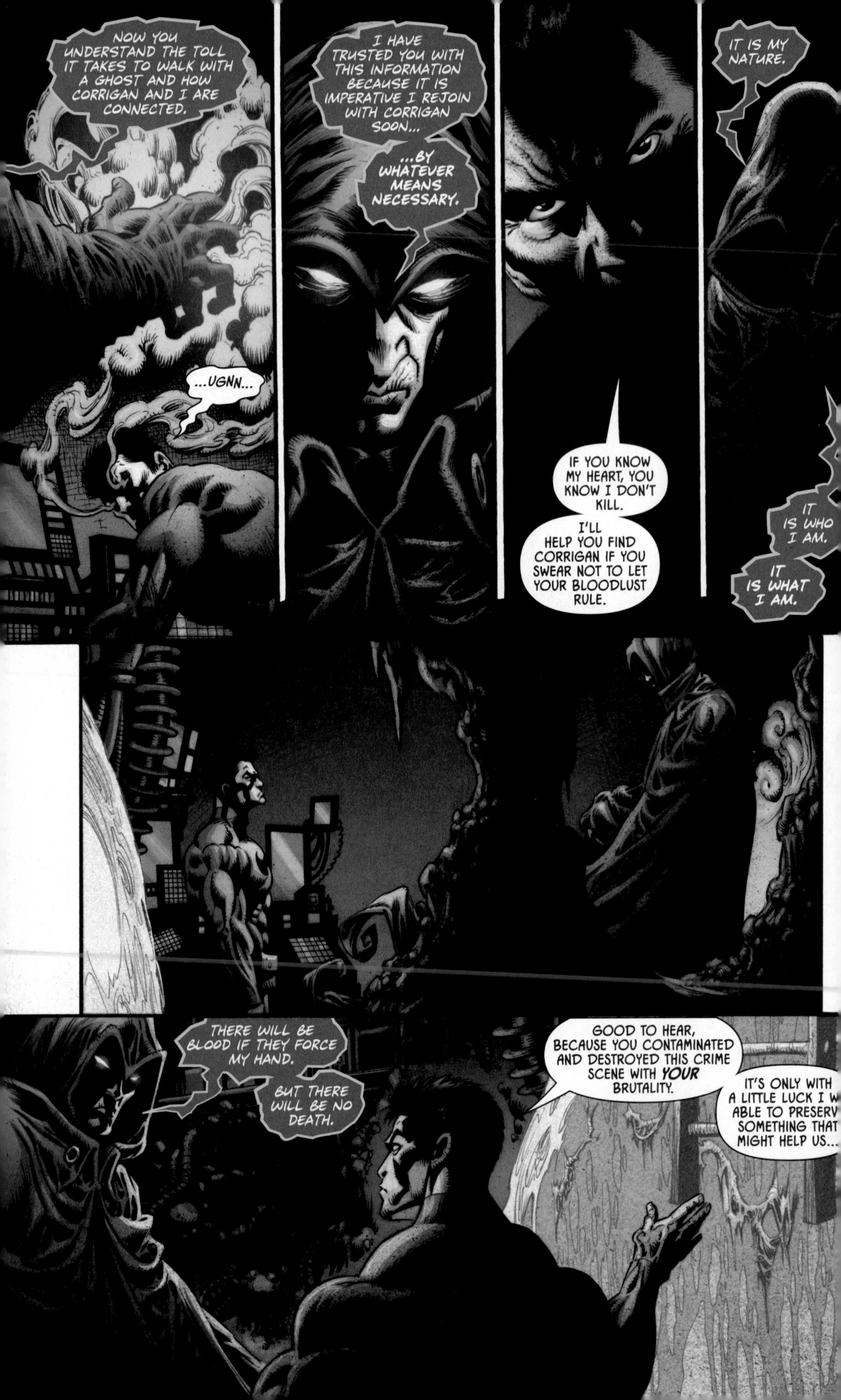
NOW YOU UNDERSTAND THE TOLL IT TAKES TO WALK WITH A GHOST AND HOW CORRIGAN AND I ARE CONNECTED.
...UGNN...
I HAVE TRUSTED YOU WITH THIS INFORMATION BECAUSE IT IS IMPERATIVE I REJOIN WITH CORRIGAN SOON...
...BY WHATEVER MEANS NECESSARY.
IF YOU KNOW MY HEART, YOU KNOW I DON'T KILL.
I'LL HELP YOU FIND CORRIGAN IF YOU SWEAR NOT TO LET YOUR BLOODLUST RULE.
IT IS MY NATURE.
IT IS WHO I AM.
IT IS WHAT I AM.
THERE WILL BE BLOOD IF THEY FORCE MY HAND.
BUT THERE WILL BE NO DEATH.
GOOD TO HEAR, BECAUSE YOU CONTAMINATED AND DESTROYED THIS CRIME SCENE WITH YOUR BRUTALITY.
IT'S ONLY WITH A LITTLE LUCK I W ABLE TO PRESERV SOMETHING THAT MIGHT HELP US...

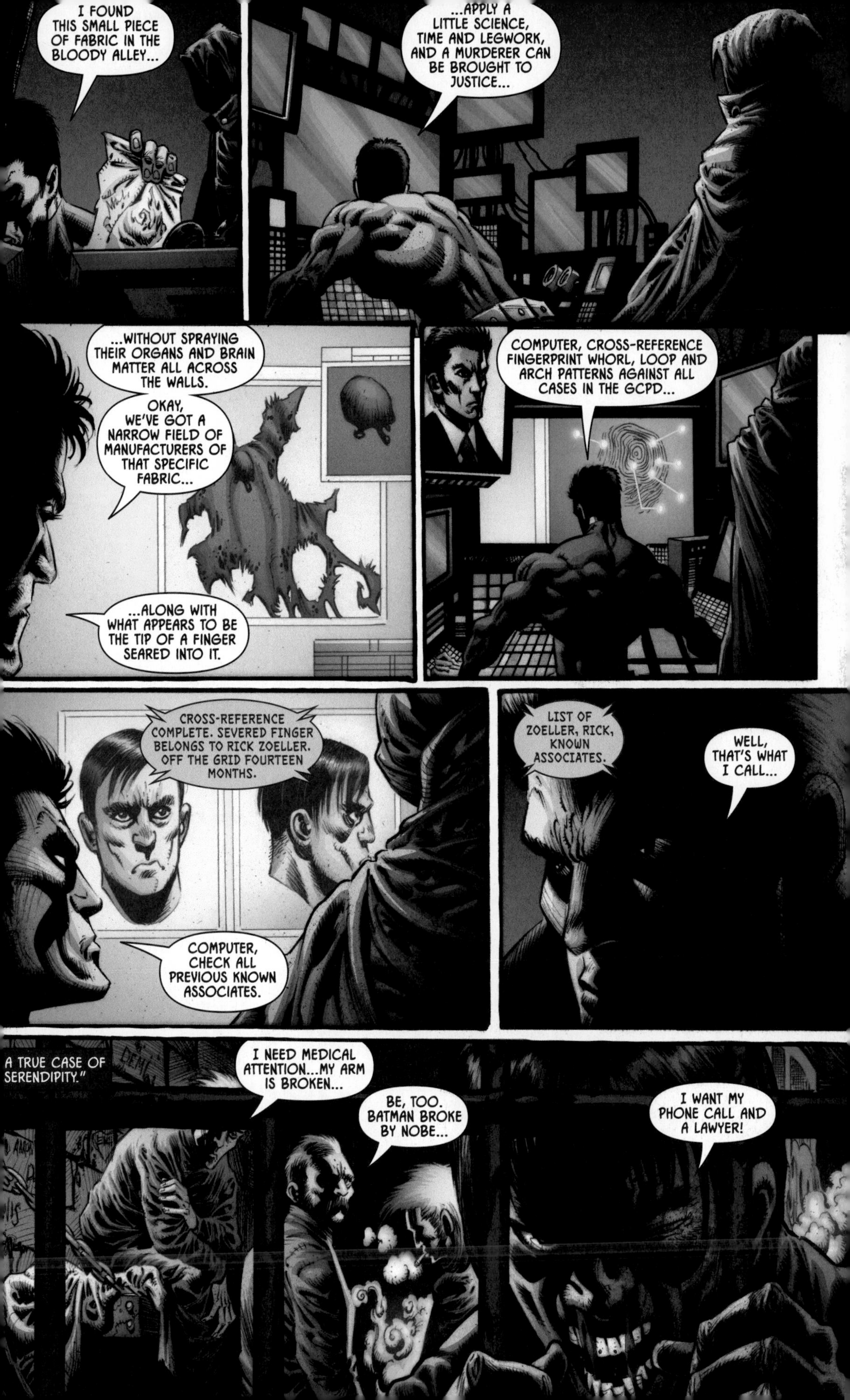
I FOUND THIS SMALL PIECE OF FABRIC IN THE BLOODY ALLEY...
...APPLY A LITTLE SCIENCE, TIME AND LEGWORK, AND A MURDERER CAN BE BROUGHT TO JUSTICE...
...WITHOUT SPRAYING THEIR ORGANS AND BRAIN MATTER ALL ACROSS THE WALLS.
OKAY, WE'VE GOT A NARROW FIELD OF MANUFACTURERS OF THAT SPECIFIC FABRIC...
...ALONG WITH WHAT APPEARS TO BE THE TIP OF A FINGER SEARED INTO IT.
COMPUTER, CROSS-REFERENCE FINGERPRINT WHORL, LOOP AND ARCH PATTERNS AGAINST ALL CASES IN THE GCPD...
CROSS-REFERENCE COMPLETE. SEVERED FINGER BELONGS TO RICK ZOELLER. OFF THE GRID FOURTEEN MONTHS.
COMPUTER, CHECK ALL PREVIOUS KNOWN ASSOCIATES.
LIST OF ZOELLER, RICK, KNOWN ASSOCIATES.
WELL, THAT'S WHAT I CALL...
A TRUE CASE OF SERENDIPITY."
I NEED MEDICAL ATTENTION...MY ARM IS BROKEN...
BE, TOO. BATMAN BROKE BY NOBE...
I WANT MY PHONE CALL AND A LAWYER!

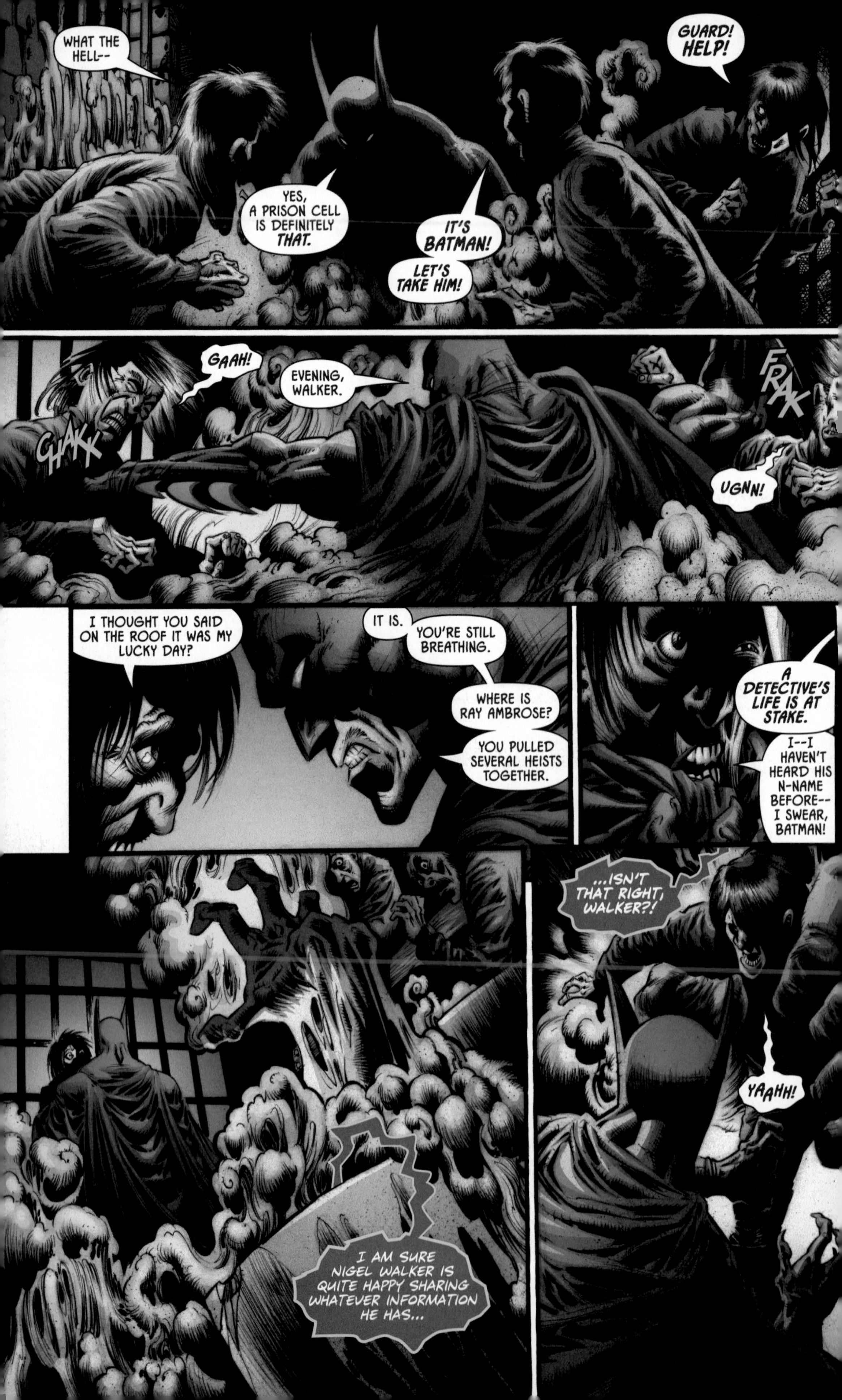

WHAT THE HELL--
GUARD! HELP!
YES, A PRISON CELL IS DEFINITELY THAT.
IT'S BATMAN!
LET'S TAKE HIM!
GAAH!
EVENING, WALKER.
CHAKK
FRAK
UGNN!
I THOUGHT YOU SAID ON THE ROOF IT WAS MY LUCKY DAY?
IT IS.
YOU'RE STILL BREATHING.
WHERE IS RAY AMBROSE?
YOU PULLED SEVERAL HEISTS TOGETHER.
A DETECTIVE'S LIFE IS AT STAKE.
I--I HAVEN'T HEARD HIS N-NAME BEFORE-- I SWEAR, BATMAN!
I AM SURE NIGEL WALKER IS QUITE HAPPY SHARING WHATEVER INFORMATION HE HAS...
...ISN'T THAT RIGHT, WALKER?!
YAAHH!

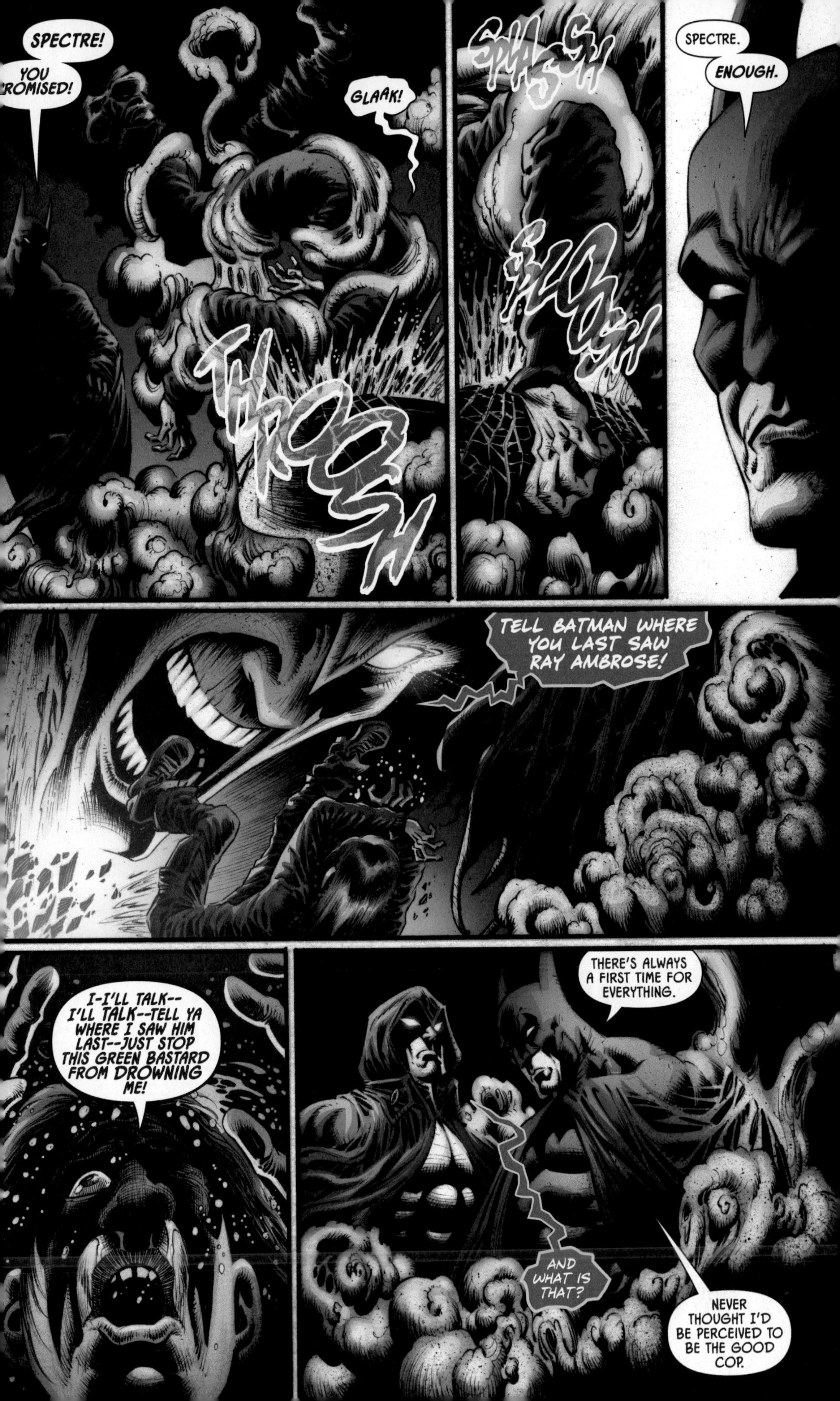
SPECTRE!
YOU
ROMISED!
GLAAK!
THROOOSH
SPLASSH
SPLOOSH
SPECTRE.
ENOUGH.
TELL BATMAN WHERE YOU LAST SAW RAY AMBROSE!
I-I'LL TALK--I'LL TALK--TELL YA WHERE I SAW HIM LAST--JUST STOP THIS GREEN BASTARD FROM DROWNING ME!
THERE'S ALWAYS A FIRST TIME FOR EVERYTHING.
AND WHAT IS THAT?
NEVER THOUGHT I'D BE PERCEIVED TO BE THE GOOD COP.

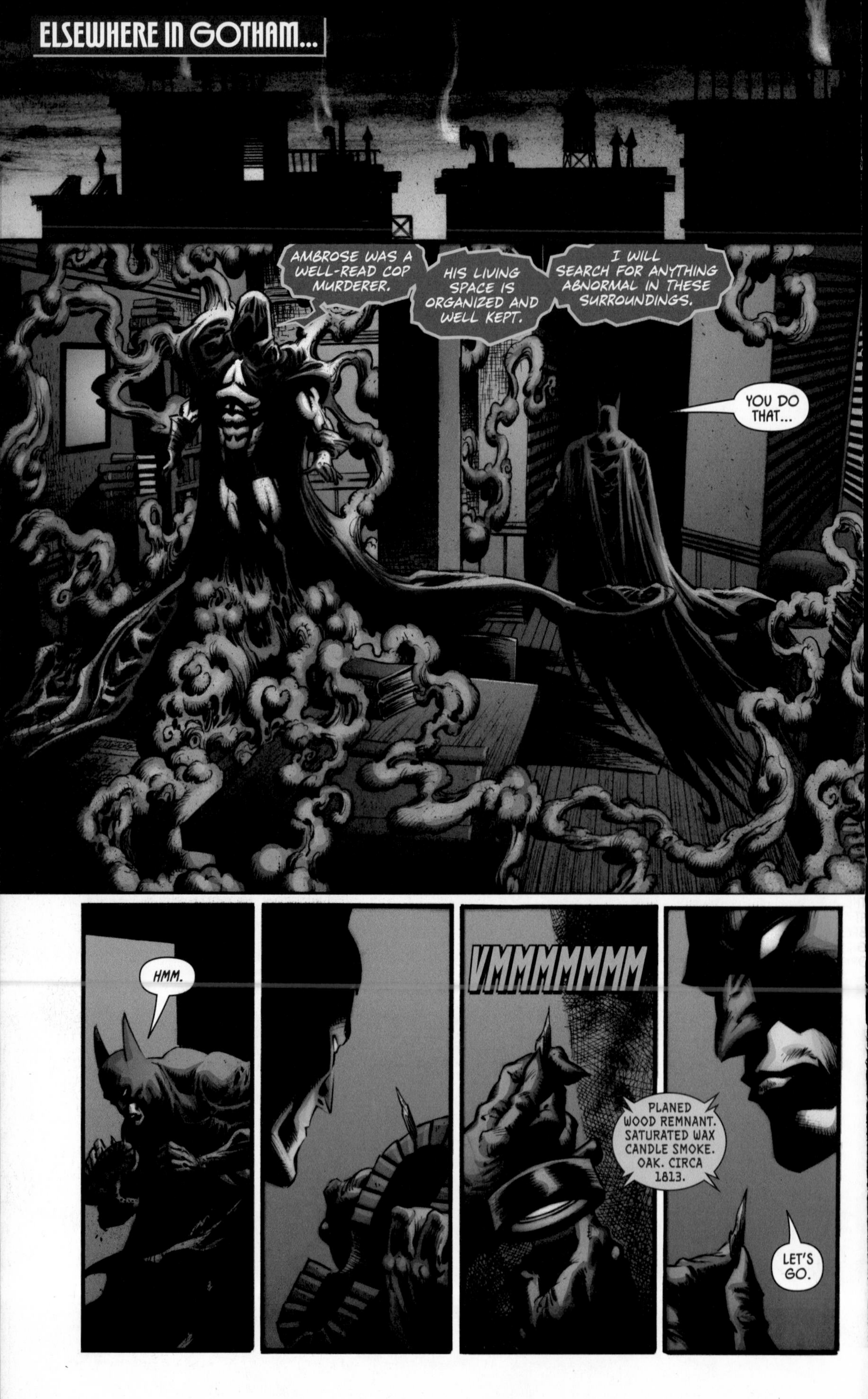

ELSEWHERE IN GOTHAM...
AMBROSE WAS A WELL-READ COP MURDERER.
HIS LIVING SPACE IS ORGANIZED AND WELL KEPT.
I WILL SEARCH FOR ANYTHING ABNORMAL IN THESE SURROUNDINGS.
YOU DO THAT...
HMM.
VMMMMMMM
PLANED WOOD REMNANT. SATURATED WAX CANDLE SMOKE. OAK. CIRCA 1813.
LET'S GO.

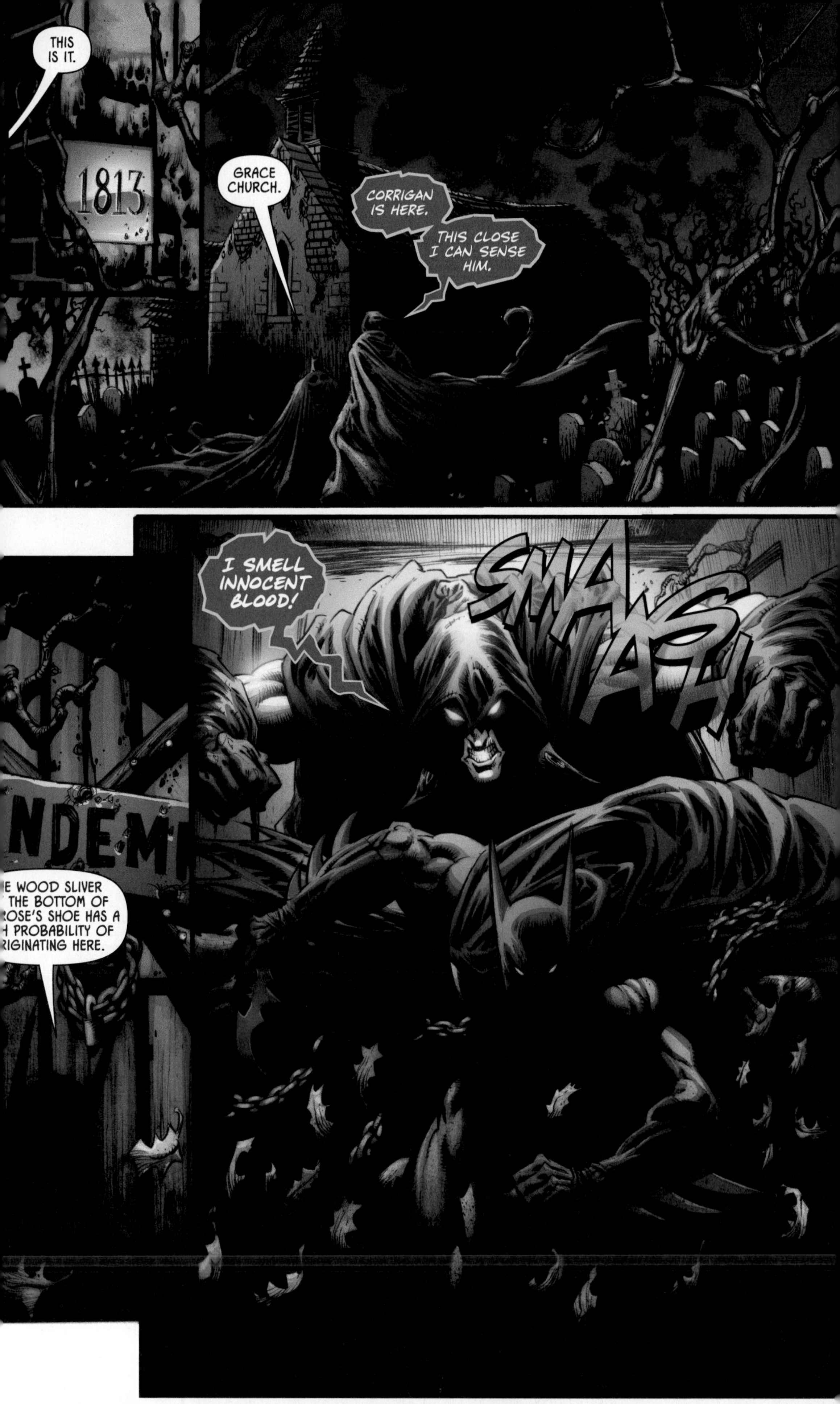
THIS IS IT.
1813
GRACE CHURCH.
CORRIGAN IS HERE.
THIS CLOSE I CAN SENSE HIM.
I SMELL INNOCENT BLOOD!
SMASH
NDEM
E WOOD SLIVER THE BOTTOM OF ROSE'S SHOE HAS A H PROBABILITY OF RIGINATING HERE.

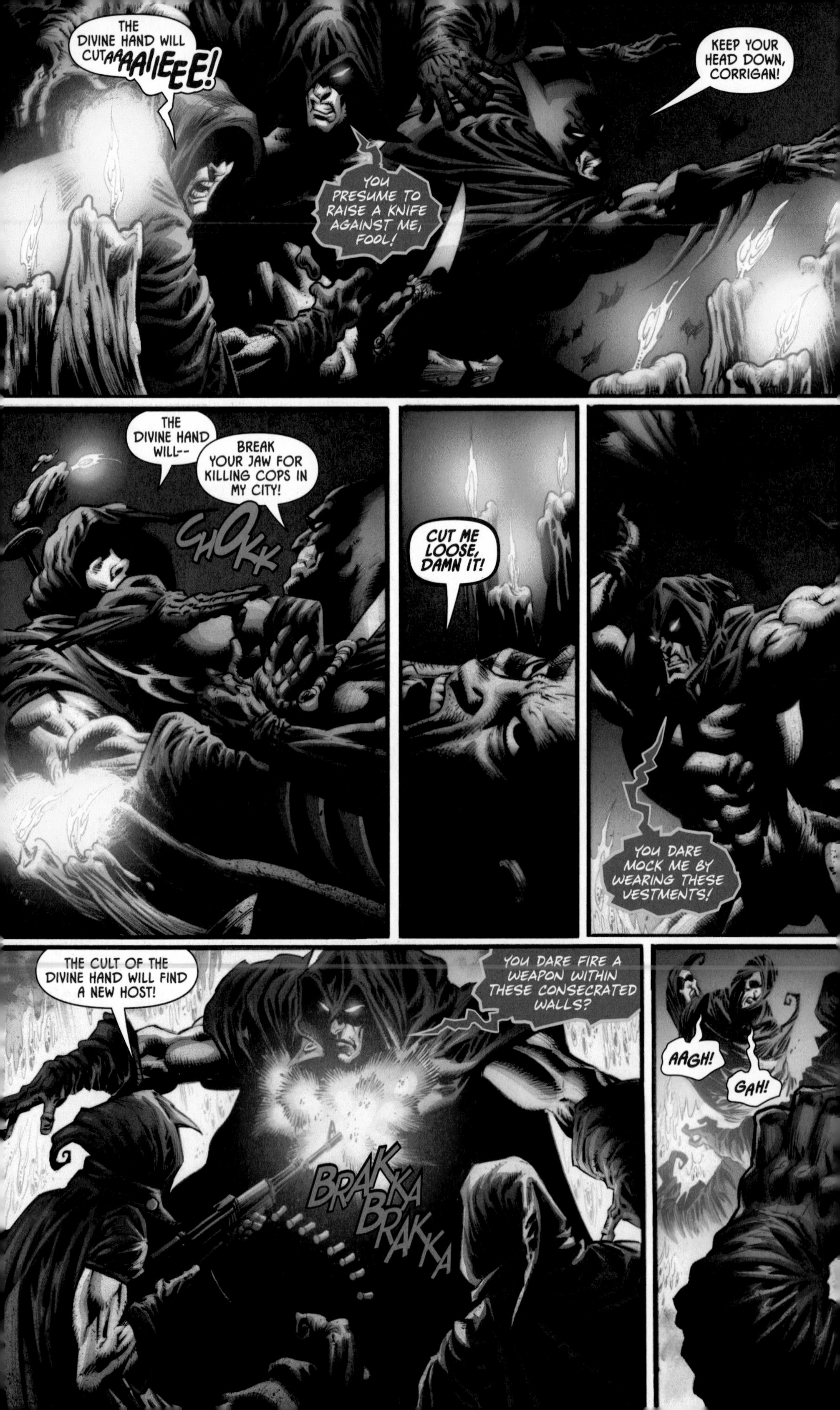
THE DIVINE HAND WILL CUTAAAAIIEEE!
YOU PRESUME TO RAISE A KNIFE AGAINST ME, FOOL!
KEEP YOUR HEAD DOWN, CORRIGAN!
THE DIVINE HAND WILL--
BREAK YOUR JAW FOR KILLING COPS IN MY CITY!
CHOKK
CUT ME LOOSE, DAMN IT!
YOU DARE MOCK ME BY WEARING THESE VESTMENTS!
THE CULT OF THE DIVINE HAND WILL FIND A NEW HOST!
YOU DARE FIRE A WEAPON WITHIN THESE CONSECRATED WALLS?
BRAKKA BRAKKA
AAGH!
GAH!

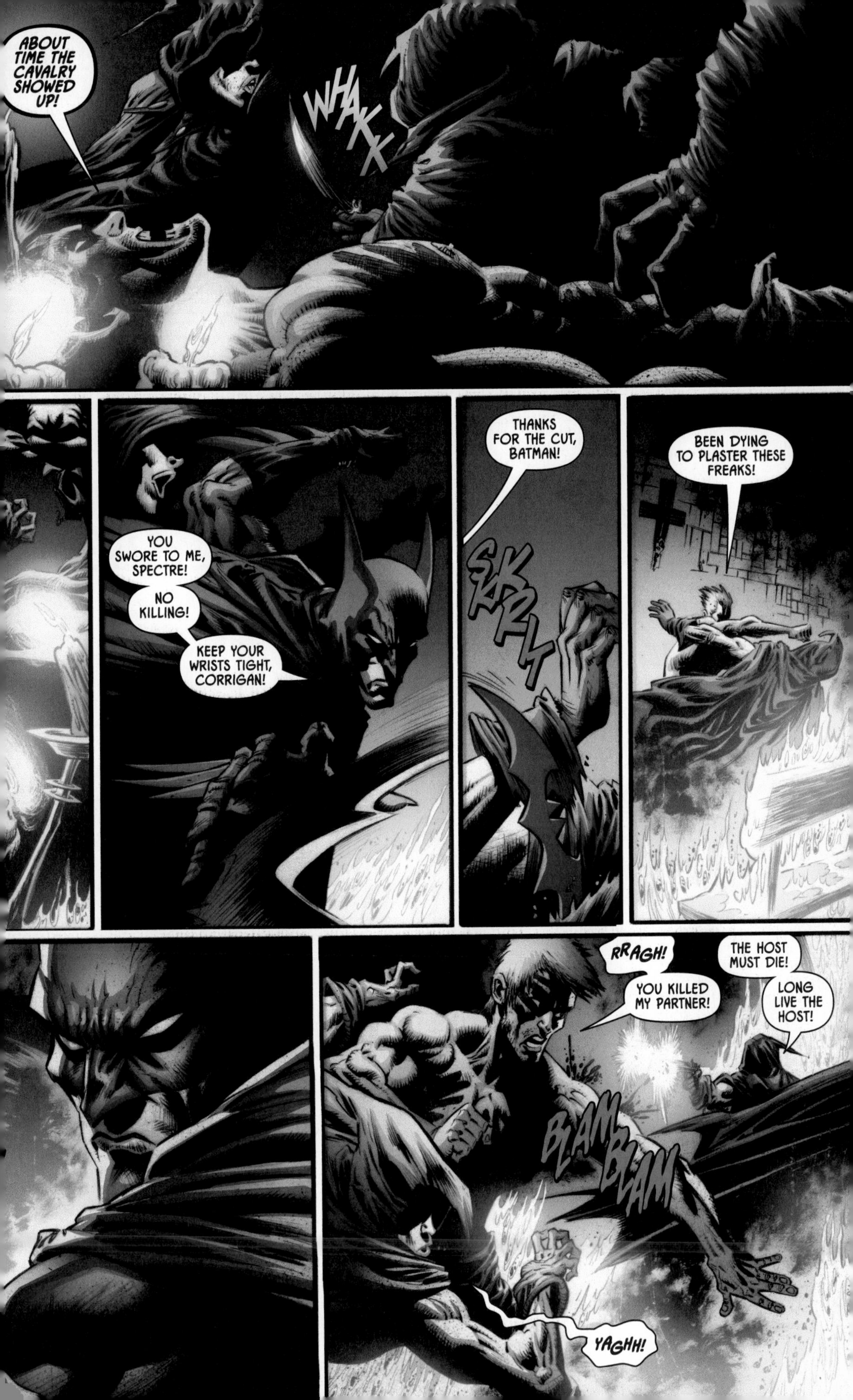
ABOUT TIME THE CAVALRY SHOWED UP!
WHAKK
YOU SWORE TO ME, SPECTRE!
NO KILLING!
KEEP YOUR WRISTS TIGHT, CORRIGAN!
THANKS FOR THE CUT, BATMAN!
SKRKK
BEEN DYING TO PLASTER THESE FREAKS!
RRAGH!
YOU KILLED MY PARTNER!
THE HOST MUST DIE!
LONG LIVE THE HOST!
BLAM BLAM
YAGHH!

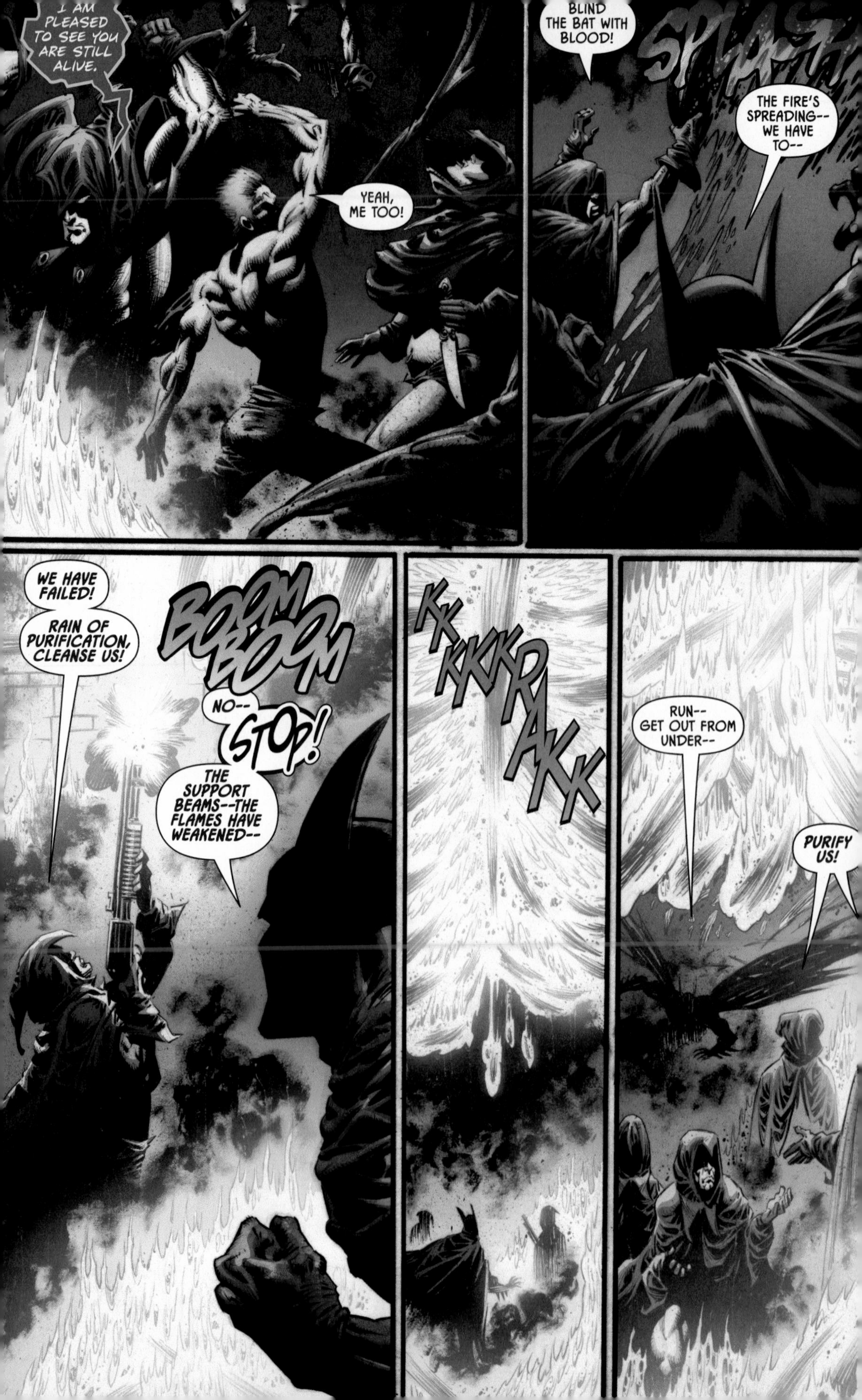
I AM PLEASED TO SEE YOU ARE STILL ALIVE.
YEAH, ME TOO!
BLIND THE BAT WITH BLOOD!
SPLASH
THE FIRE'S SPREADING-- WE HAVE TO--
WE HAVE FAILED!
RAIN OF PURIFICATION, CLEANSE US!
BOOM BOOM
NO--
STOP!
THE SUPPORT BEAMS--THE FLAMES HAVE WEAKENED--
KKKKKRAKK
RUN-- GET OUT FROM UNDER--
PURIFY US!

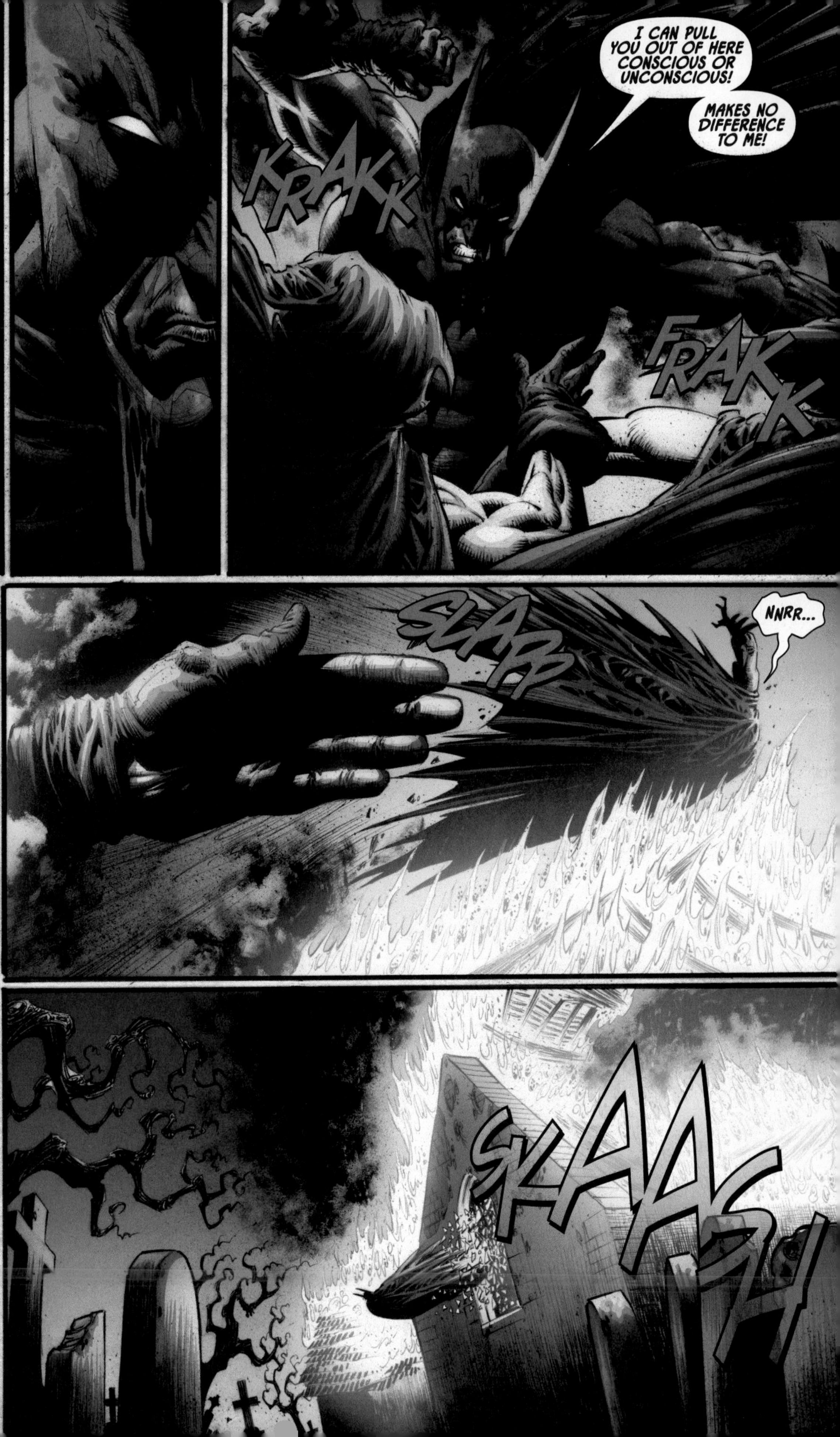
KRAKK
I CAN PULL YOU OUT OF HERE CONSCIOUS OR UNCONSCIOUS!
MAKES NO DIFFERENCE TO ME!
FRAKK
SLAPP
NNRR...
SKAAASHH

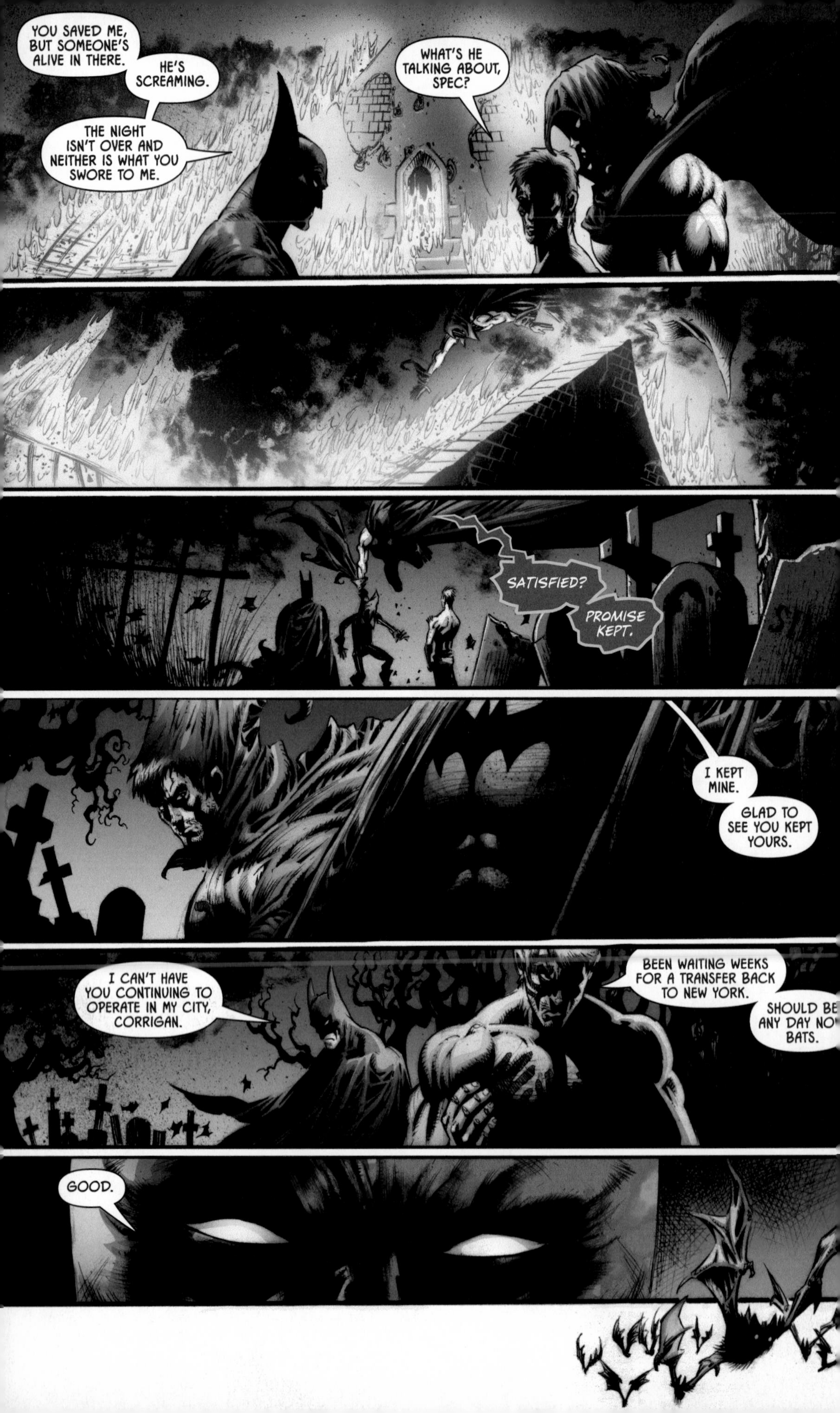
YOU SAVED ME, BUT SOMEONE'S ALIVE IN THERE.
HE'S SCREAMING.
THE NIGHT ISN'T OVER AND NEITHER IS WHAT YOU SWORE TO ME.
WHAT'S HE TALKING ABOUT, SPEC?
SATISFIED?
PROMISE KEPT.
I KEPT MINE.
GLAD TO SEE YOU KEPT YOURS.
I CAN'T HAVE YOU CONTINUING TO OPERATE IN MY CITY, CORRIGAN.
BEEN WAITING WEEKS FOR A TRANSFER BACK TO NEW YORK.
GOOD.

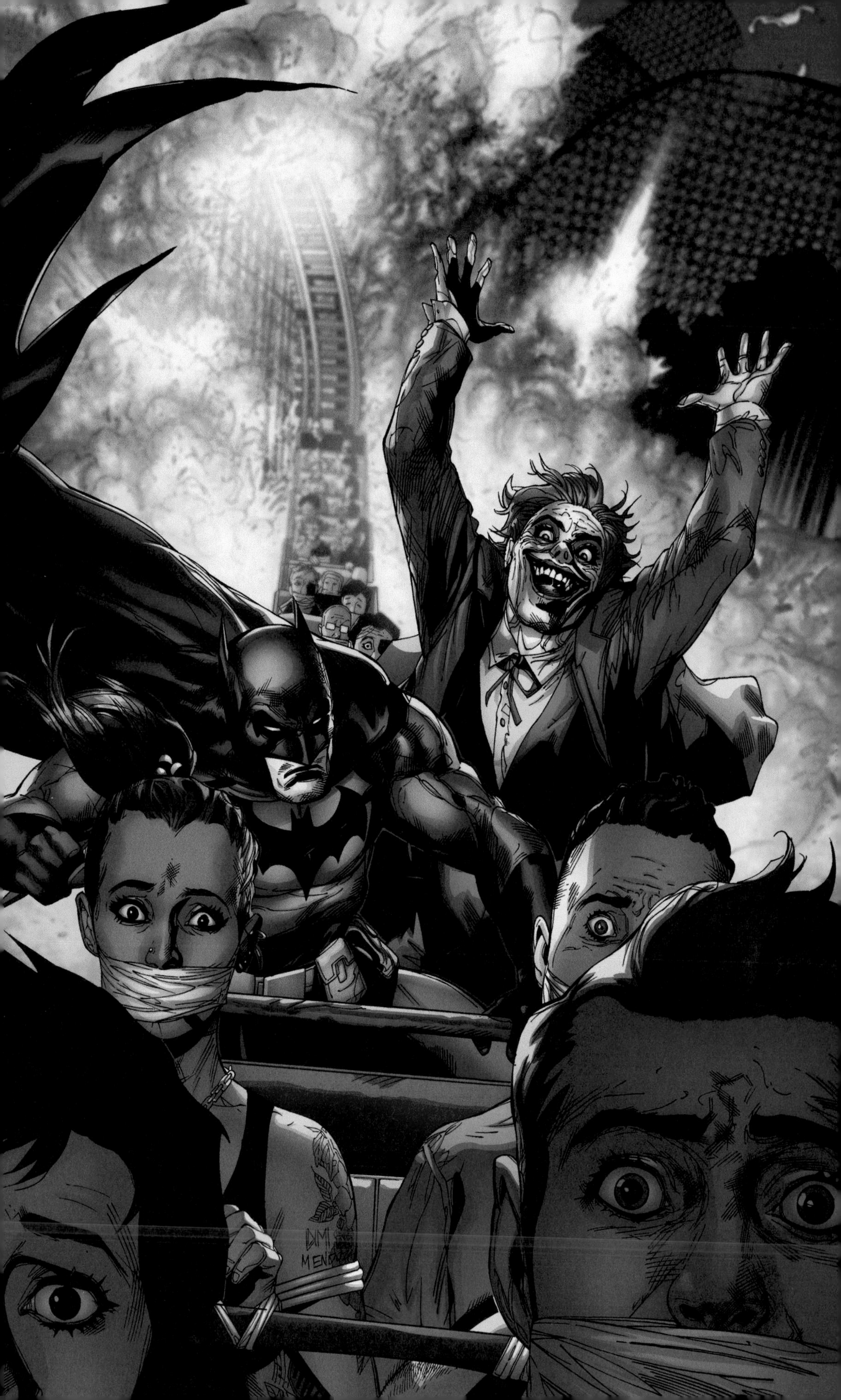

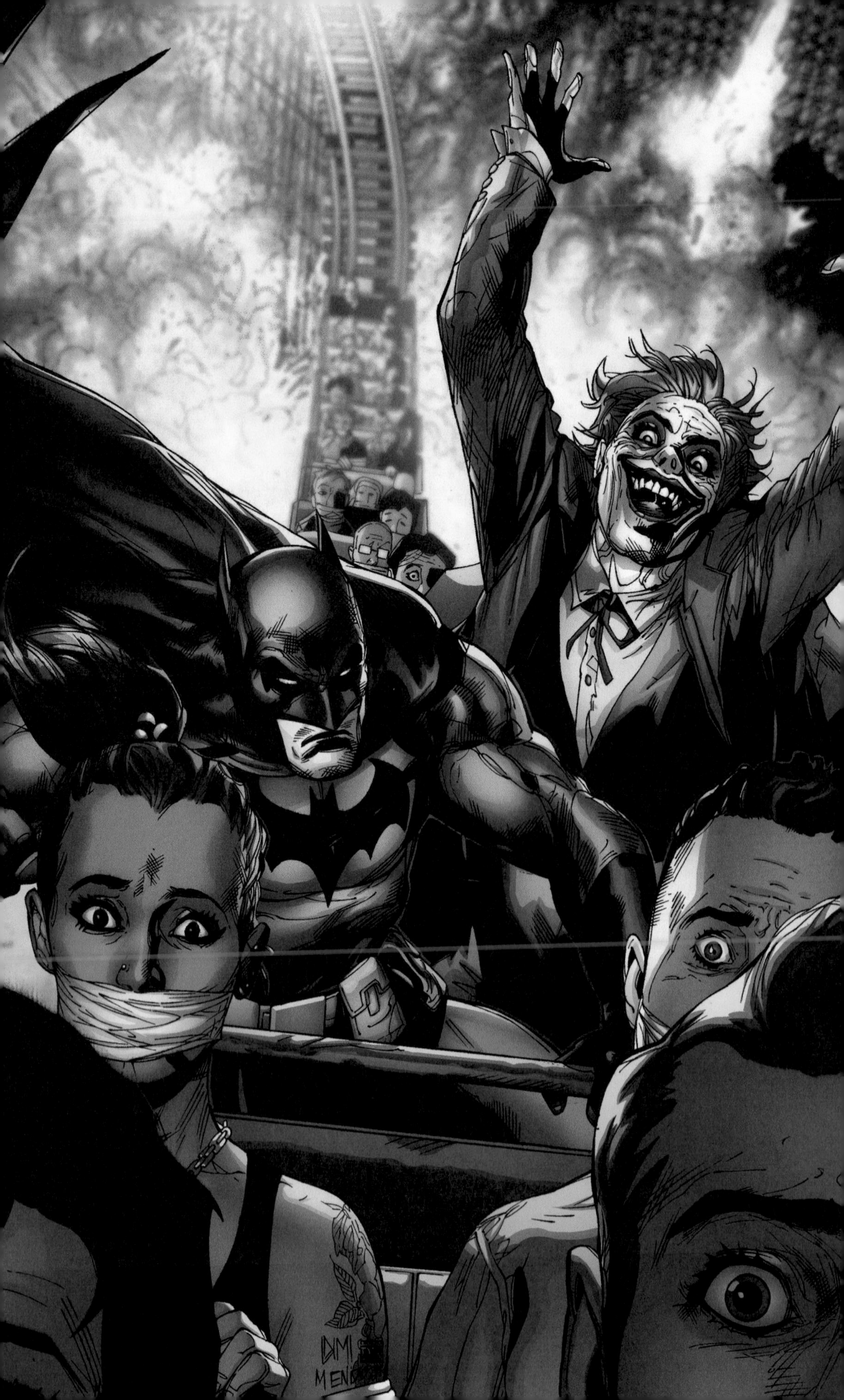

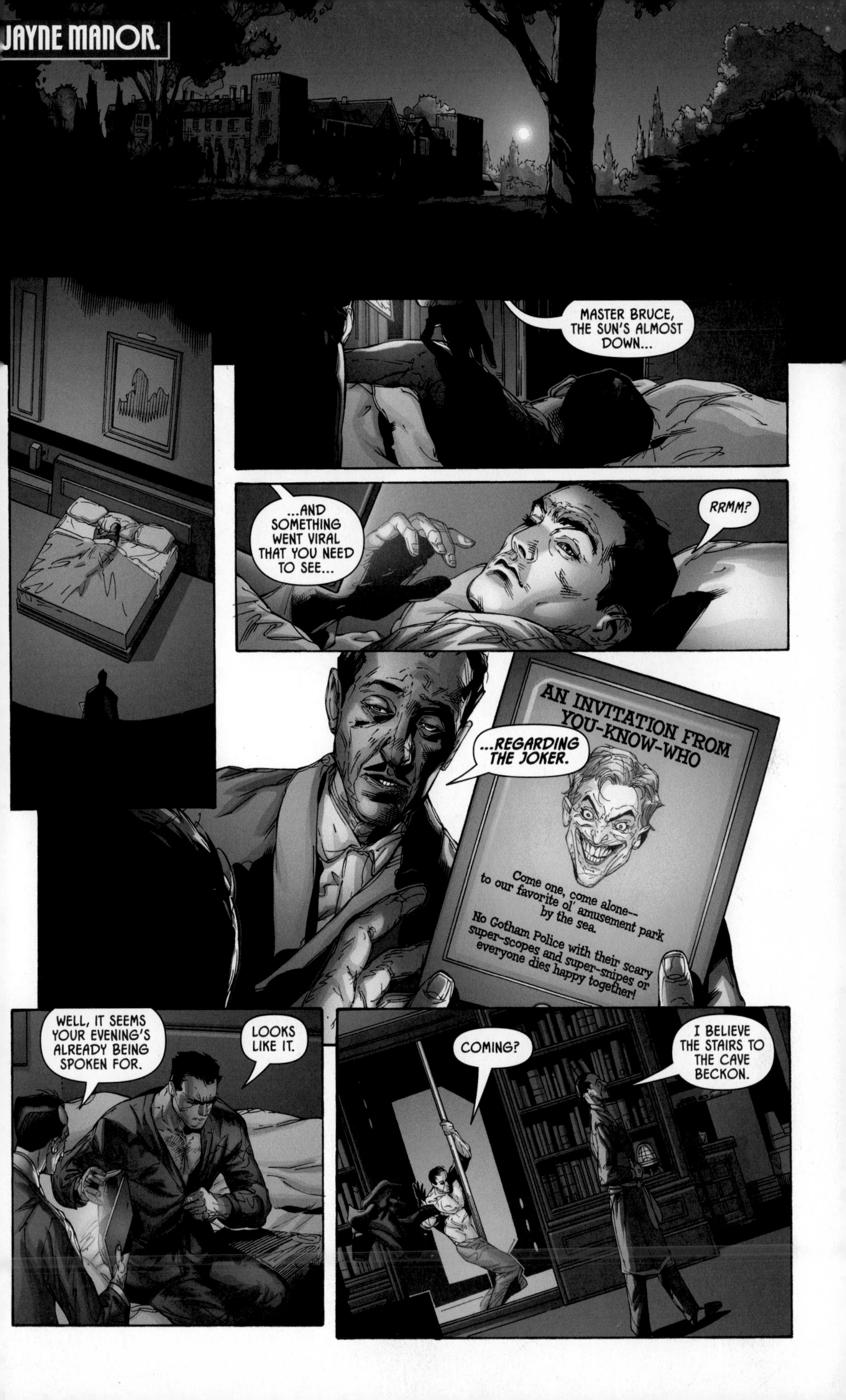
JAYNE MANOR.
MASTER BRUCE, THE SUN'S ALMOST DOWN...
...AND SOMETHING WENT VIRAL THAT YOU NEED TO SEE...
RRMM?
...REGARDING THE JOKER.
AN INVITATION FROM YOU-KNOW-WHO
Come one, come alone-- to our favorite ol' amusement park by the sea.
No Gotham Police with their scary super-scopes and super-snipes or everyone dies happy together!
WELL, IT SEEMS YOUR EVENING'S ALREADY BEING SPOKEN FOR.
LOOKS LIKE IT.
COMING?
I BELIEVE THE STAIRS TO THE CAVE BECKON.

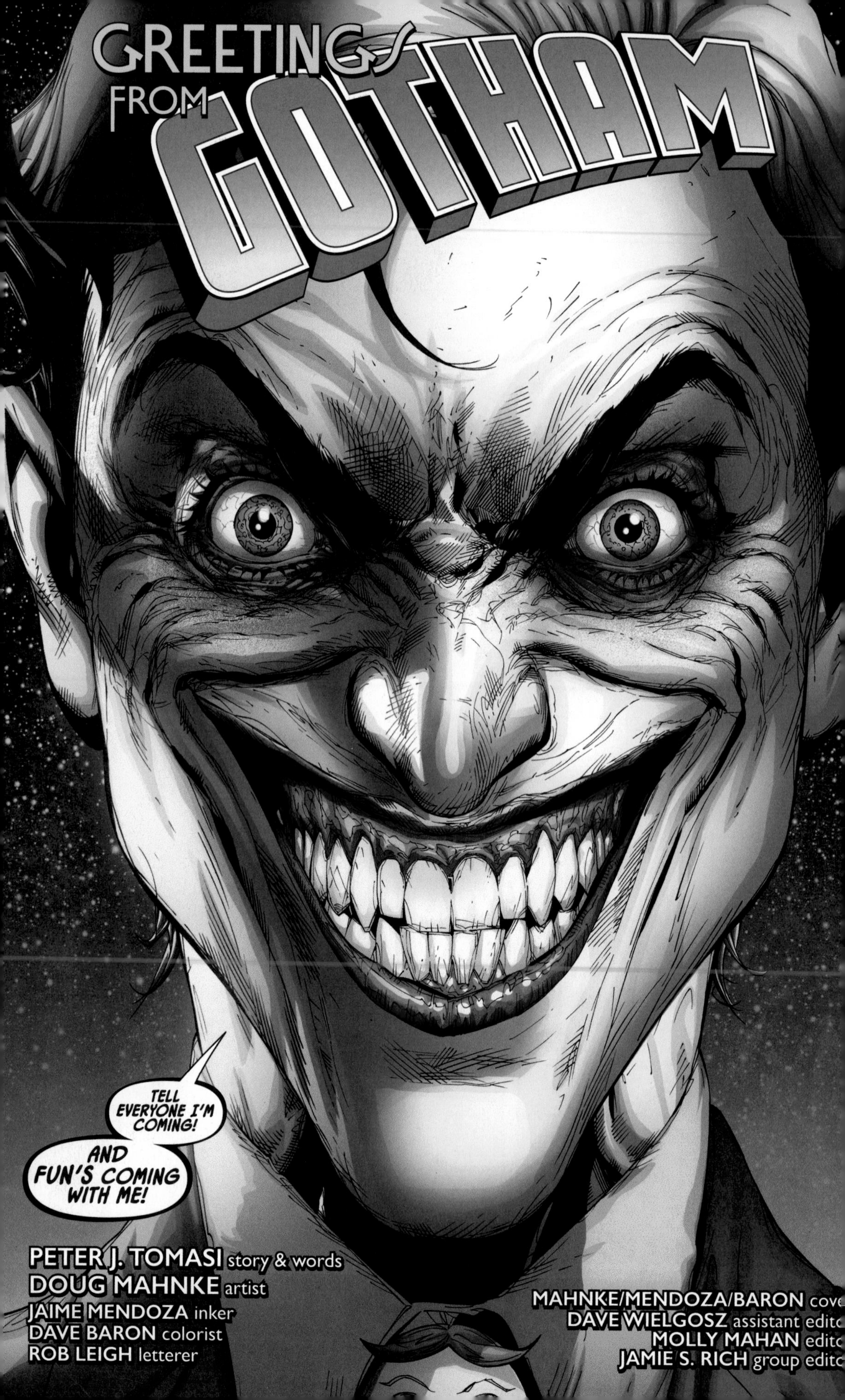
GREETINGS FROM GOTHAM
TELL EVERYONE I'M COMING!
AND FUN'S COMING WITH ME!
PETER J. TOMASI story & words
DOUG MAHNKE artist
JAIME MENDOZA inker
DAVE BARON colorist
ROB LEIGH letterer
MAHNKE/MENDOZA/BARON cove
DAVE WIELGOSZ assistant edito
MOLLY MAHAN edito
JAMIE S. RICH group edito

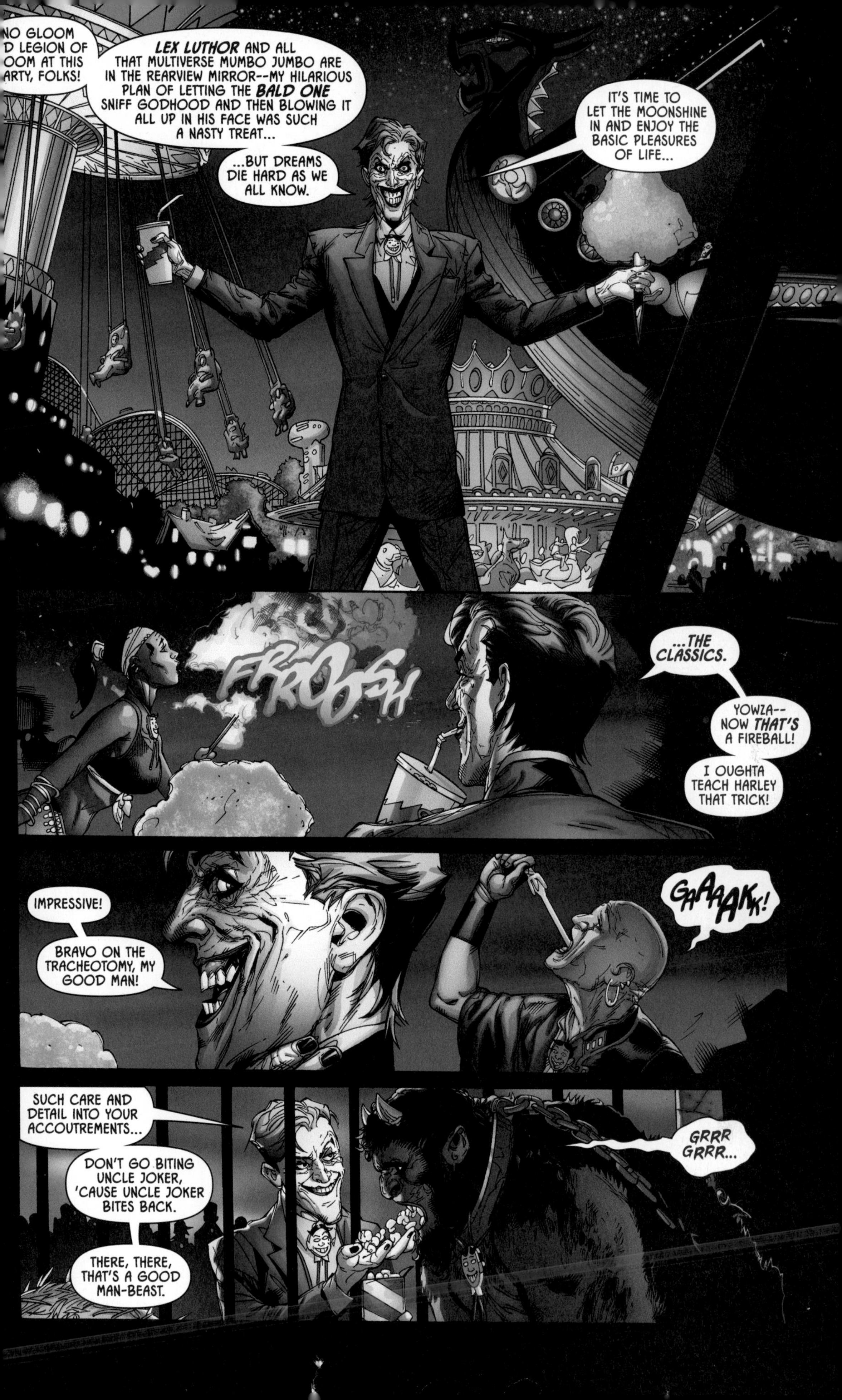
NO GLOOM
D LEGION OF
OOM AT THIS
ARTY, FOLKS!
LEX LUTHOR AND ALL THAT MULTIVERSE MUMBO JUMBO ARE IN THE REARVIEW MIRROR--MY HILARIOUS PLAN OF LETTING THE BALD ONE SNIFF GODHOOD AND THEN BLOWING IT ALL UP IN HIS FACE WAS SUCH A NASTY TREAT...
...BUT DREAMS DIE HARD AS WE ALL KNOW.
IT'S TIME TO LET THE MOONSHINE IN AND ENJOY THE BASIC PLEASURES OF LIFE...
FRROOSH
...THE CLASSICS.
YOWZA--NOW THAT'S A FIREBALL!
I OUGHTA TEACH HARLEY THAT TRICK!
IMPRESSIVE!
BRAVO ON THE TRACHEOTOMY, MY GOOD MAN!
GAAAAKK!
SUCH CARE AND DETAIL INTO YOUR ACCOUTREMENTS...
DON'T GO BITING UNCLE JOKER, 'CAUSE UNCLE JOKER BITES BACK.
THERE, THERE, THAT'S A GOOD MAN-BEAST.
GRRR GRRR...

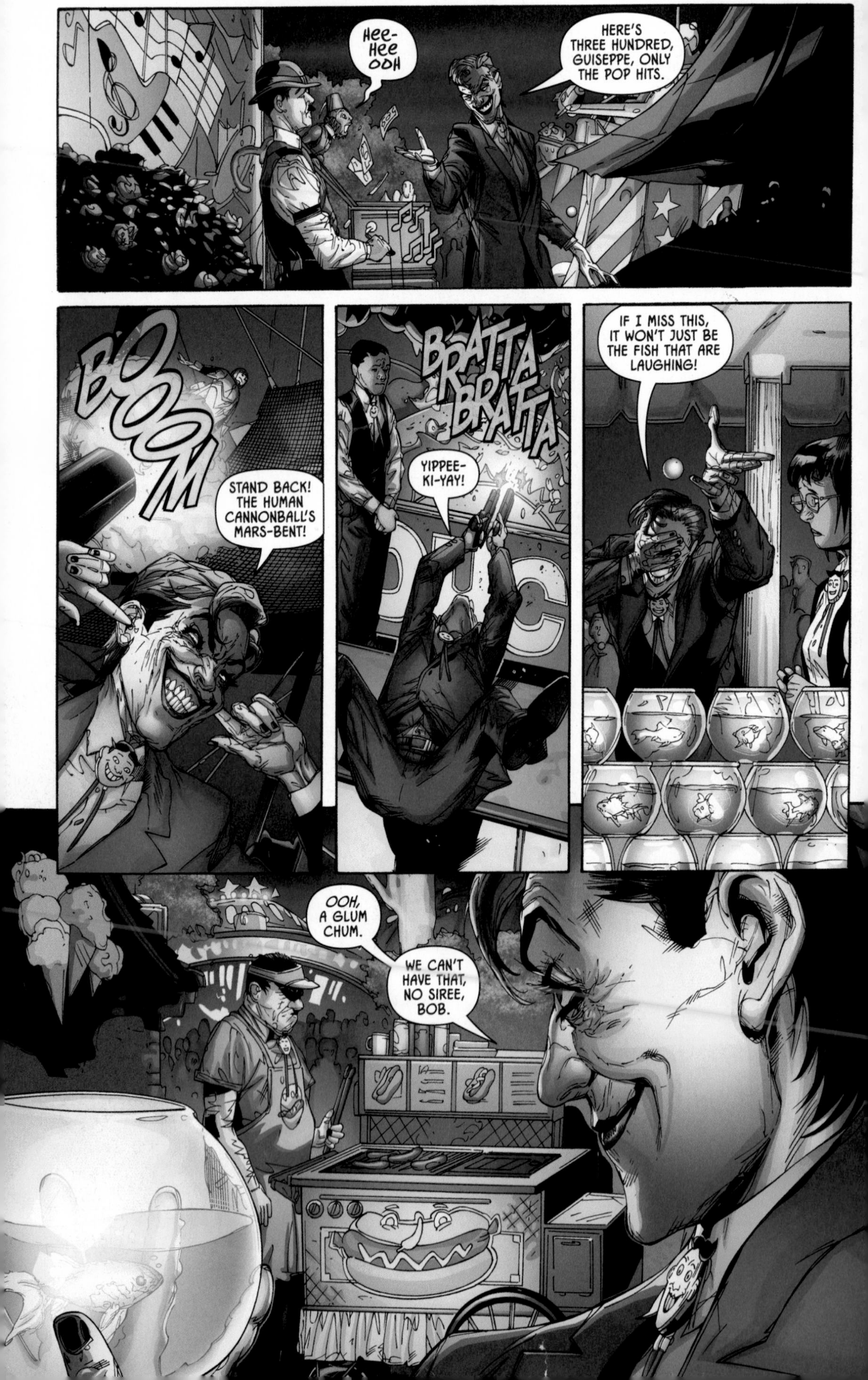
HEE-HEE OOH
HERE'S THREE HUNDRED, GUISEPPE, ONLY THE POP HITS.
BOOOM
STAND BACK! THE HUMAN CANNONBALL'S MARS-BENT!
BRATTA BRATTA BRATTA
YIPPEE-KI-YAY!
IF I MISS THIS, IT WON'T JUST BE THE FISH THAT ARE LAUGHING!
OOH, A GLUM CHUM.
WE CAN'T HAVE THAT, NO SIREE, BOB.

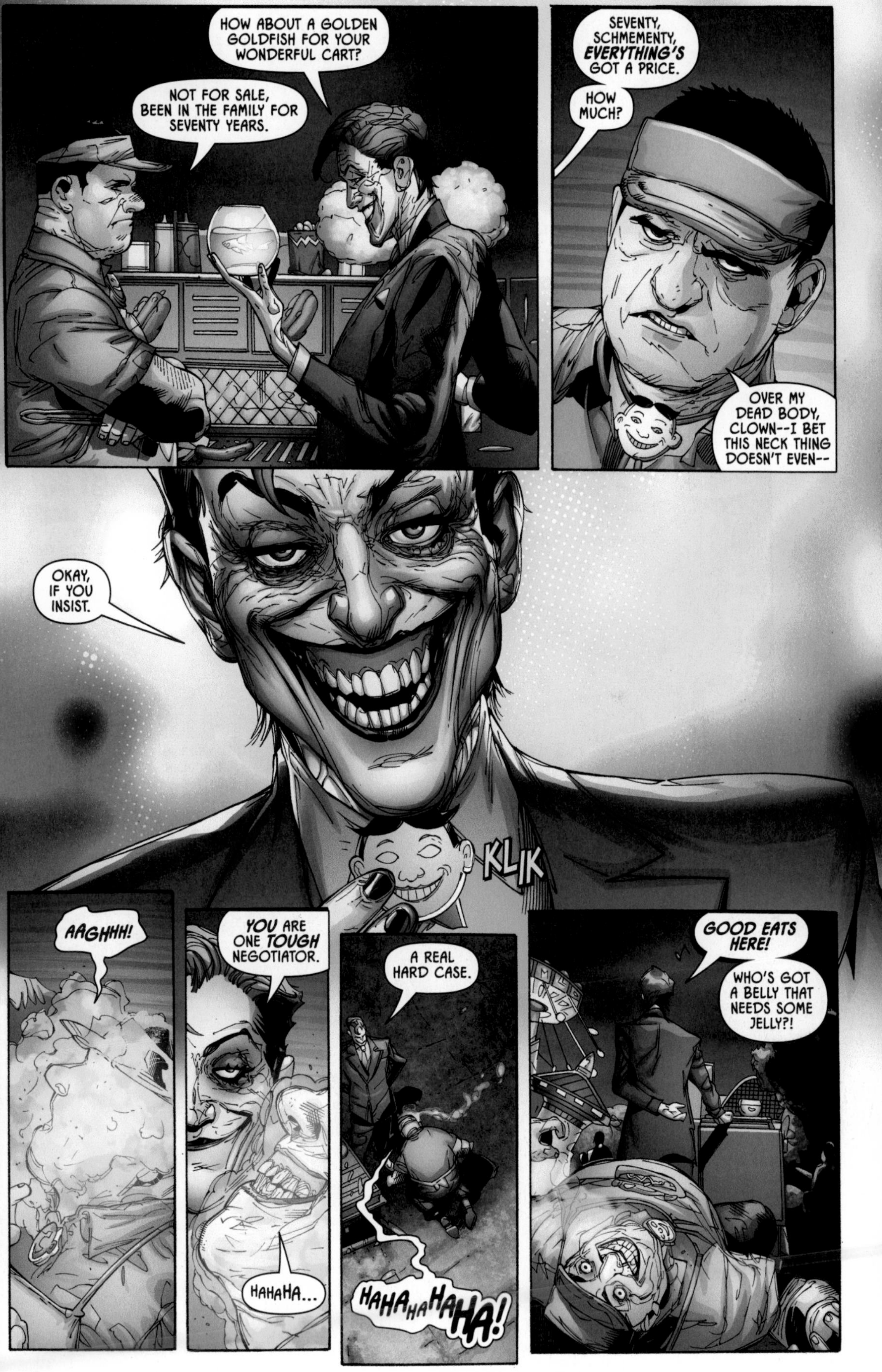
HOW ABOUT A GOLDEN GOLDFISH FOR YOUR WONDERFUL CART?
NOT FOR SALE, BEEN IN THE FAMILY FOR SEVENTY YEARS.
SEVENTY, SCHMEMENTY, EVERYTHING'S GOT A PRICE.
HOW MUCH?
OVER MY DEAD BODY, CLOWN--I BET THIS NECK THING DOESN'T EVEN--
OKAY, IF YOU INSIST.
KLIK
AAGHHH!
YOU ARE ONE TOUGH NEGOTIATOR.
HAHAHA...
A REAL HARD CASE.
HAHAHAHAHA!
GOOD EATS HERE!
WHO'S GOT A BELLY THAT NEEDS SOME JELLY?!

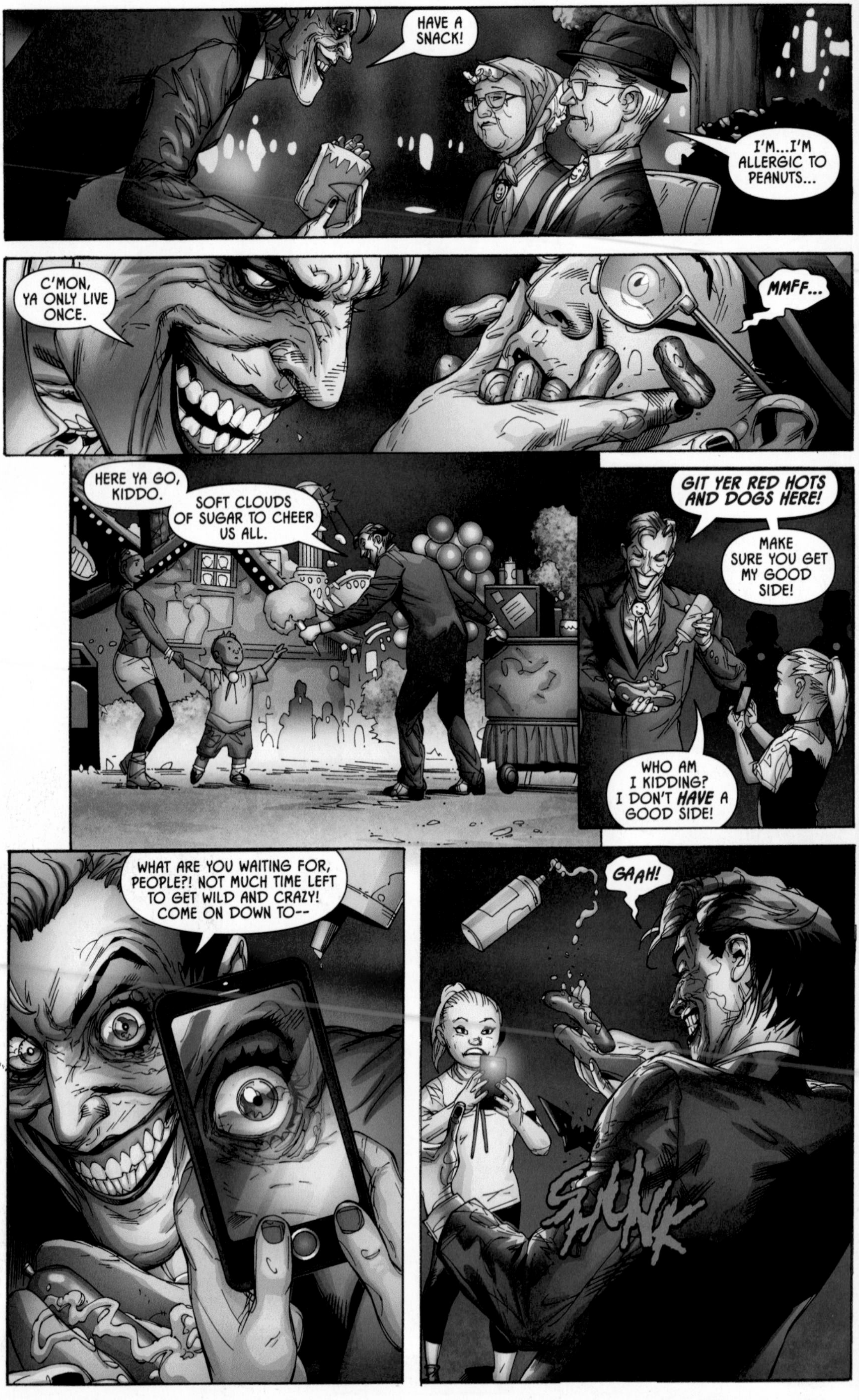

HAVE A SNACK!
I'M...I'M ALLERGIC TO PEANUTS...
C'MON, YA ONLY LIVE ONCE.
MMFF...
HERE YA GO, KIDDO.
SOFT CLOUDS OF SUGAR TO CHEER US ALL.
GIT YER RED HOTS AND DOGS HERE!
MAKE SURE YOU GET MY GOOD SIDE!
WHO AM I KIDDING? I DON'T HAVE A GOOD SIDE!
WHAT ARE YOU WAITING FOR, PEOPLE?! NOT MUCH TIME LEFT TO GET WILD AND CRAZY! COME ON DOWN TO--
GAAH!
SHUNK

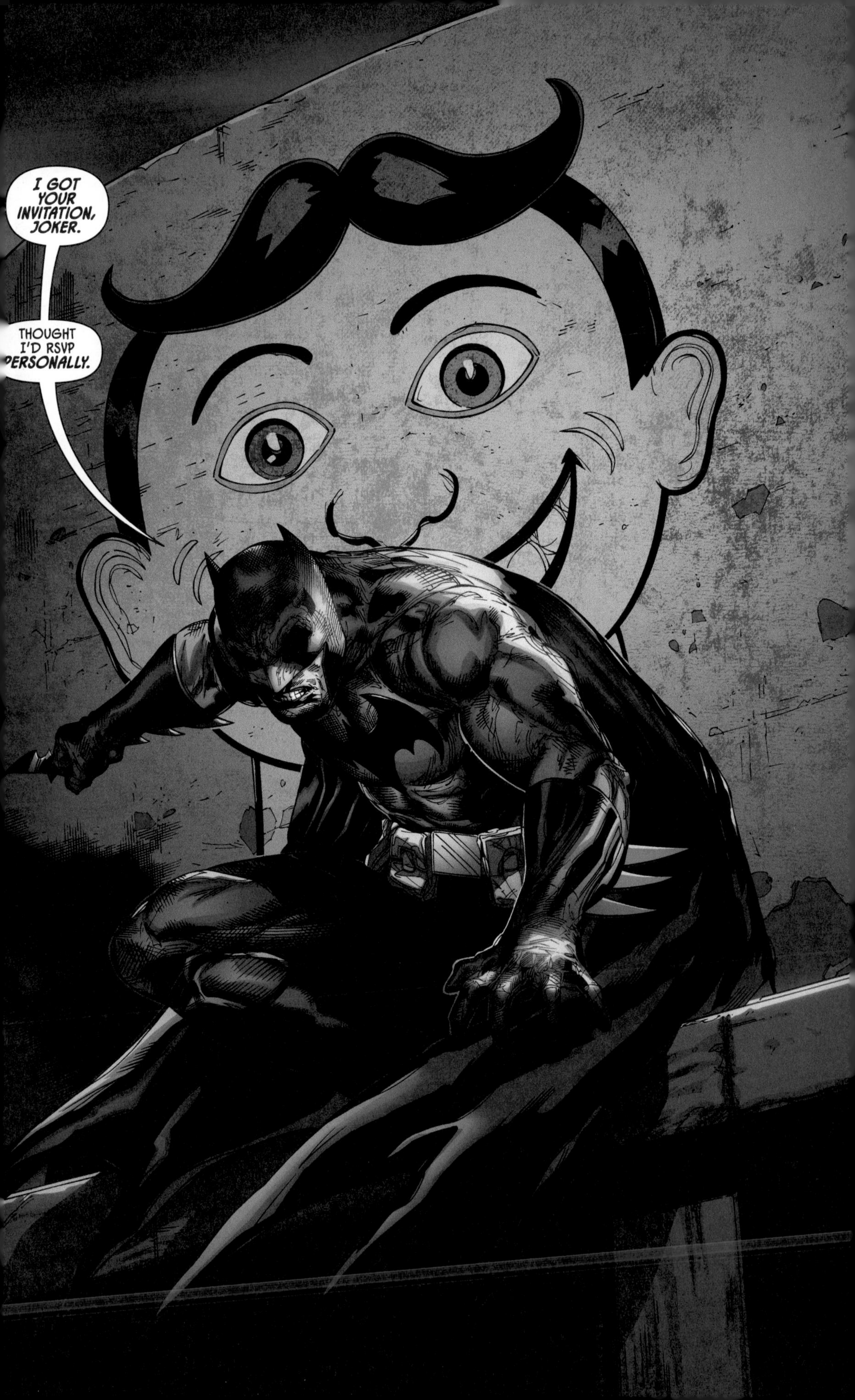
I GOT YOUR INVITATION, JOKER.
THOUGHT I'D RSVP PERSONALLY.

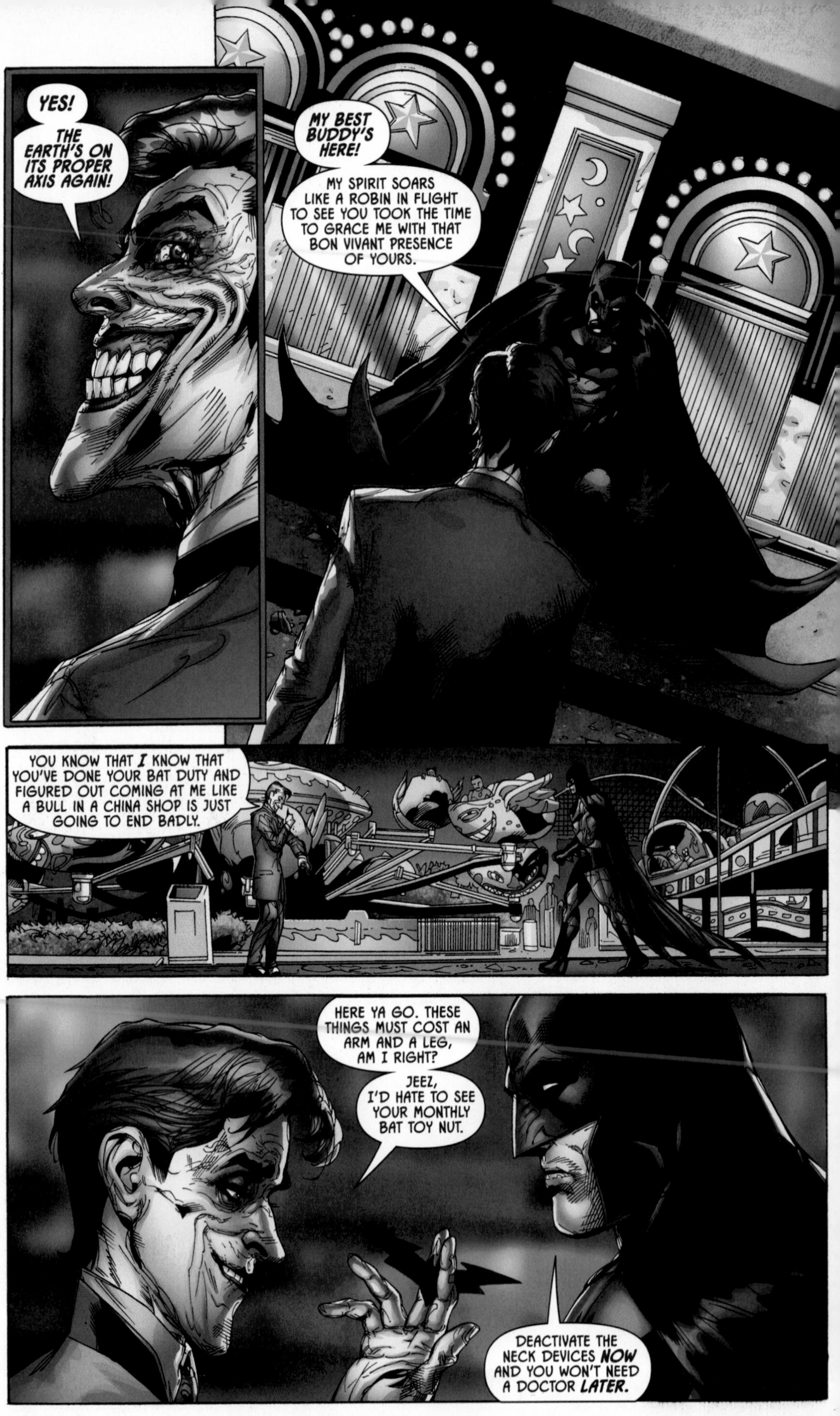
YES!
THE EARTH'S ON ITS PROPER AXIS AGAIN!
MY BEST BUDDY'S HERE!
MY SPIRIT SOARS LIKE A ROBIN IN FLIGHT TO SEE YOU TOOK THE TIME TO GRACE ME WITH THAT BON VIVANT PRESENCE OF YOURS.
YOU KNOW THAT I KNOW THAT YOU'VE DONE YOUR BAT DUTY AND FIGURED OUT COMING AT ME LIKE A BULL IN A CHINA SHOP IS JUST GOING TO END BADLY.
HERE YA GO. THESE THINGS MUST COST AN ARM AND A LEG, AM I RIGHT?
JEEZ, I'D HATE TO SEE YOUR MONTHLY BAT TOY NUT.
DEACTIVATE THE NECK DEVICES NOW AND YOU WON'T NEED A DOCTOR LATER.

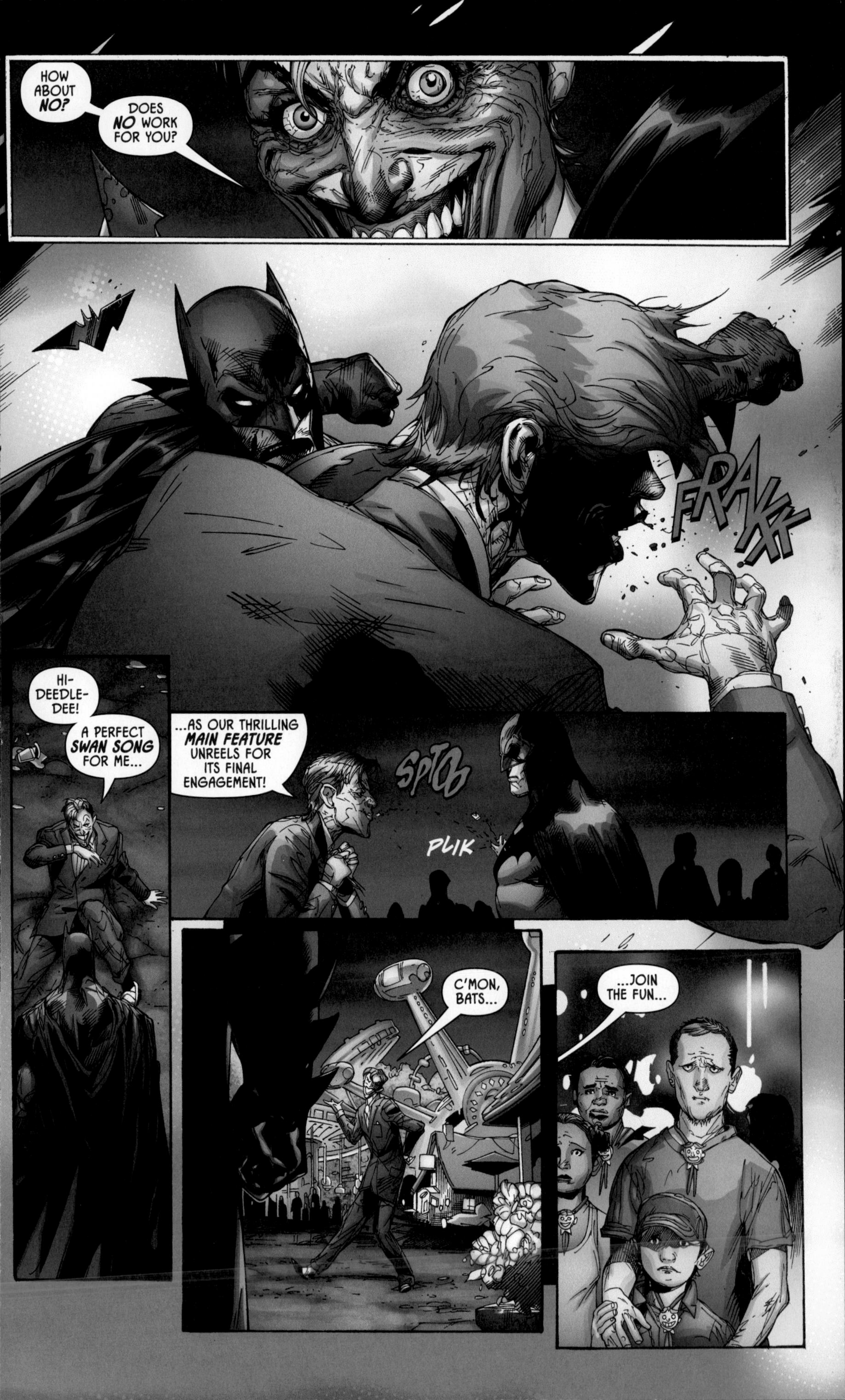
HOW ABOUT NO?
DOES NO WORK FOR YOU?
FRAKK
HI-DEEDLE-DEE!
A PERFECT SWAN SONG FOR ME...
...AS OUR THRILLING MAIN FEATURE UNREELS FOR ITS FINAL ENGAGEMENT!
SPTOO
PLIK
C'MON, BATS...
...JOIN THE FUN...

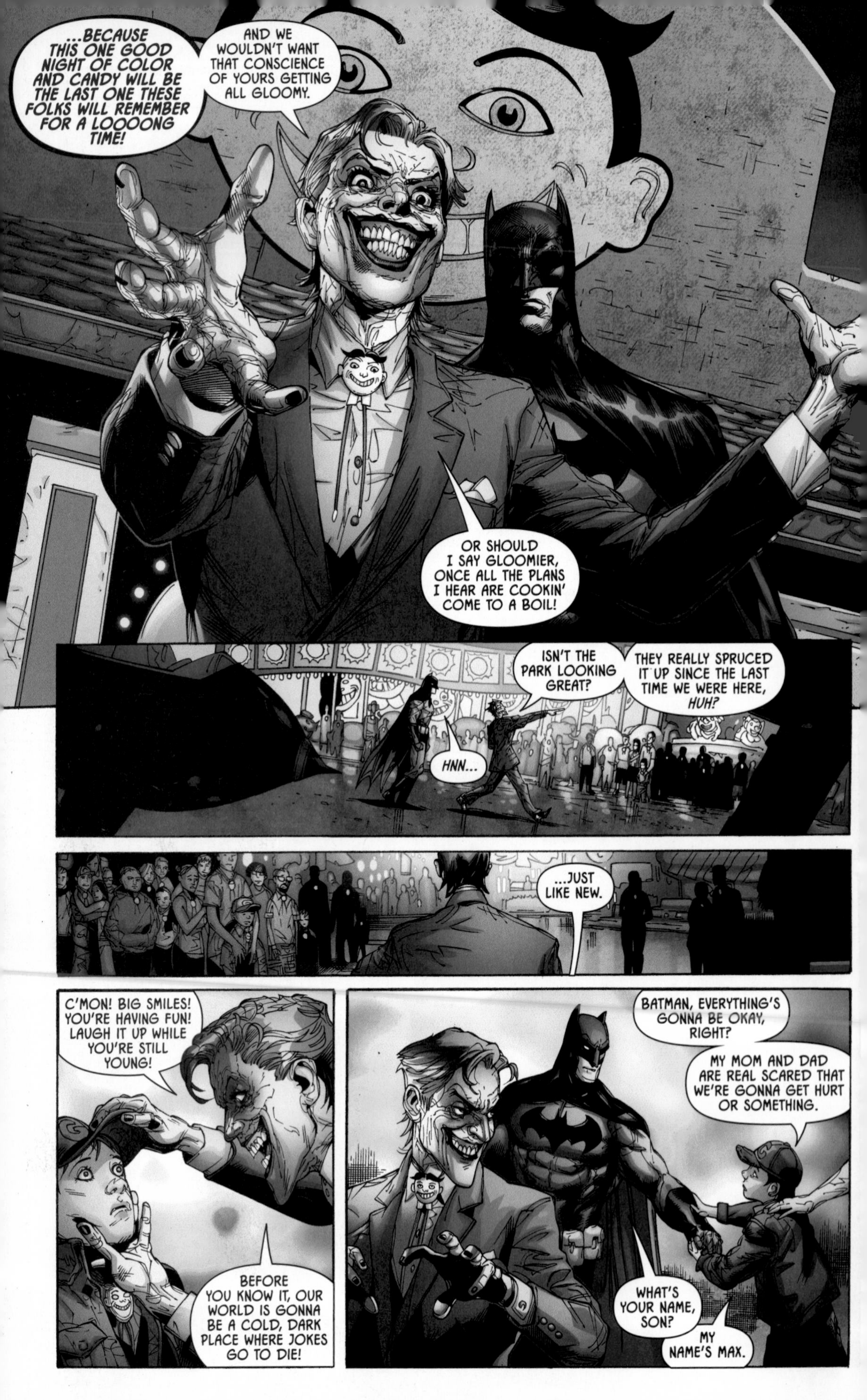
...BECAUSE THIS ONE GOOD NIGHT OF COLOR AND CANDY WILL BE THE LAST ONE THESE FOLKS WILL REMEMBER FOR A LOOOONG TIME!
AND WE WOULDN'T WANT THAT CONSCIENCE OF YOURS GETTING ALL GLOOMY.
OR SHOULD I SAY GLOOMIER, ONCE ALL THE PLANS I HEAR ARE COOKIN' COME TO A BOIL!
ISN'T THE PARK LOOKING GREAT?
THEY REALLY SPRUCED IT UP SINCE THE LAST TIME WE WERE HERE, *HUH?*
HNN...
...JUST LIKE NEW.
C'MON! BIG SMILES! YOU'RE HAVING FUN! LAUGH IT UP WHILE YOU'RE STILL YOUNG!
BEFORE YOU KNOW IT, OUR WORLD IS GONNA BE A COLD, DARK PLACE WHERE JOKES GO TO DIE!
BATMAN, EVERYTHING'S GONNA BE OKAY, RIGHT?
MY MOM AND DAD ARE REAL SCARED THAT WE'RE GONNA GET HURT OR SOMETHING.
WHAT'S YOUR NAME, SON?
MY NAME'S MAX.

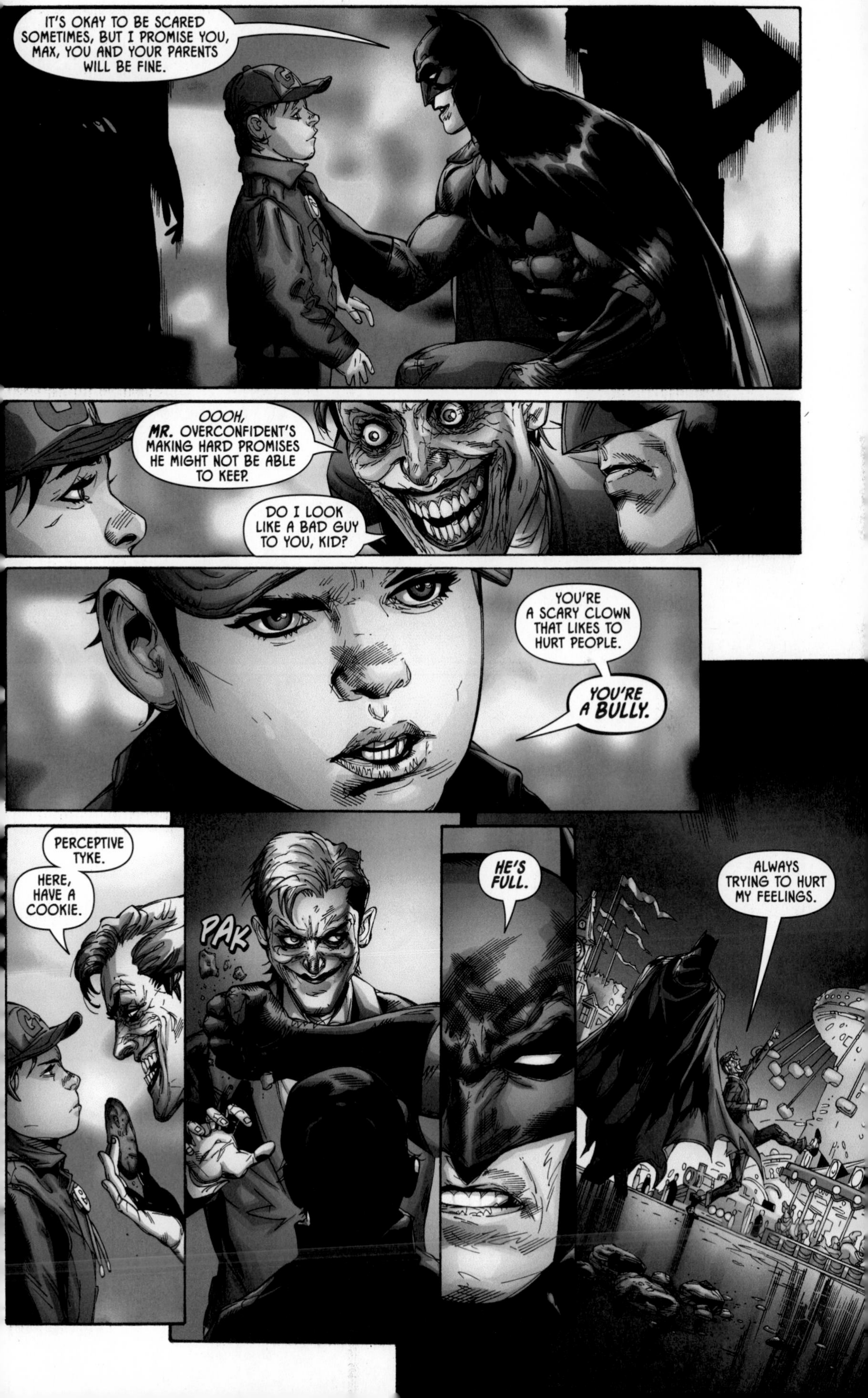
IT'S OKAY TO BE SCARED SOMETIMES, BUT I PROMISE YOU, MAX, YOU AND YOUR PARENTS WILL BE FINE.
OOOH, MR. OVERCONFIDENT'S MAKING HARD PROMISES HE MIGHT NOT BE ABLE TO KEEP.
DO I LOOK LIKE A BAD GUY TO YOU, KID?
YOU'RE A SCARY CLOWN THAT LIKES TO HURT PEOPLE.
YOU'RE A BULLY.
PERCEPTIVE TYKE.
HERE, HAVE A COOKIE.
PAK
HE'S FULL.
ALWAYS TRYING TO HURT MY FEELINGS.

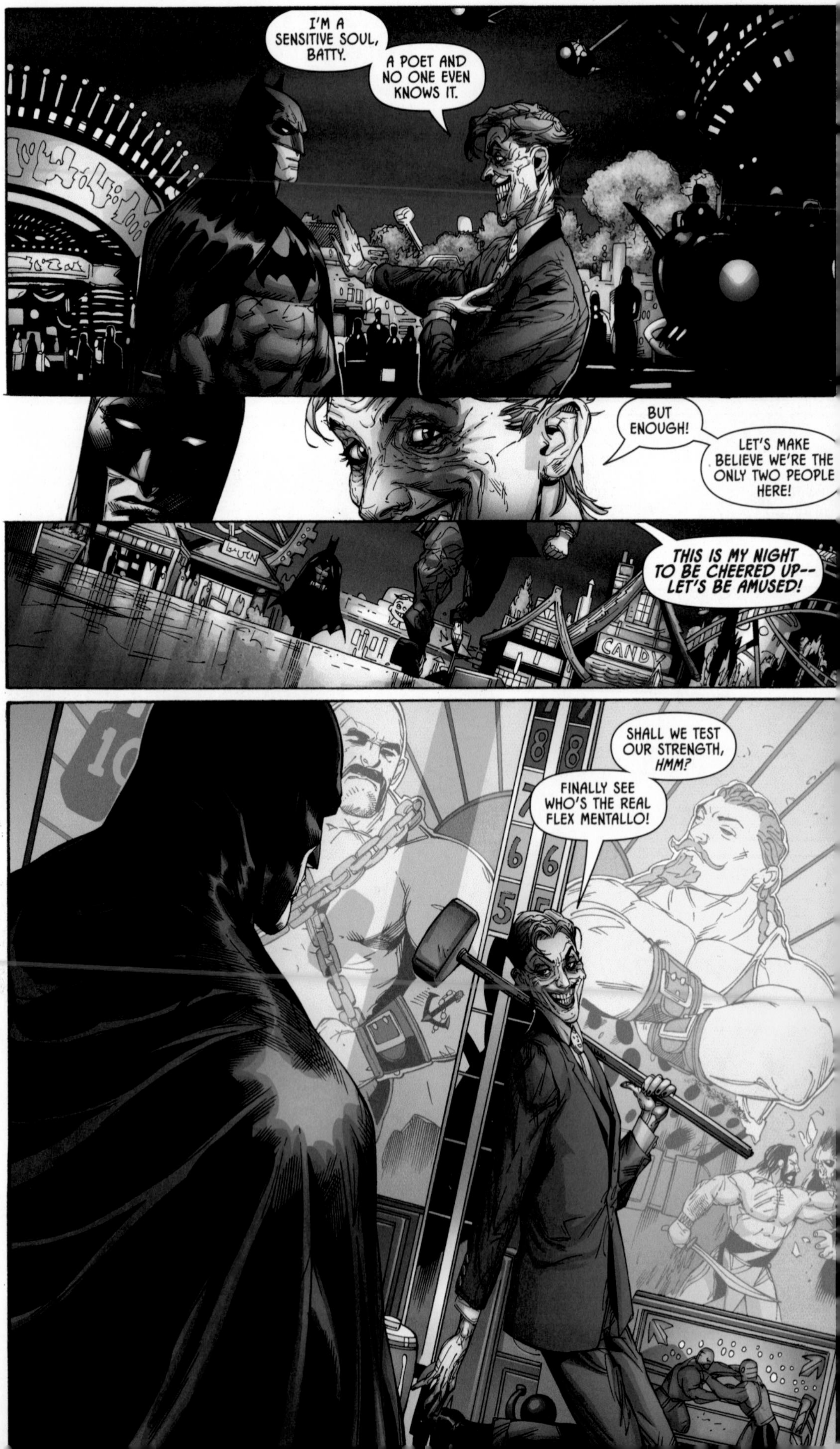

I'M A SENSITIVE SOUL, BATTY.
A POET AND NO ONE EVEN KNOWS IT.
BUT ENOUGH!
LET'S MAKE BELIEVE WE'RE THE ONLY TWO PEOPLE HERE!
THIS IS MY NIGHT TO BE CHEERED UP-- LET'S BE AMUSED!
CANDY
SHALL WE TEST OUR STRENGTH, HMM?
FINALLY SEE WHO'S THE REAL FLEX MENTALLO!

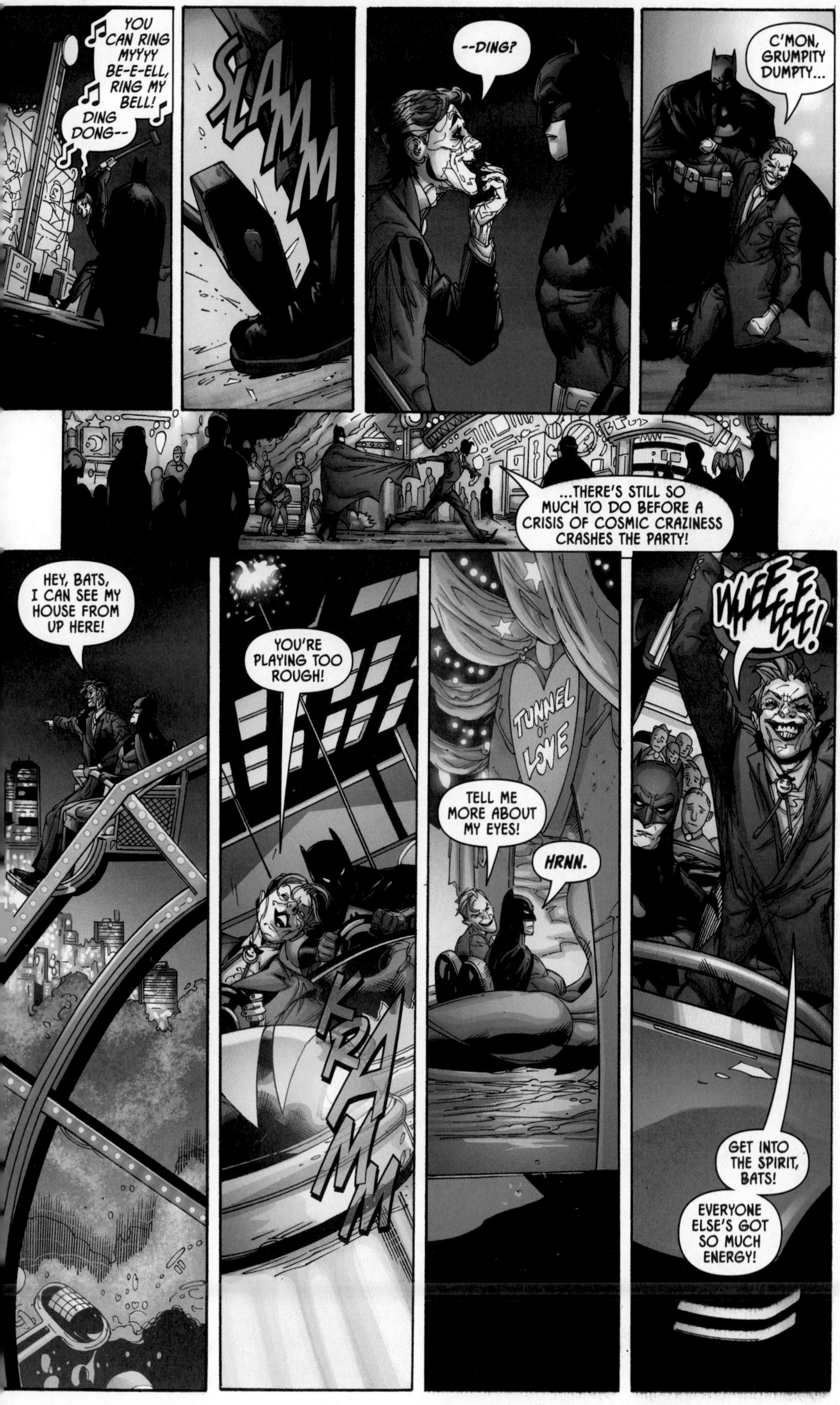
YOU CAN RING MYYYY BE-E-ELL, RING MY BELL!
DING DONG--
SLAMM
--DING?
C'MON, GRUMPITY DUMPTY...
...THERE'S STILL SO MUCH TO DO BEFORE A CRISIS OF COSMIC CRAZINESS CRASHES THE PARTY!
HEY, BATS, I CAN SEE MY HOUSE FROM UP HERE!
YOU'RE PLAYING TOO ROUGH!
KRAMM
TUNNEL OF LOVE
TELL ME MORE ABOUT MY EYES!
HRNN.
WHEEEEE!
GET INTO THE SPIRIT, BATS!
EVERYONE ELSE'S GOT SO MUCH ENERGY!

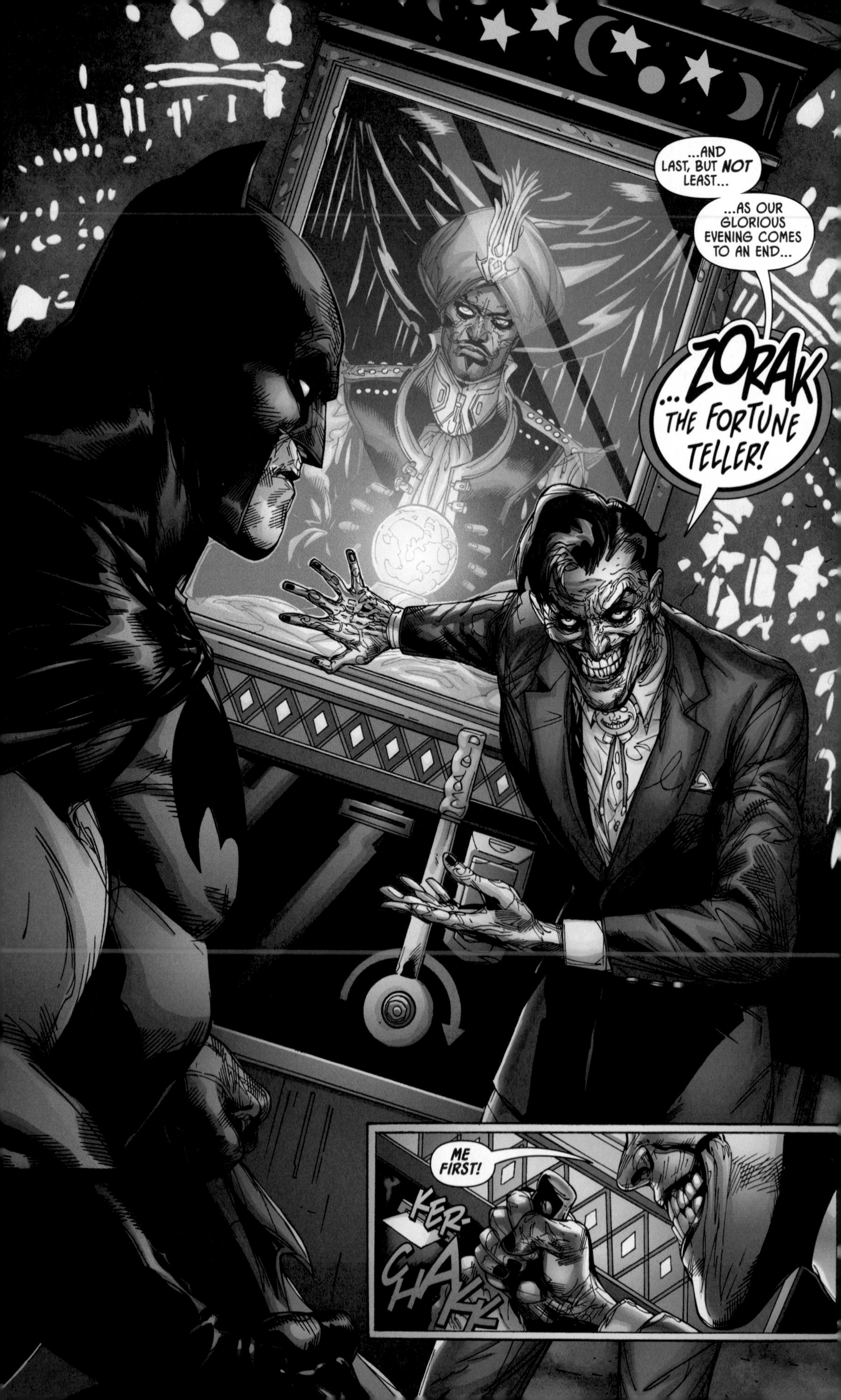
...AND LAST, BUT NOT LEAST...
...AS OUR GLORIOUS EVENING COMES TO AN END...
...ZORAK THE FORTUNE TELLER!
ME FIRST!
KER-CHAKK

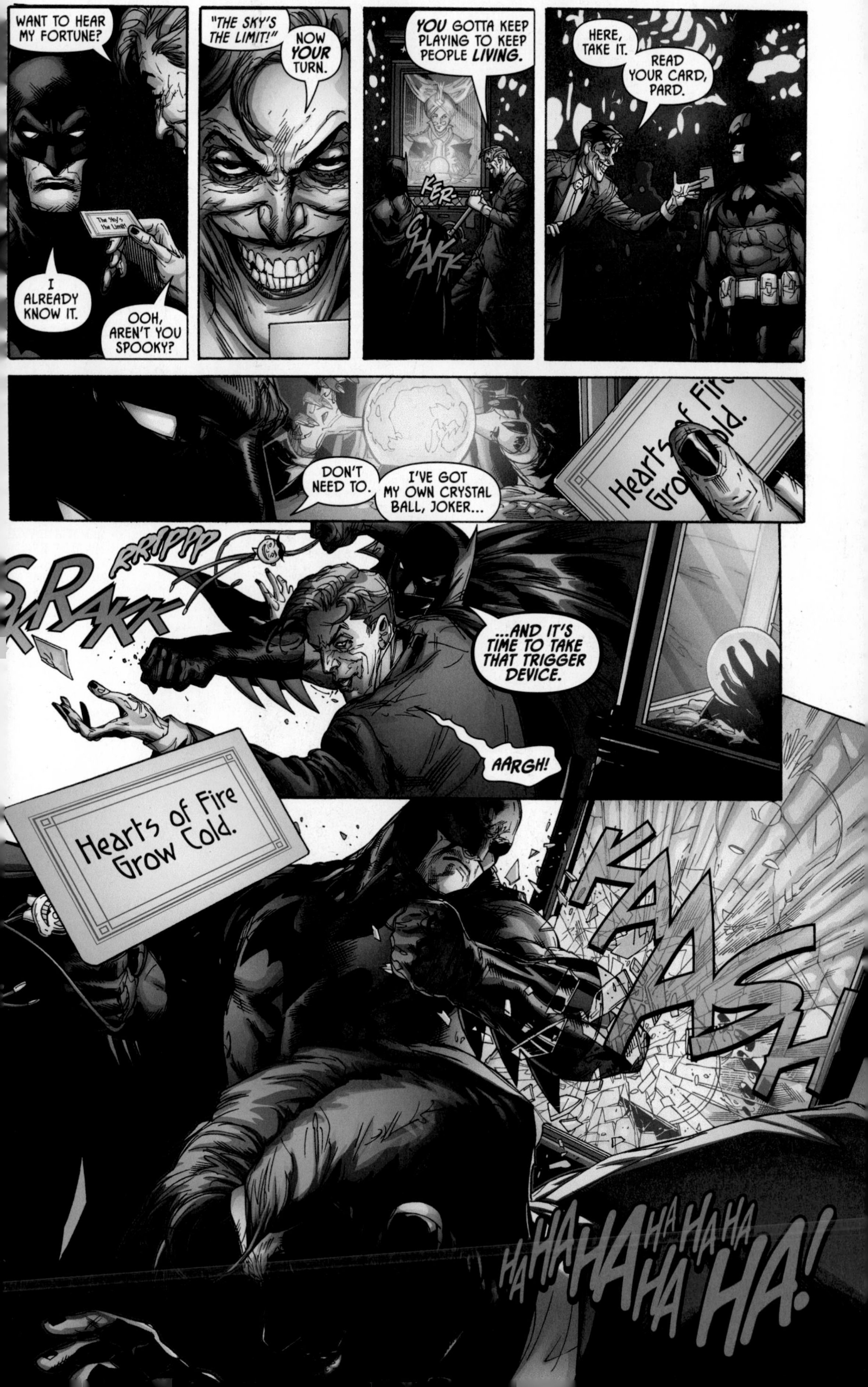
WANT TO HEAR MY FORTUNE?
The Sky's the Limit!
I ALREADY KNOW IT.
OOH, AREN'T YOU SPOOKY?
"THE SKY'S THE LIMIT!"
NOW YOUR TURN.
YOU GOTTA KEEP PLAYING TO KEEP PEOPLE LIVING.
KER-CHAKK
HERE, TAKE IT.
READ YOUR CARD, PARD.
DON'T NEED TO.
I'VE GOT MY OWN CRYSTAL BALL, JOKER...
SRAKK
RRIPPP
...AND IT'S TIME TO TAKE THAT TRIGGER DEVICE.
AARGH!
Hearts of Fire Grow Cold.
KRAASH
HA HA HA HA HA HA HA HA HA HA!

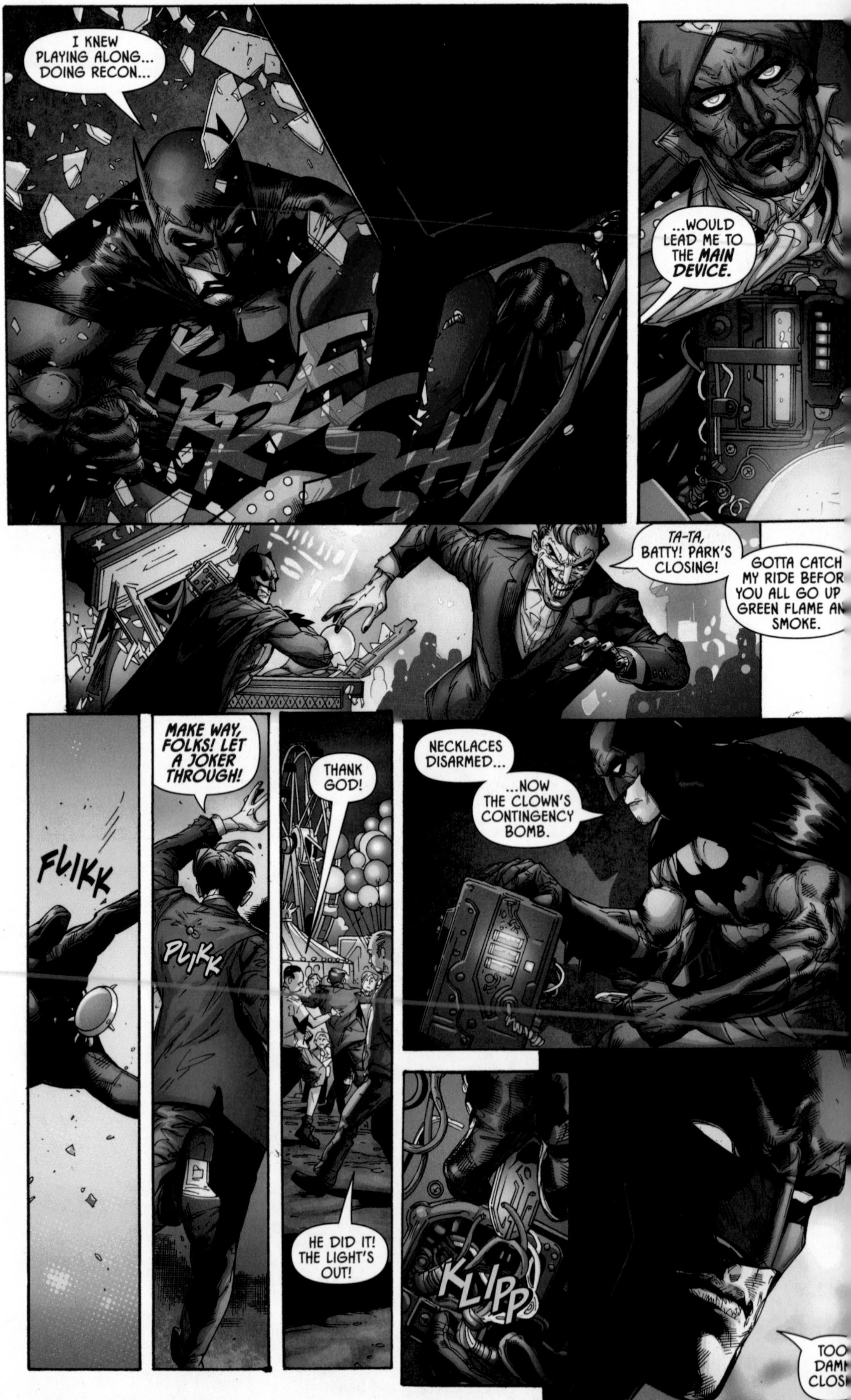
I KNEW PLAYING ALONG... DOING RECON...
...WOULD LEAD ME TO THE MAIN DEVICE.
TA-TA, BATTY! PARK'S CLOSING!
GOTTA CATCH MY RIDE BEFOR YOU ALL GO UP GREEN FLAME AN SMOKE.
FLIKK
MAKE WAY, FOLKS! LET A JOKER THROUGH!
PLIKK
THANK GOD!
HE DID IT! THE LIGHT'S OUT!
NECKLACES DISARMED...
...NOW THE CLOWN'S CONTINGENCY BOMB.
KLIPP
TOO DAM CLOS

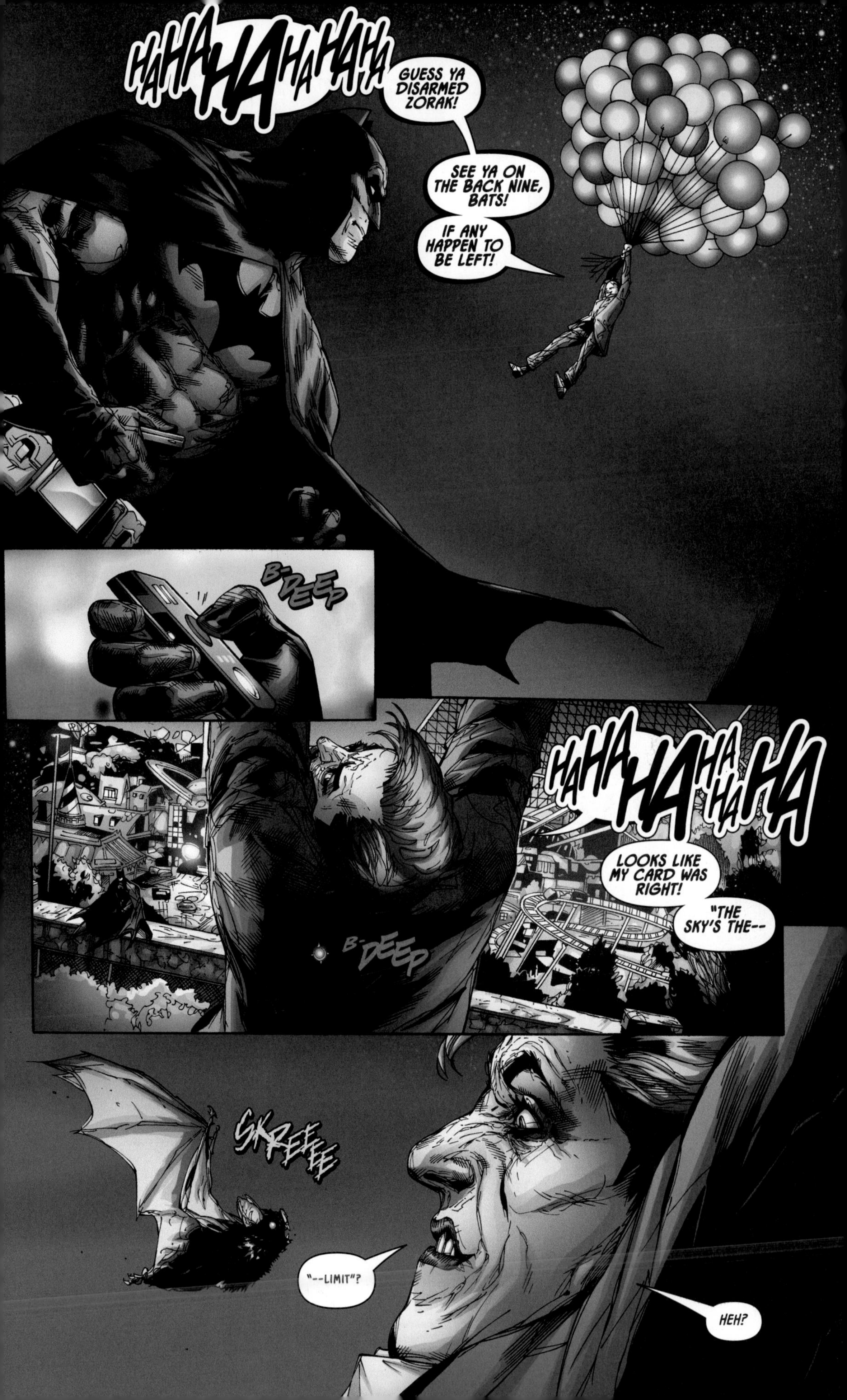
HAHAHAHAHAHAHA
GUESS YA DISARMED ZORAK!
SEE YA ON THE BACK NINE, BATS!
IF ANY HAPPEN TO BE LEFT!
B-DEEP
HAHAHAHAHAHAHA
LOOKS LIKE MY CARD WAS RIGHT!
"THE SKY'S THE--
B-DEEP
SKREEEE
"--LIMIT"?
HEH?

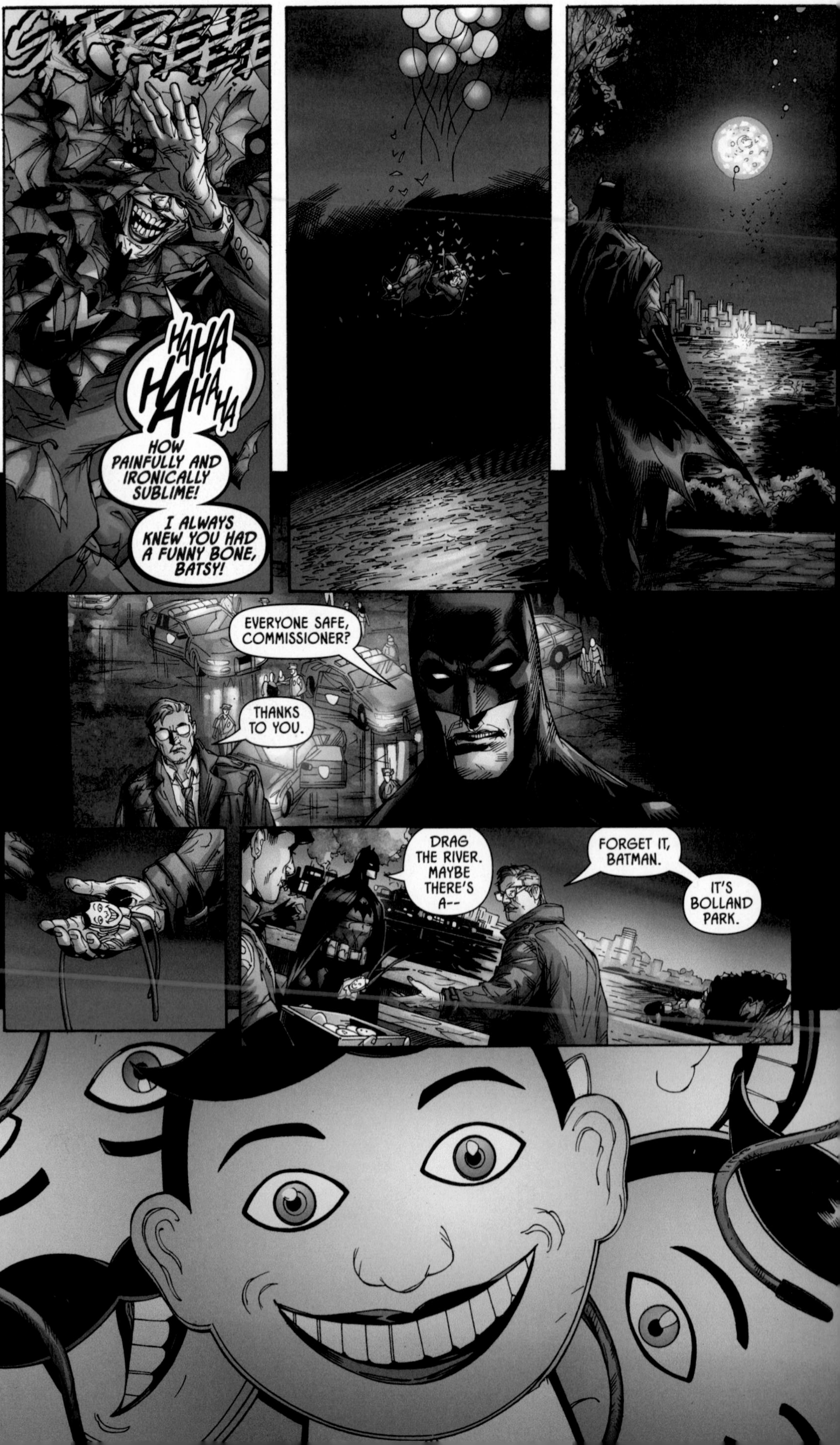
HAHA HA HAHAHA
HOW PAINFULLY AND IRONICALLY SUBLIME!
I ALWAYS KNEW YOU HAD A FUNNY BONE, BATSY!
EVERYONE SAFE, COMMISSIONER?
THANKS TO YOU.
DRAG THE RIVER. MAYBE THERE'S A--
FORGET IT, BATMAN.
IT'S BOLLAND PARK.

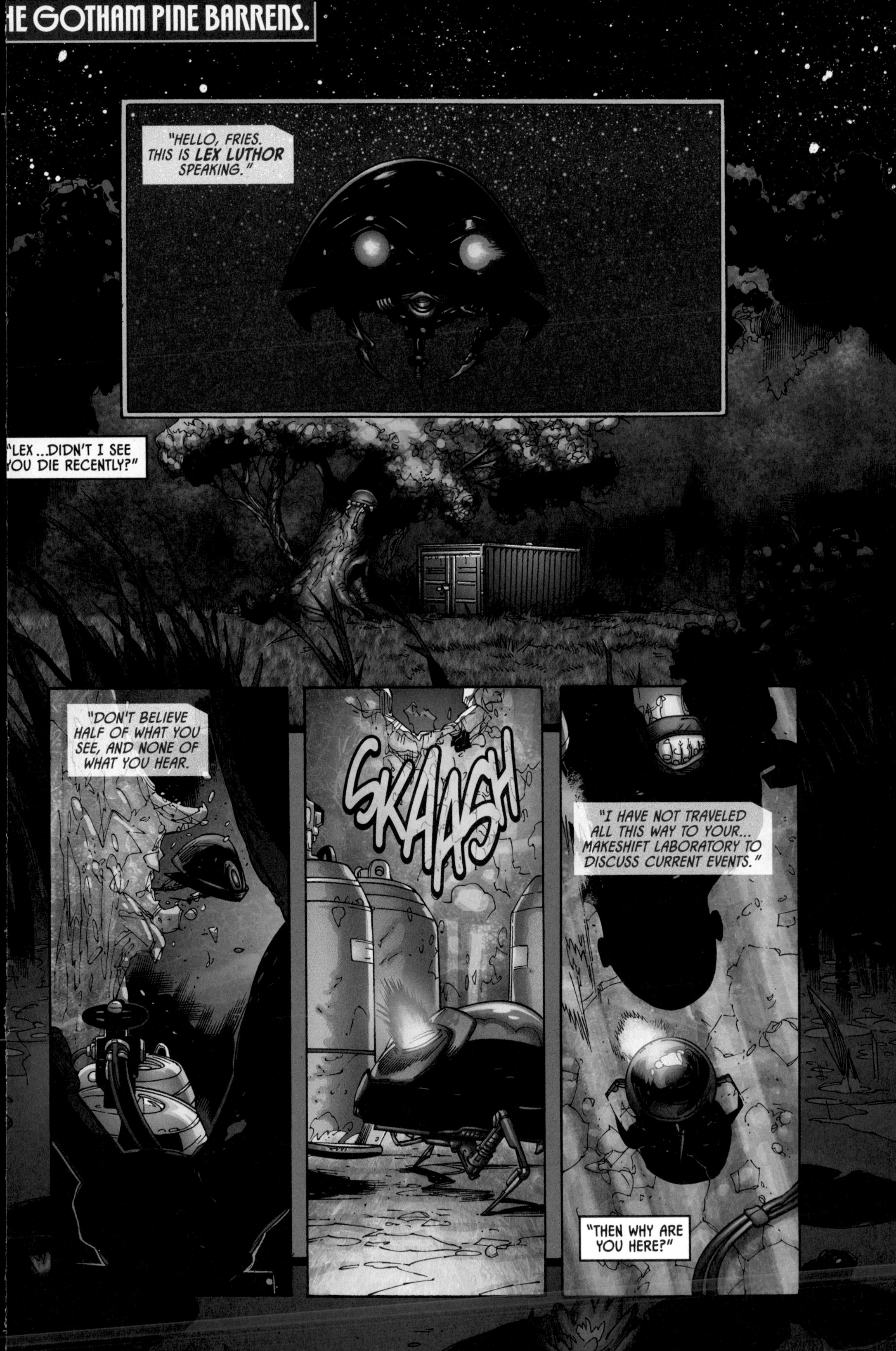
HE GOTHAM PINE BARRENS.
"HELLO, FRIES. THIS IS LEX LUTHOR SPEAKING."
"LEX...DIDN'T I SEE YOU DIE RECENTLY?"
"DON'T BELIEVE HALF OF WHAT YOU SEE, AND NONE OF WHAT YOU HEAR.
SKAASH
"I HAVE NOT TRAVELED ALL THIS WAY TO YOUR... MAKESHIFT LABORATORY TO DISCUSS CURRENT EVENTS."
"THEN WHY ARE YOU HERE?"

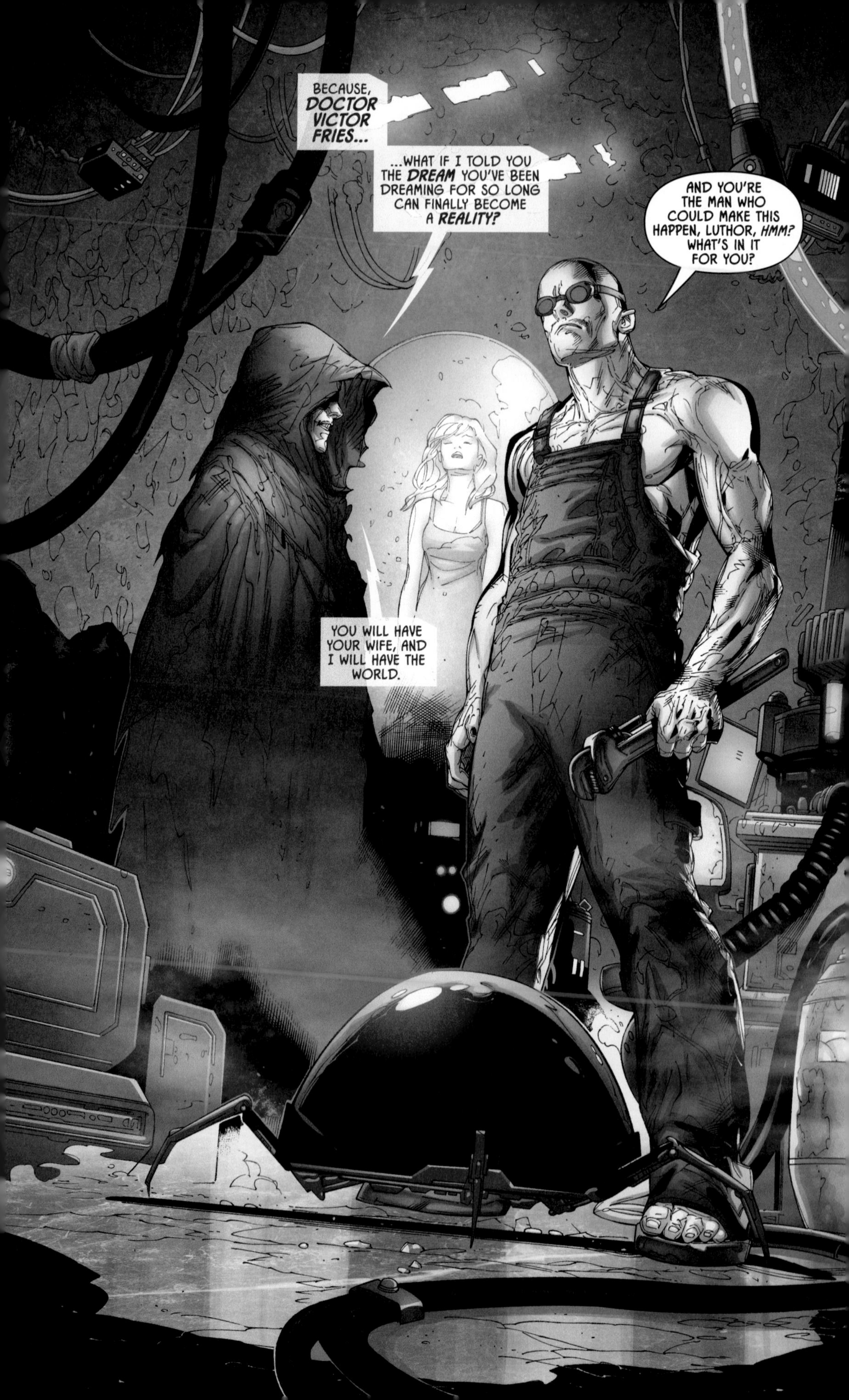
BECAUSE, DOCTOR VICTOR FRIES...
...WHAT IF I TOLD YOU THE DREAM YOU'VE BEEN DREAMING FOR SO LONG CAN FINALLY BECOME A REALITY?
AND YOU'RE THE MAN WHO COULD MAKE THIS HAPPEN, LUTHOR, HMM? WHAT'S IN IT FOR YOU?
YOU WILL HAVE YOUR WIFE, AND I WILL HAVE THE WORLD.

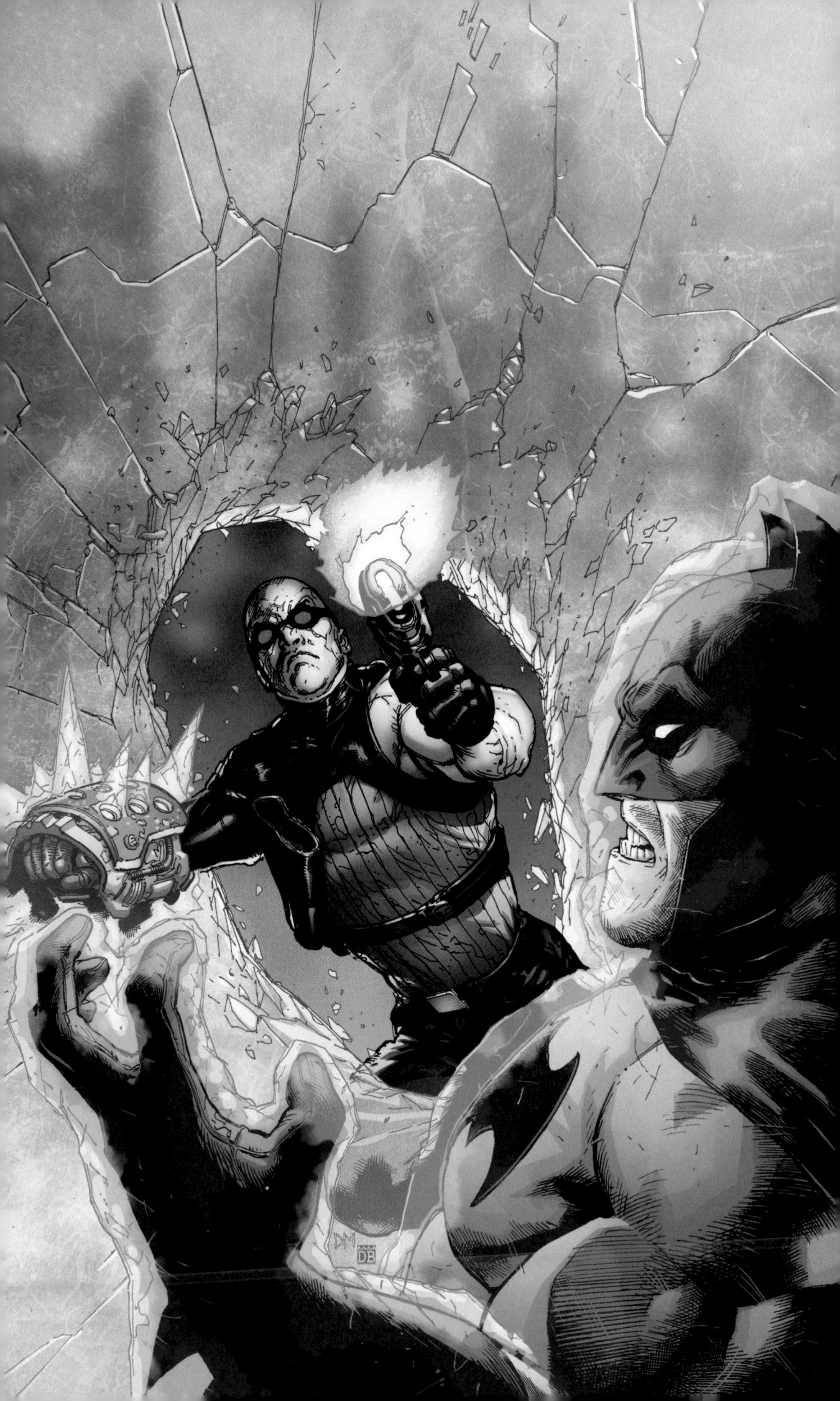

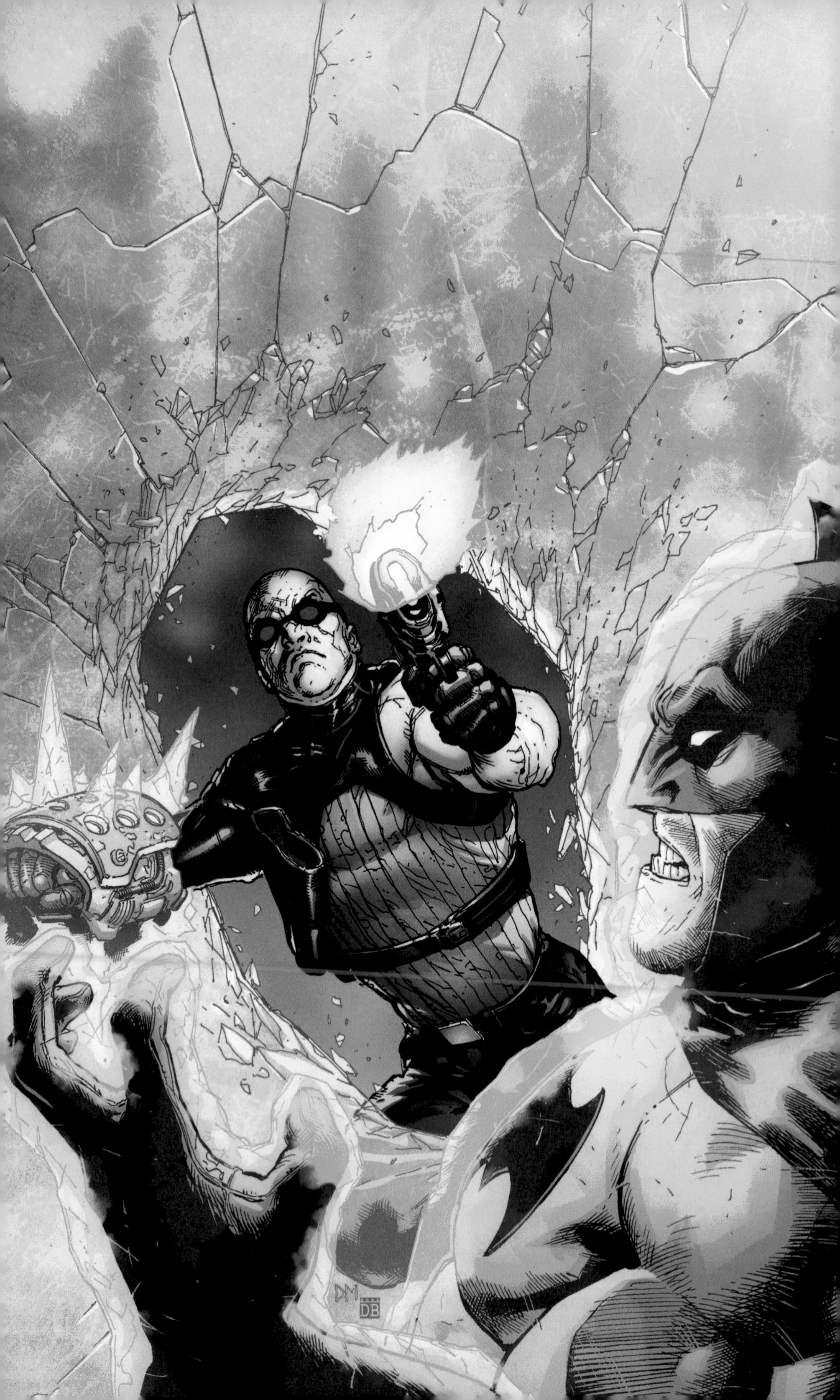

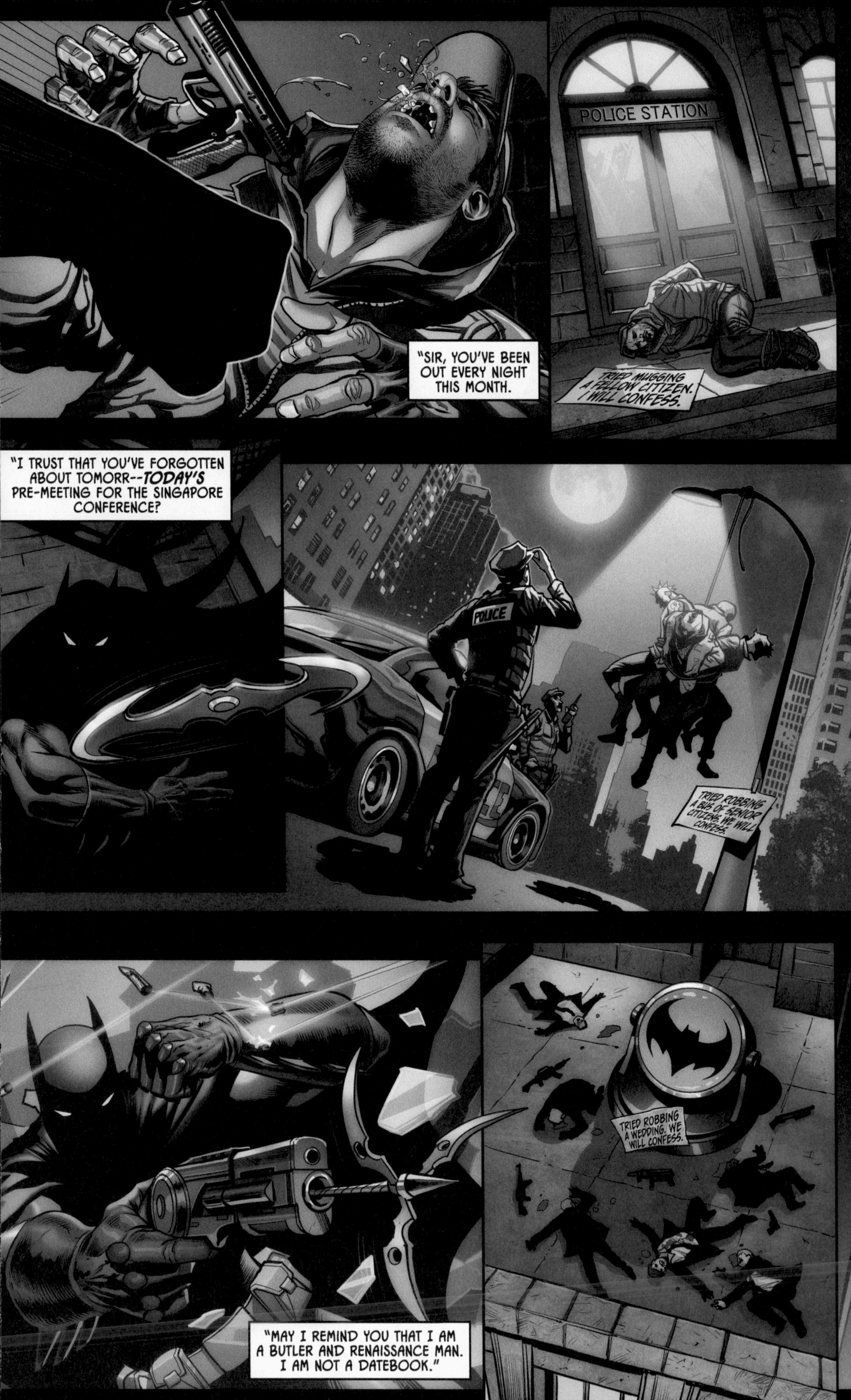
"SIR, YOU'VE BEEN OUT EVERY NIGHT THIS MONTH.
POLICE STATION
TRIED MUGGING A FELLOW CITIZEN. I WILL CONFESS.
"I TRUST THAT YOU'VE FORGOTTEN ABOUT TOMORR--TODAY'S PRE-MEETING FOR THE SINGAPORE CONFERENCE?
POLICE
TRIED ROBBING A BUS OF SENIOR CITIZENS. WE WILL CONFESS.
TRIED ROBBING A WEDDING. WE WILL CONFESS.
"MAY I REMIND YOU THAT I AM A BUTLER AND RENAISSANCE MAN. I AM NOT A DATEBOOK."

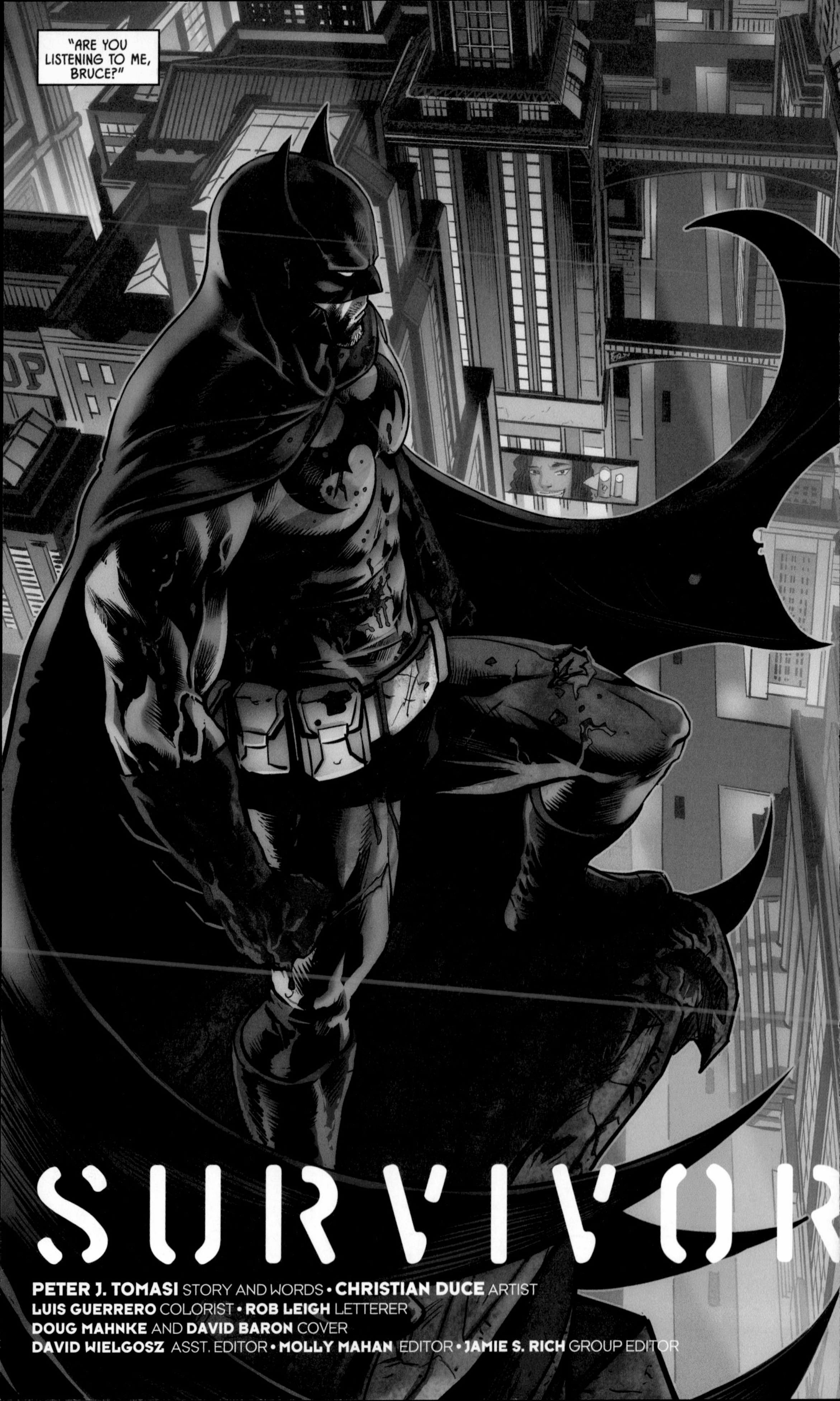
"ARE YOU LISTENING TO ME, BRUCE?"
SURVIVOR
PETER J. TOMASI STORY AND WORDS • CHRISTIAN DUCE ARTIST
LUIS GUERRERO COLORIST • ROB LEIGH LETTERER
DOUG MAHNKE AND DAVID BARON COVER
DAVID WIELGOSZ ASST. EDITOR • MOLLY MAHAN EDITOR • JAMIE S. RICH GROUP EDITOR

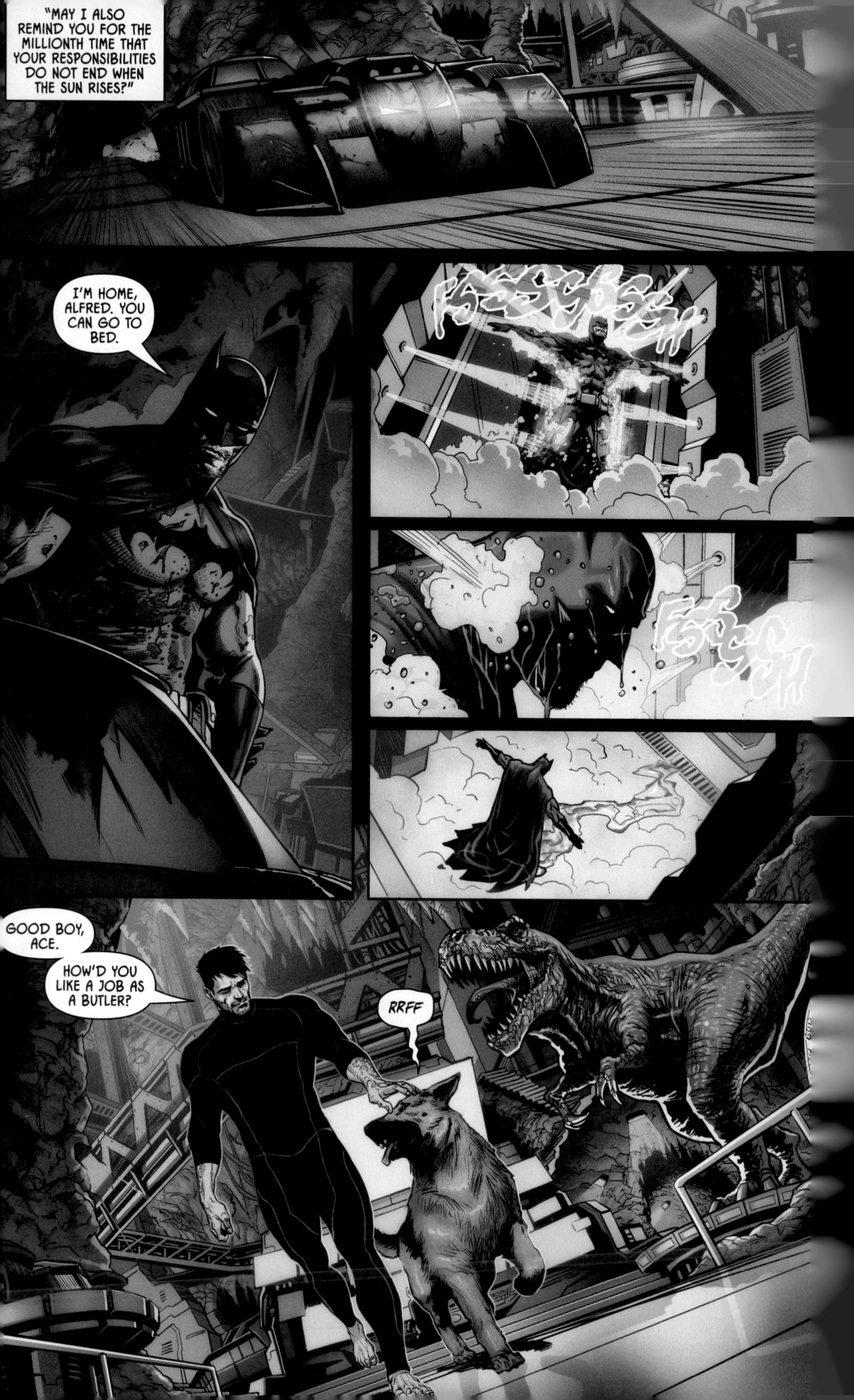
"MAY I ALSO REMIND YOU FOR THE MILLIONTH TIME THAT YOUR RESPONSIBILITIES DO NOT END WHEN THE SUN RISES?"
I'M HOME, ALFRED. YOU CAN GO TO BED.
FSSSCHSSCH
FSSCH
GOOD BOY, ACE.
HOW'D YOU LIKE A JOB AS A BUTLER?
RRFF

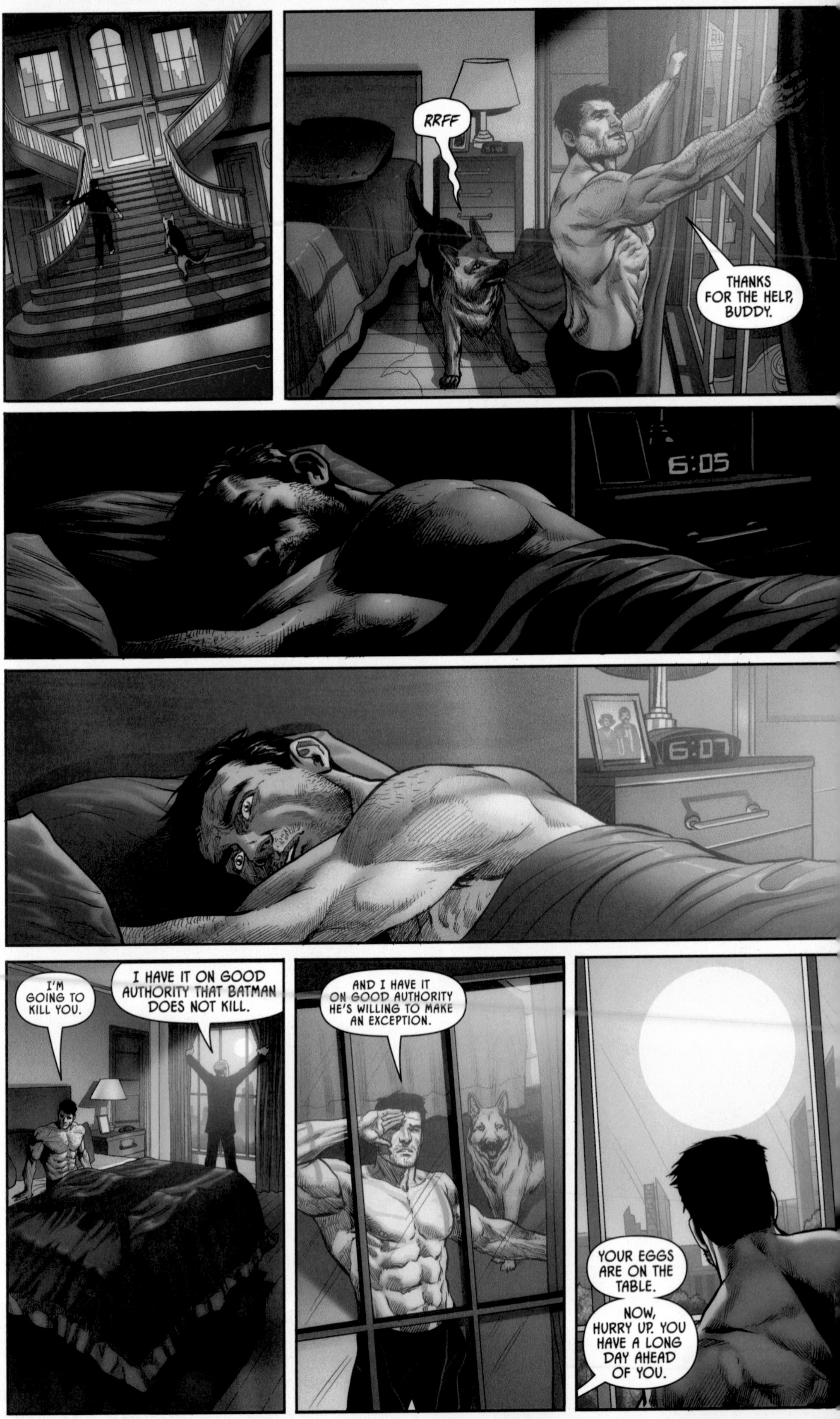
RRFF
THANKS FOR THE HELP, BUDDY.
6:05
6:07
I'M GOING TO KILL YOU.
I HAVE IT ON GOOD AUTHORITY THAT BATMAN DOES NOT KILL.
AND I HAVE IT ON GOOD AUTHORITY HE'S WILLING TO MAKE AN EXCEPTION.
YOUR EGGS ARE ON THE TABLE.
NOW, HURRY UP. YOU HAVE A LONG DAY AHEAD OF YOU.

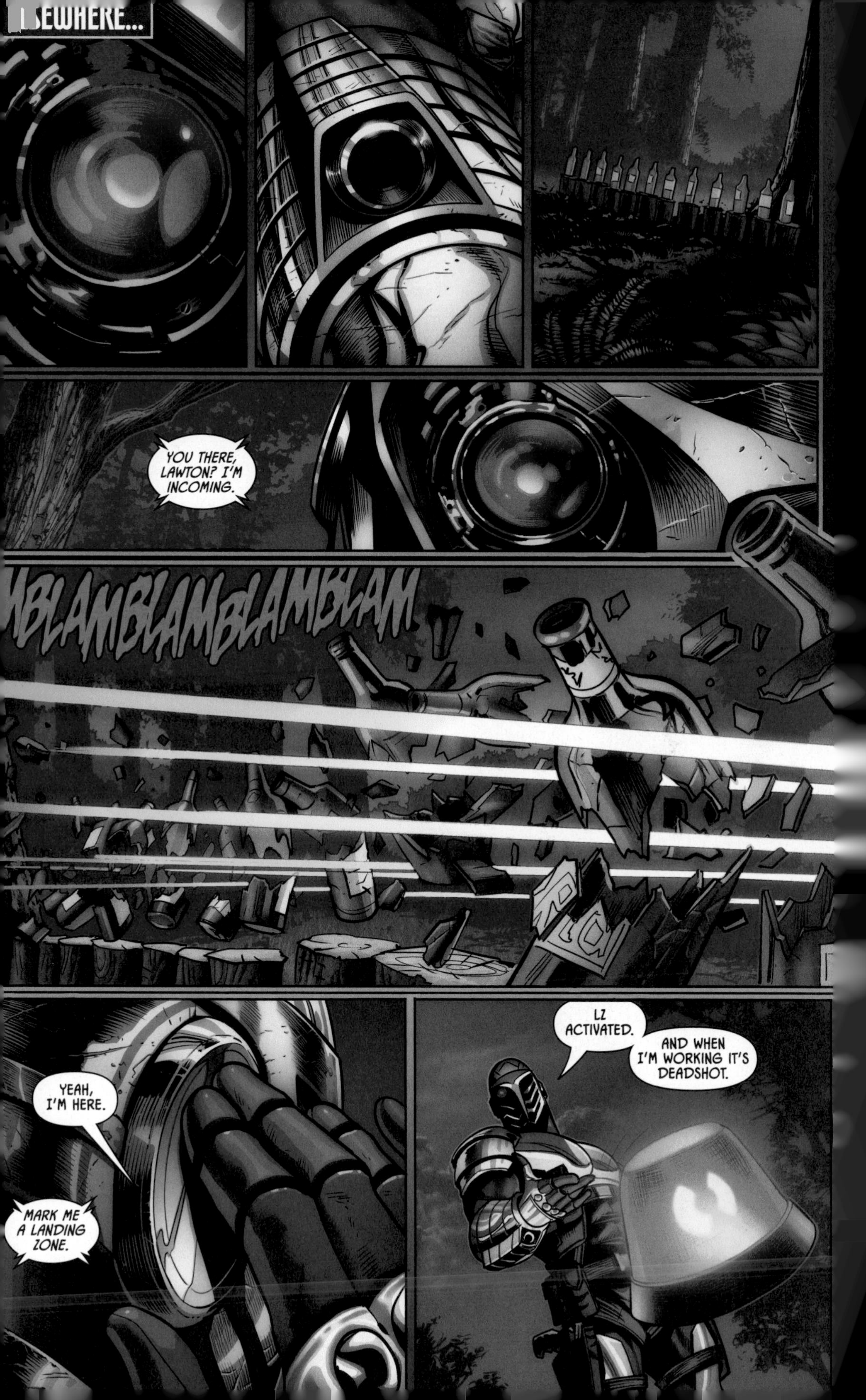

ELSEWHERE...
YOU THERE, LAWTON? I'M INCOMING.
BLAMBLAMBLAMBLAMBLAM
YEAH, I'M HERE.
MARK ME A LANDING ZONE.
LZ ACTIVATED.
AND WHEN I'M WORKING IT'S DEADSHOT.

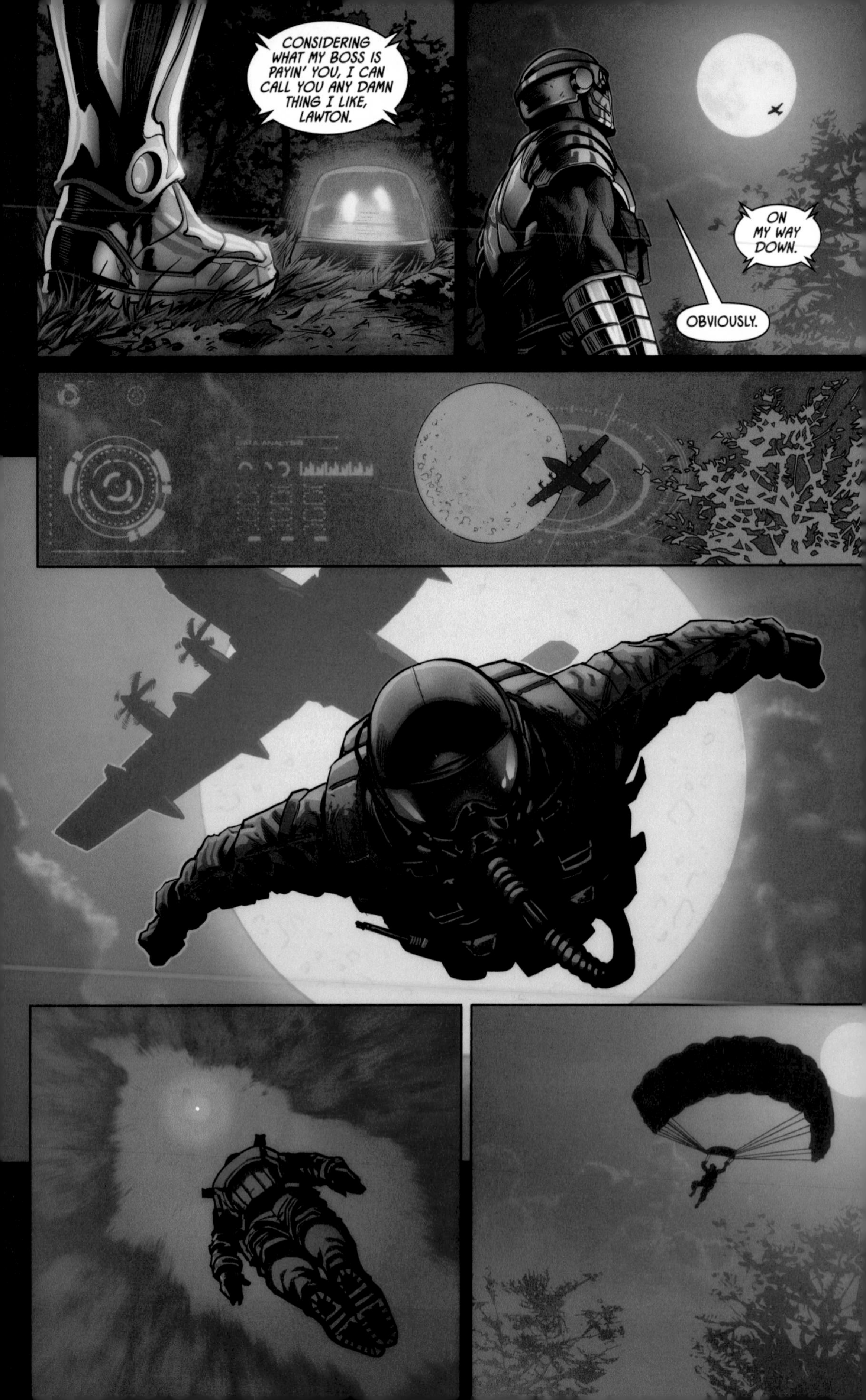
CONSIDERING WHAT MY BOSS IS PAYIN' YOU, I CAN CALL YOU ANY DAMN THING I LIKE, LAWTON.
OBVIOUSLY.
ON MY WAY DOWN.

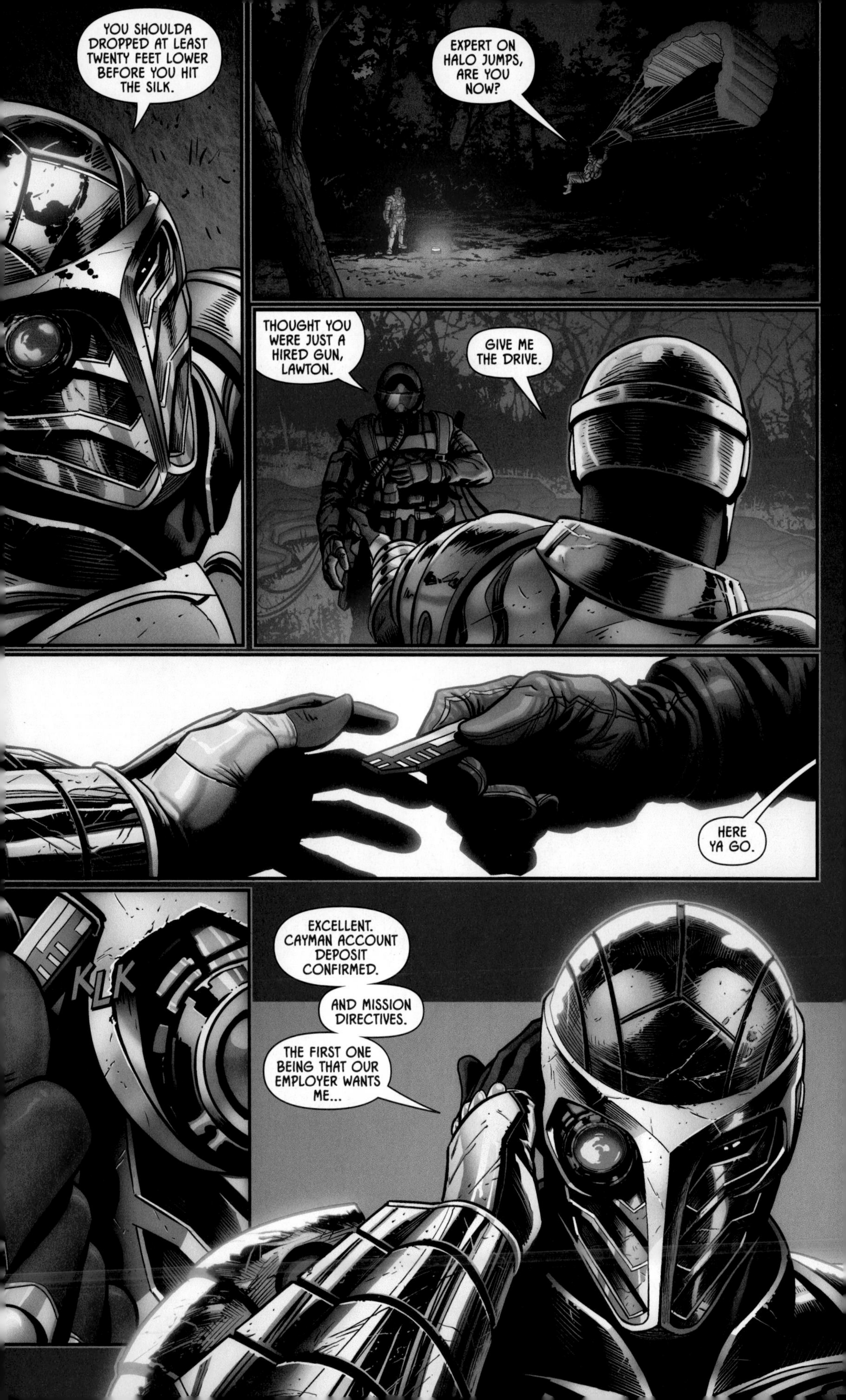
YOU SHOULDA DROPPED AT LEAST TWENTY FEET LOWER BEFORE YOU HIT THE SILK.
EXPERT ON HALO JUMPS, ARE YOU NOW?
THOUGHT YOU WERE JUST A HIRED GUN, LAWTON.
GIVE ME THE DRIVE.
HERE YA GO.
KLK
EXCELLENT. CAYMAN ACCOUNT DEPOSIT CONFIRMED.
AND MISSION DIRECTIVES.
THE FIRST ONE BEING THAT OUR EMPLOYER WANTS ME...

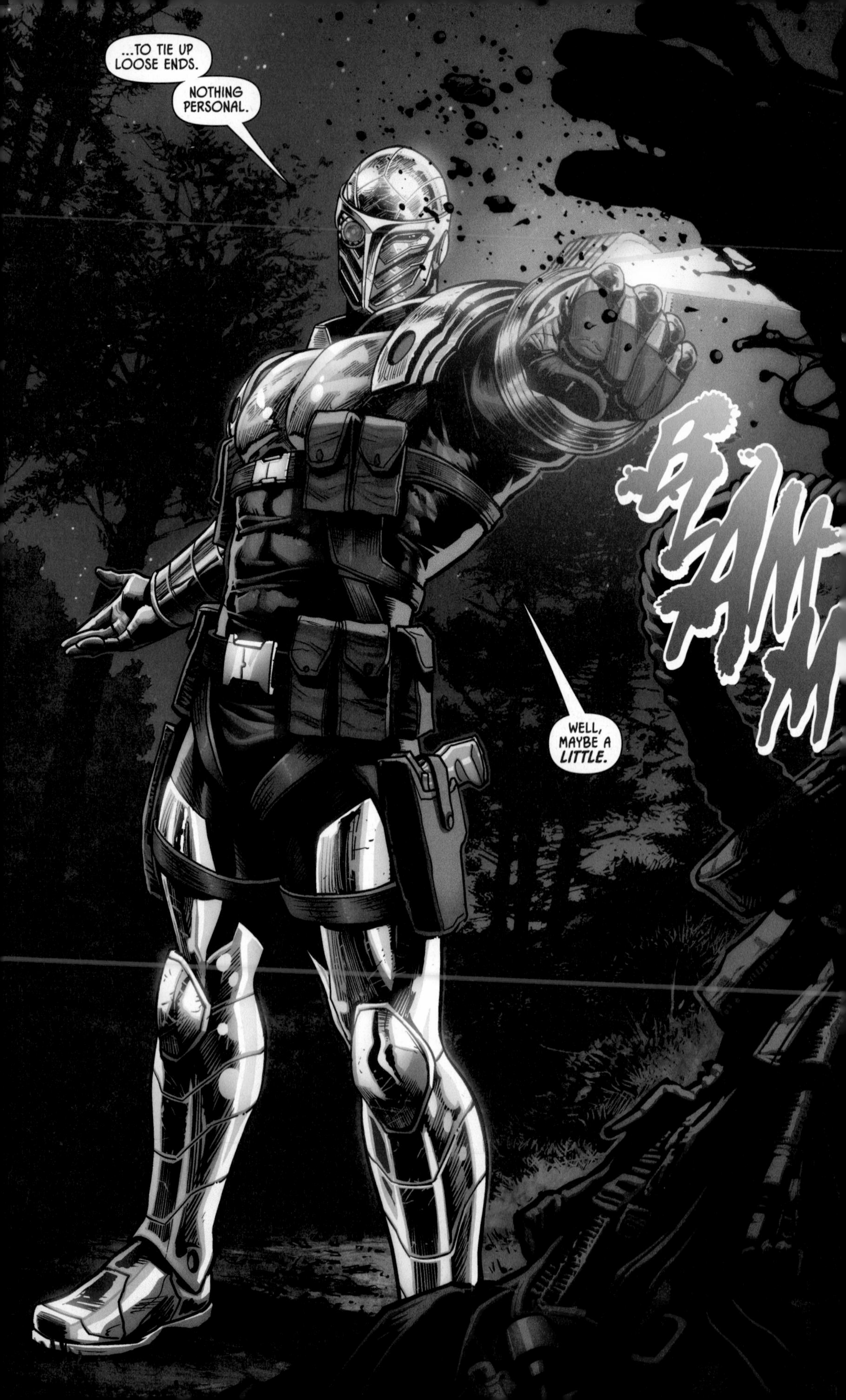
...TO TIE UP LOOSE ENDS.
NOTHING PERSONAL.
WELL, MAYBE A LITTLE.
BLAM

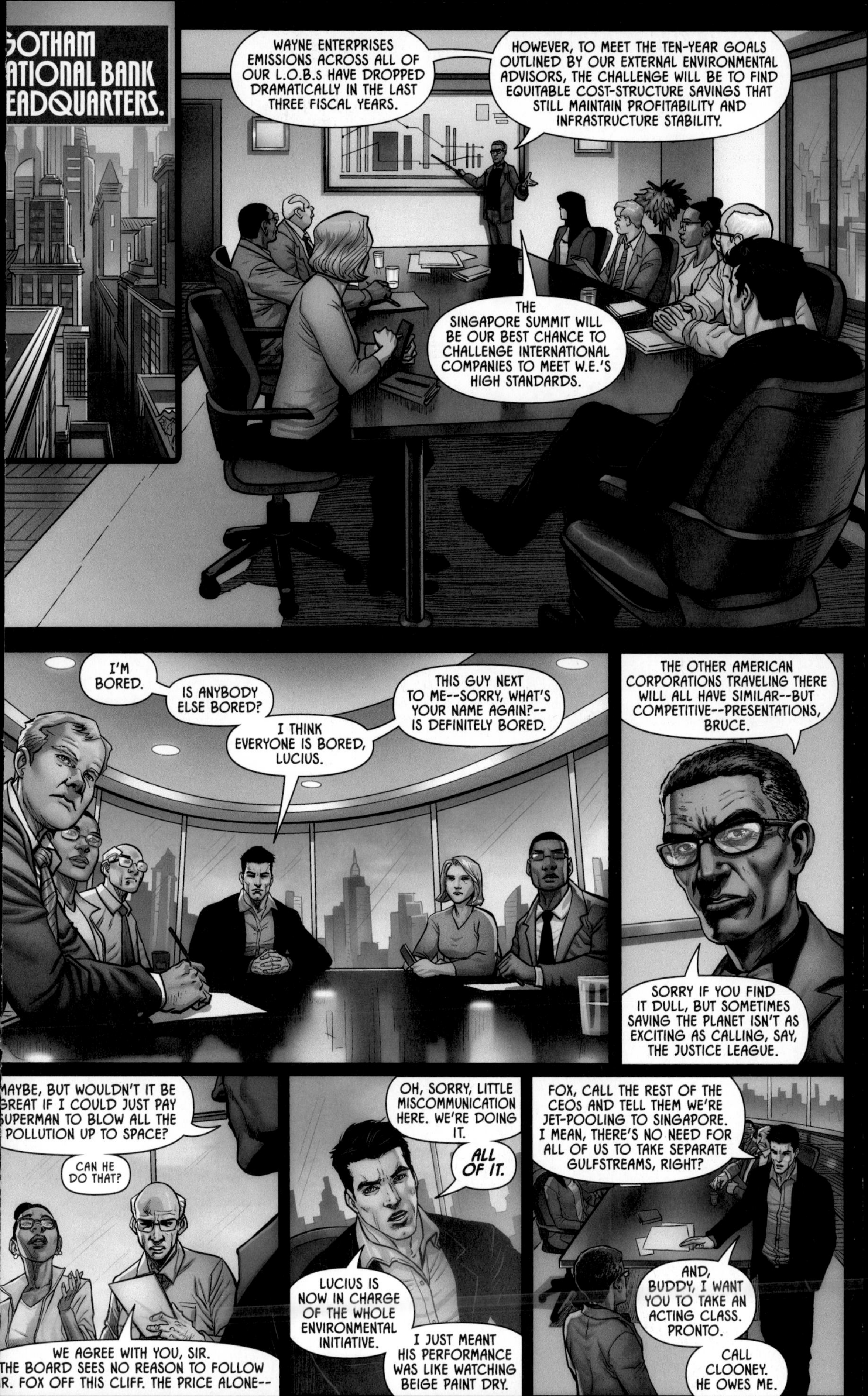
GOTHAM
ATIONAL BANK
EADQUARTERS.
WAYNE ENTERPRISES EMISSIONS ACROSS ALL OF OUR L.O.B.s HAVE DROPPED DRAMATICALLY IN THE LAST THREE FISCAL YEARS.
HOWEVER, TO MEET THE TEN-YEAR GOALS OUTLINED BY OUR EXTERNAL ENVIRONMENTAL ADVISORS, THE CHALLENGE WILL BE TO FIND EQUITABLE COST-STRUCTURE SAVINGS THAT STILL MAINTAIN PROFITABILITY AND INFRASTRUCTURE STABILITY.
THE SINGAPORE SUMMIT WILL BE OUR BEST CHANCE TO CHALLENGE INTERNATIONAL COMPANIES TO MEET W.E.'S HIGH STANDARDS.
I'M BORED.
IS ANYBODY ELSE BORED?
I THINK EVERYONE IS BORED, LUCIUS.
THIS GUY NEXT TO ME--SORRY, WHAT'S YOUR NAME AGAIN?--IS DEFINITELY BORED.
THE OTHER AMERICAN CORPORATIONS TRAVELING THERE WILL ALL HAVE SIMILAR--BUT COMPETITIVE--PRESENTATIONS, BRUCE.
SORRY IF YOU FIND IT DULL, BUT SOMETIMES SAVING THE PLANET ISN'T AS EXCITING AS CALLING, SAY, THE JUSTICE LEAGUE.
MAYBE, BUT WOULDN'T IT BE GREAT IF I COULD JUST PAY SUPERMAN TO BLOW ALL THE POLLUTION UP TO SPACE?
CAN HE DO THAT?
WE AGREE WITH YOU, SIR. THE BOARD SEES NO REASON TO FOLLOW R. FOX OFF THIS CLIFF. THE PRICE ALONE--
OH, SORRY, LITTLE MISCOMMUNICATION HERE. WE'RE DOING IT.
ALL OF IT.
LUCIUS IS NOW IN CHARGE OF THE WHOLE ENVIRONMENTAL INITIATIVE.
I JUST MEANT HIS PERFORMANCE WAS LIKE WATCHING BEIGE PAINT DRY.
FOX, CALL THE REST OF THE CEOs AND TELL THEM WE'RE JET-POOLING TO SINGAPORE. I MEAN, THERE'S NO NEED FOR ALL OF US TO TAKE SEPARATE GULFSTREAMS, RIGHT?
AND, BUDDY, I WANT YOU TO TAKE AN ACTING CLASS. PRONTO.
CALL CLOONEY. HE OWES ME.

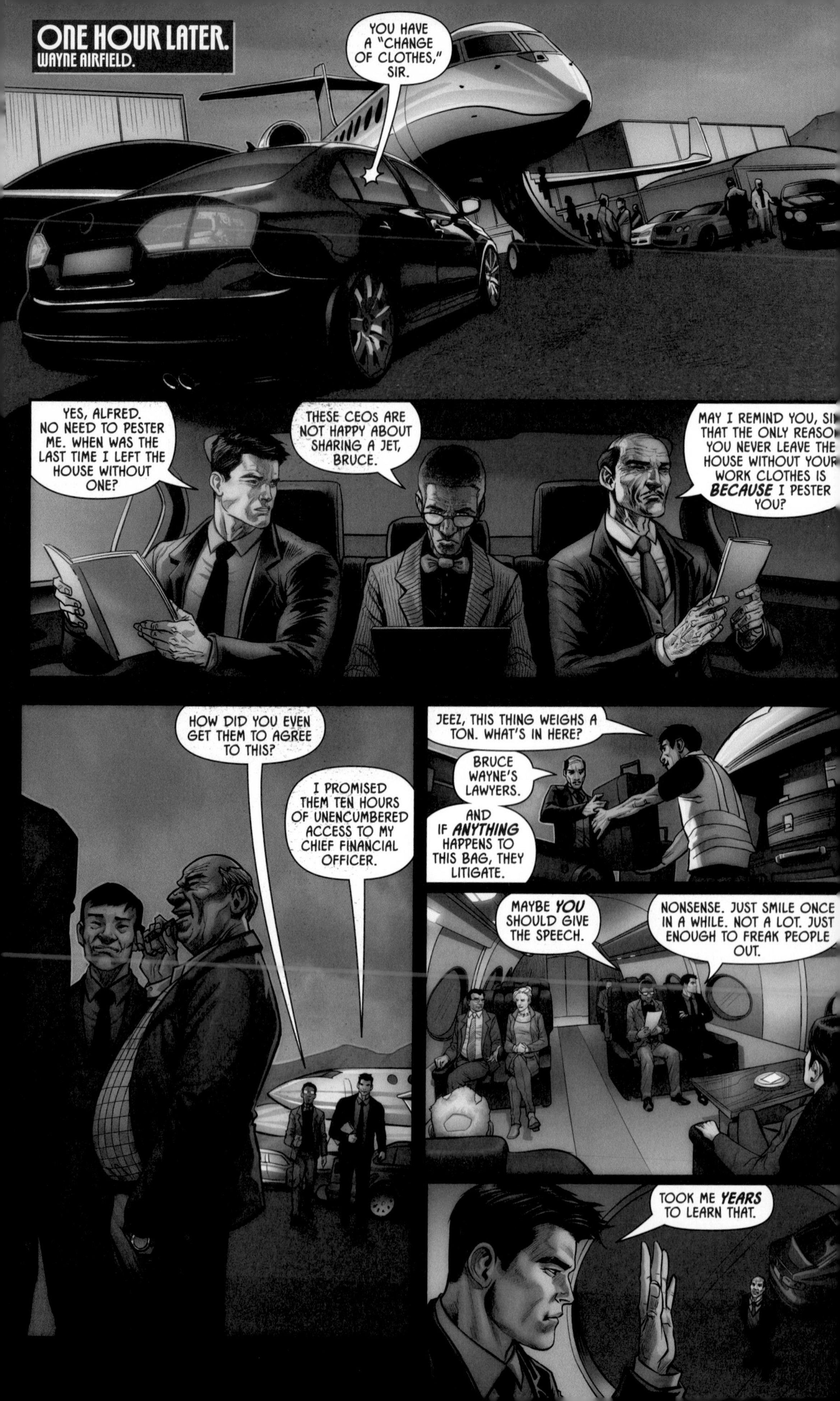
ONE HOUR LATER.
WAYNE AIRFIELD.
YOU HAVE A "CHANGE OF CLOTHES," SIR.
YES, ALFRED. NO NEED TO PESTER ME. WHEN WAS THE LAST TIME I LEFT THE HOUSE WITHOUT ONE?
THESE CEOs ARE NOT HAPPY ABOUT SHARING A JET, BRUCE.
MAY I REMIND YOU, SI THAT THE ONLY REASO YOU NEVER LEAVE THE HOUSE WITHOUT YOUR WORK CLOTHES IS *BECAUSE* I PESTER YOU?
HOW DID YOU EVEN GET THEM TO AGREE TO THIS?
I PROMISED THEM TEN HOURS OF UNENCUMBERED ACCESS TO MY CHIEF FINANCIAL OFFICER.
JEEZ, THIS THING WEIGHS A TON. WHAT'S IN HERE?
BRUCE WAYNE'S LAWYERS.
AND IF *ANYTHING* HAPPENS TO THIS BAG, THEY LITIGATE.
MAYBE *YOU* SHOULD GIVE THE SPEECH.
NONSENSE. JUST SMILE ONCE IN A WHILE. NOT A LOT. JUST ENOUGH TO FREAK PEOPLE OUT.
TOOK ME *YEARS* TO LEARN THAT.

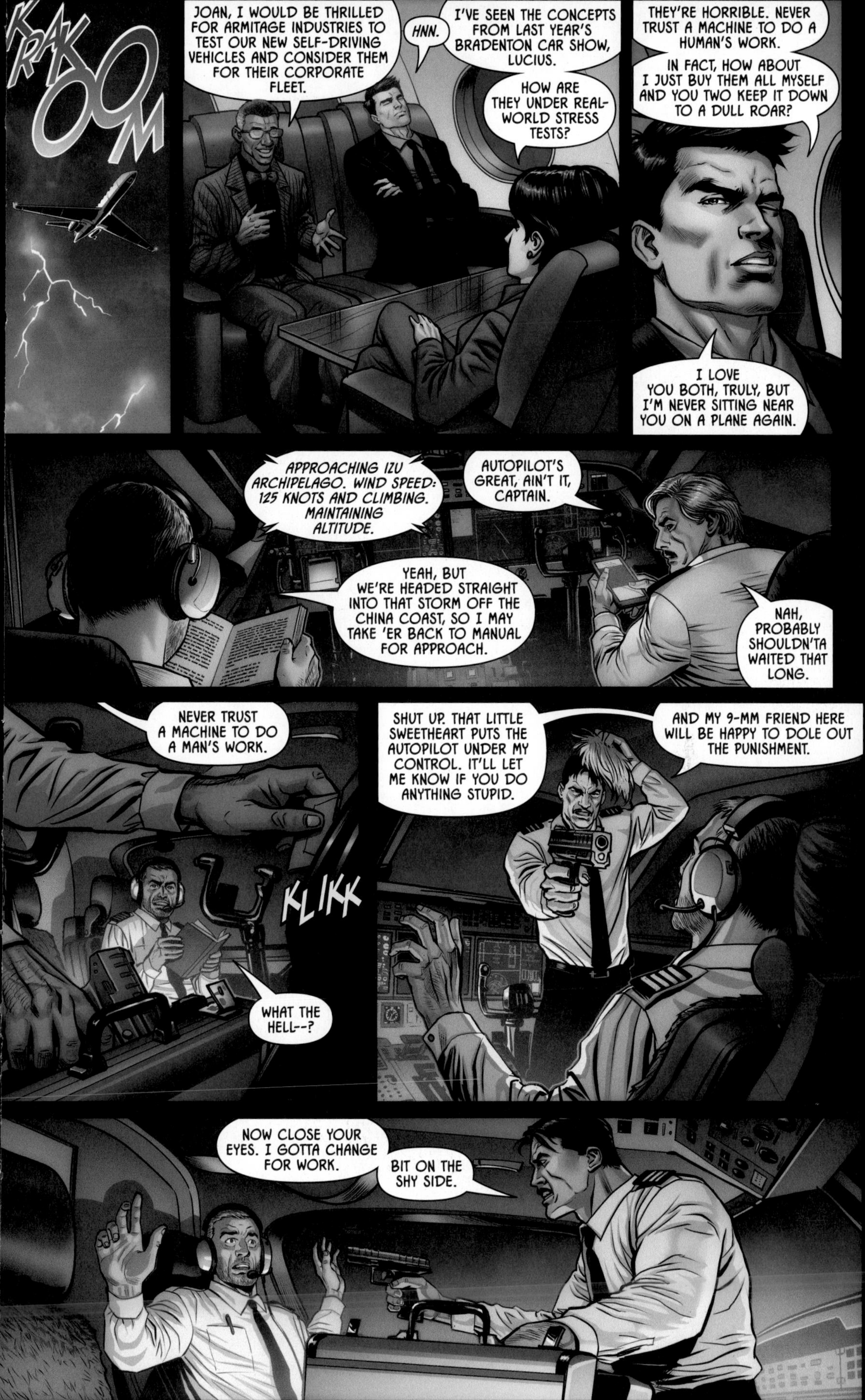
KRAKOOM
JOAN, I WOULD BE THRILLED FOR ARMITAGE INDUSTRIES TO TEST OUR NEW SELF-DRIVING VEHICLES AND CONSIDER THEM FOR THEIR CORPORATE FLEET.
HNN.
I'VE SEEN THE CONCEPTS FROM LAST YEAR'S BRADENTON CAR SHOW, LUCIUS.
HOW ARE THEY UNDER REAL-WORLD STRESS TESTS?
THEY'RE HORRIBLE. NEVER TRUST A MACHINE TO DO A HUMAN'S WORK.
IN FACT, HOW ABOUT I JUST BUY THEM ALL MYSELF AND YOU TWO KEEP IT DOWN TO A DULL ROAR?
I LOVE YOU BOTH, TRULY, BUT I'M NEVER SITTING NEAR YOU ON A PLANE AGAIN.
APPROACHING IZU ARCHIPELAGO. WIND SPEED: 125 KNOTS AND CLIMBING. MAINTAINING ALTITUDE.
AUTOPILOT'S GREAT, AIN'T IT, CAPTAIN.
YEAH, BUT WE'RE HEADED STRAIGHT INTO THAT STORM OFF THE CHINA COAST, SO I MAY TAKE 'ER BACK TO MANUAL FOR APPROACH.
NAH, PROBABLY SHOULDN'TA WAITED THAT LONG.
NEVER TRUST A MACHINE TO DO A MAN'S WORK.
KLIKK
WHAT THE HELL--?
SHUT UP. THAT LITTLE SWEETHEART PUTS THE AUTOPILOT UNDER MY CONTROL. IT'LL LET ME KNOW IF YOU DO ANYTHING STUPID.
AND MY 9-MM FRIEND HERE WILL BE HAPPY TO DOLE OUT THE PUNISHMENT.
NOW CLOSE YOUR EYES. I GOTTA CHANGE FOR WORK.
BIT ON THE SHY SIDE.

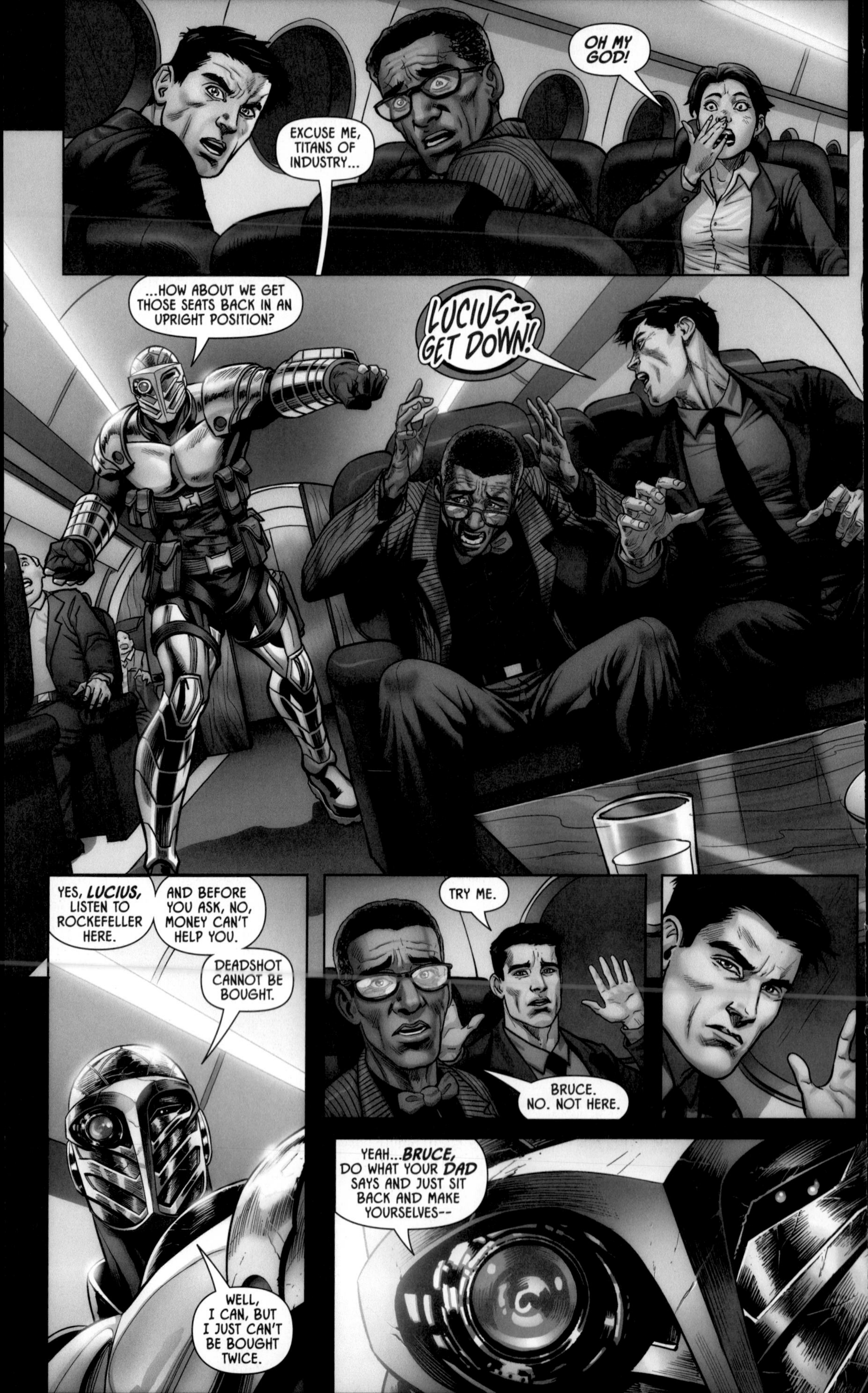
OH MY GOD!
EXCUSE ME, TITANS OF INDUSTRY...
...HOW ABOUT WE GET THOSE SEATS BACK IN AN UPRIGHT POSITION?
LUCIUS-- GET DOWN!!
YES, LUCIUS, LISTEN TO ROCKEFELLER HERE.
AND BEFORE YOU ASK, NO, MONEY CAN'T HELP YOU.
DEADSHOT CANNOT BE BOUGHT.
WELL, I CAN, BUT I JUST CAN'T BE BOUGHT TWICE.
TRY ME.
BRUCE. NO. NOT HERE.
YEAH...BRUCE, DO WHAT YOUR DAD SAYS AND JUST SIT BACK AND MAKE YOURSELVES--

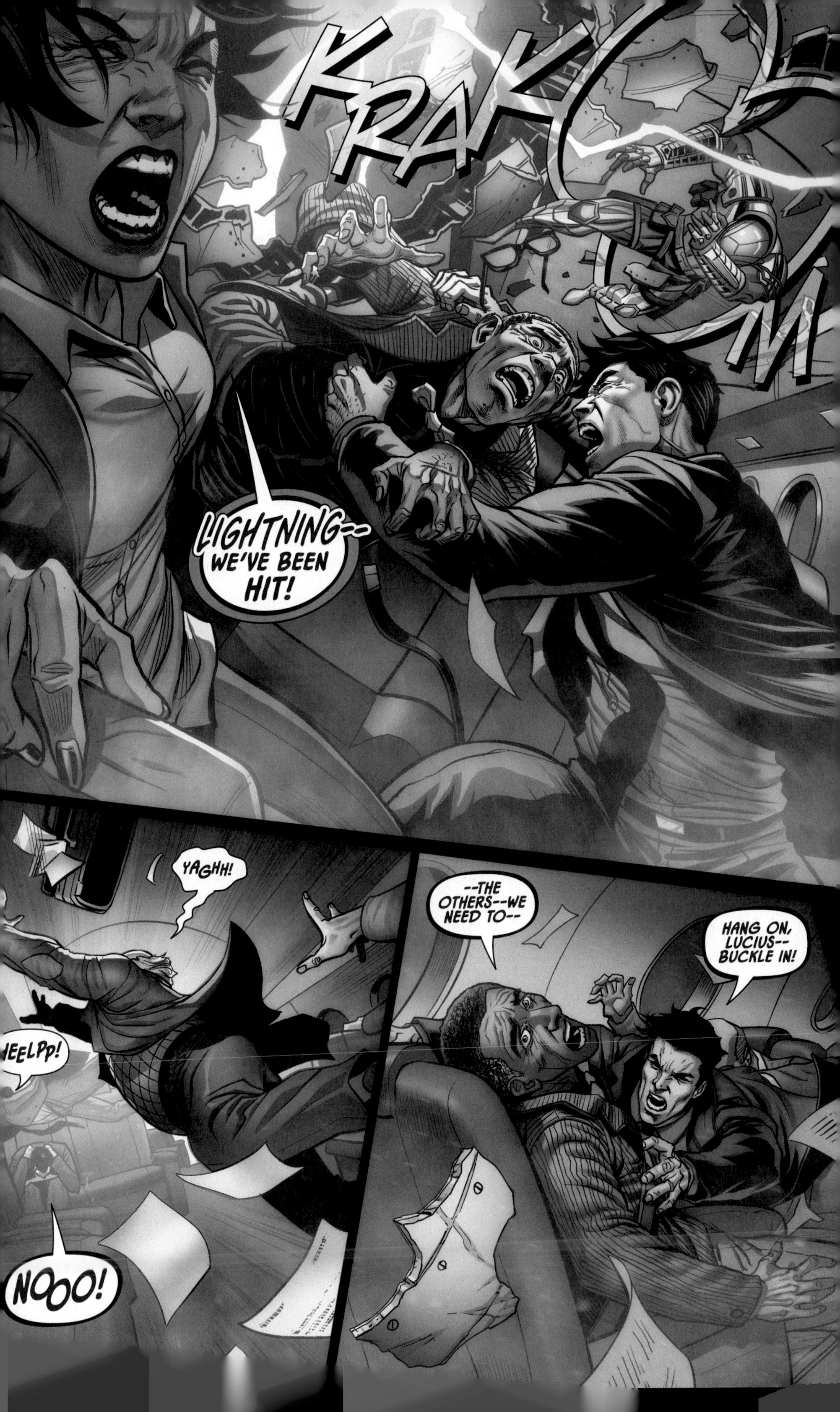
KRAKKOOM
LIGHTNING-- WE'VE BEEN HIT!
YAGHH!
HEELPP!
NOOO!
--THE OTHERS--WE NEED TO--
HANG ON, LUCIUS-- BUCKLE IN!

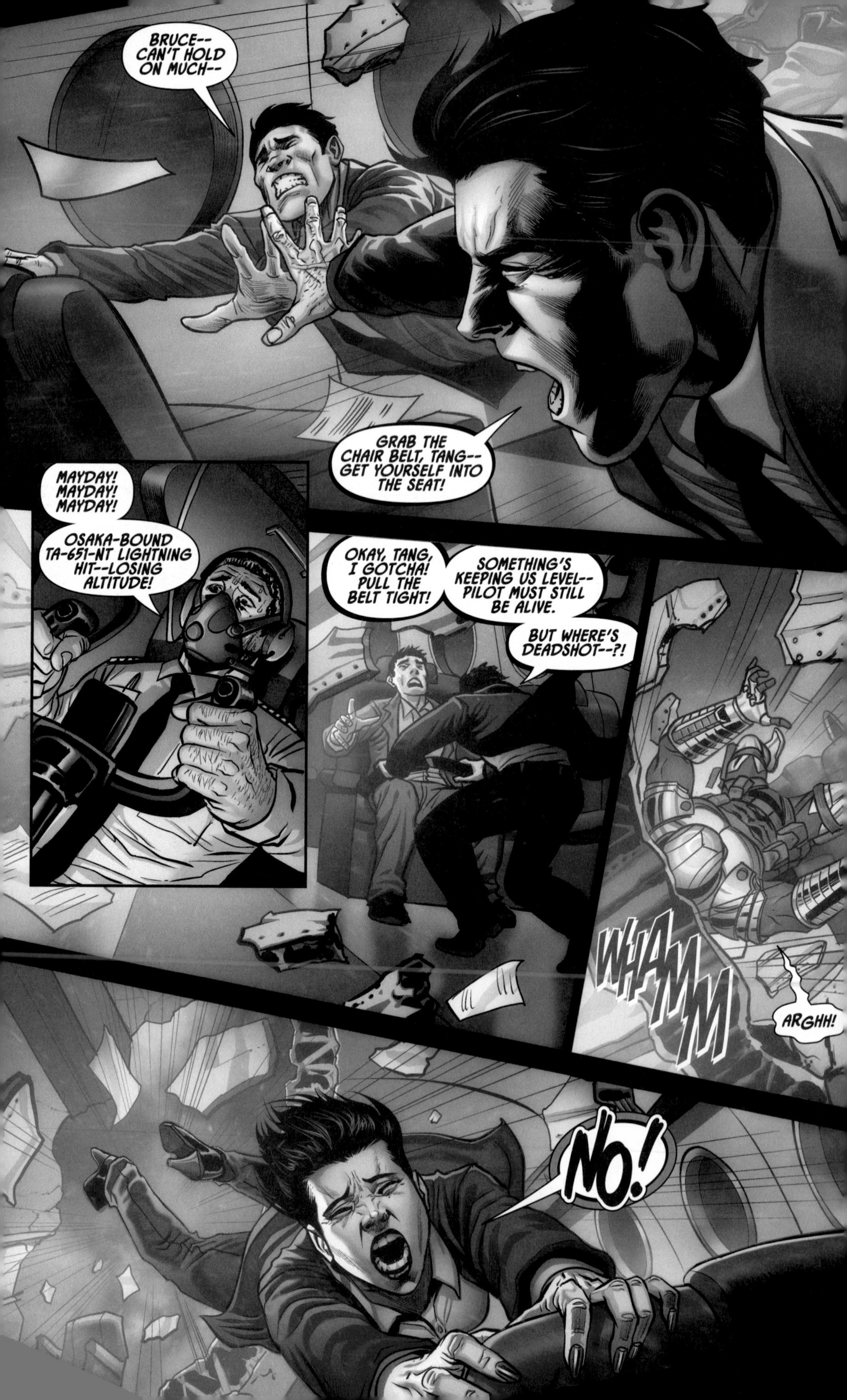
BRUCE--
CAN'T HOLD
ON MUCH--
GRAB THE
CHAIR BELT, TANG--
GET YOURSELF INTO
THE SEAT!
MAYDAY!
MAYDAY!
MAYDAY!
OSAKA-BOUND
TA-651-NT LIGHTNING
HIT--LOSING
ALTITUDE!
OKAY, TANG,
I GOTCHA!
PULL THE
BELT TIGHT!
SOMETHING'S
KEEPING US LEVEL--
PILOT MUST STILL
BE ALIVE.
BUT WHERE'S
DEADSHOT--?!
WHAMM
ARGHH!
NO!

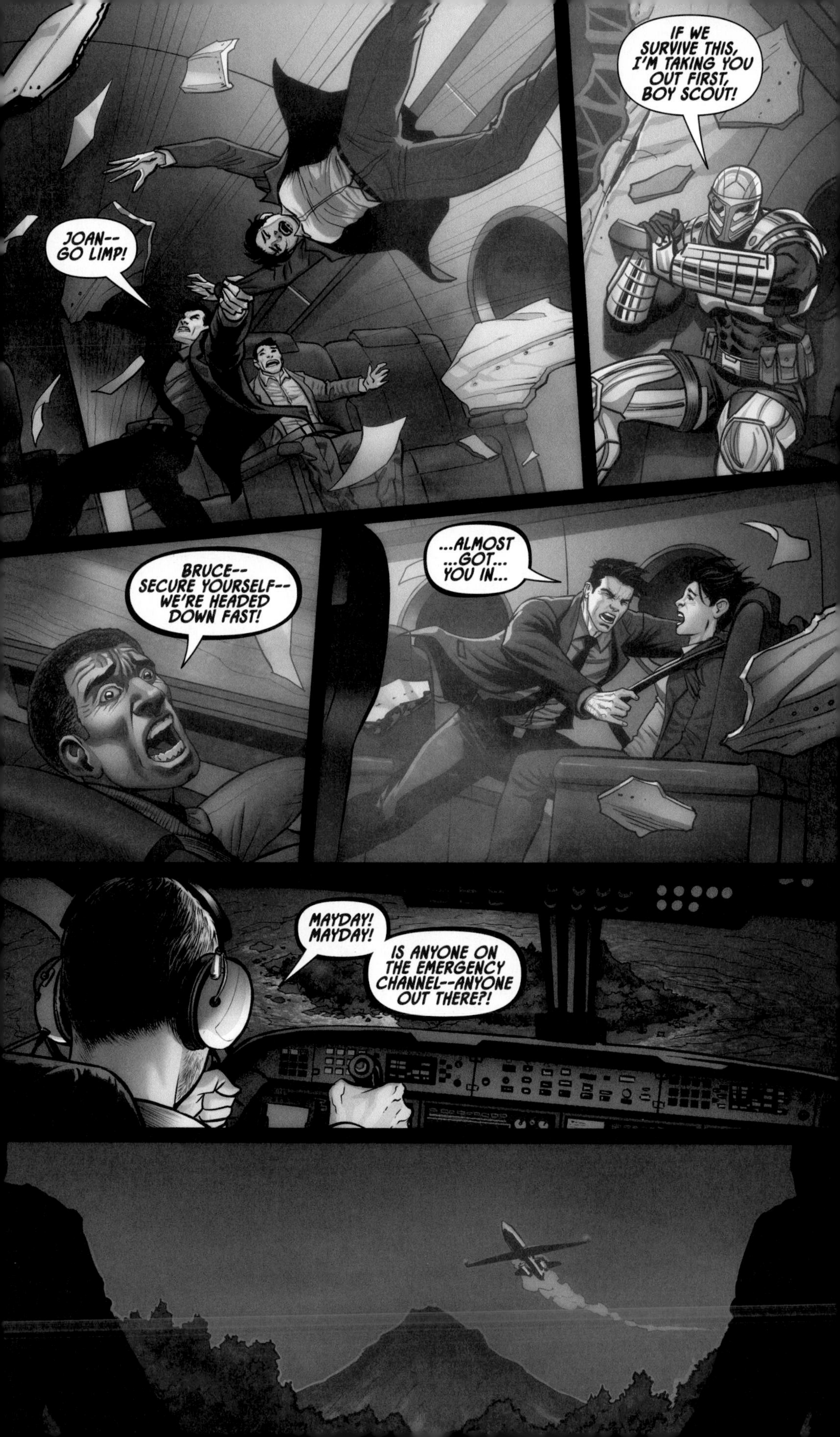
JOAN--
GO LIMP!
IF WE SURVIVE THIS, I'M TAKING YOU OUT FIRST, BOY SCOUT!
BRUCE-- SECURE YOURSELF-- WE'RE HEADED DOWN FAST!
...ALMOST ...GOT... YOU IN...
MAYDAY! MAYDAY!
IS ANYONE ON THE EMERGENCY CHANNEL--ANYONE OUT THERE?!

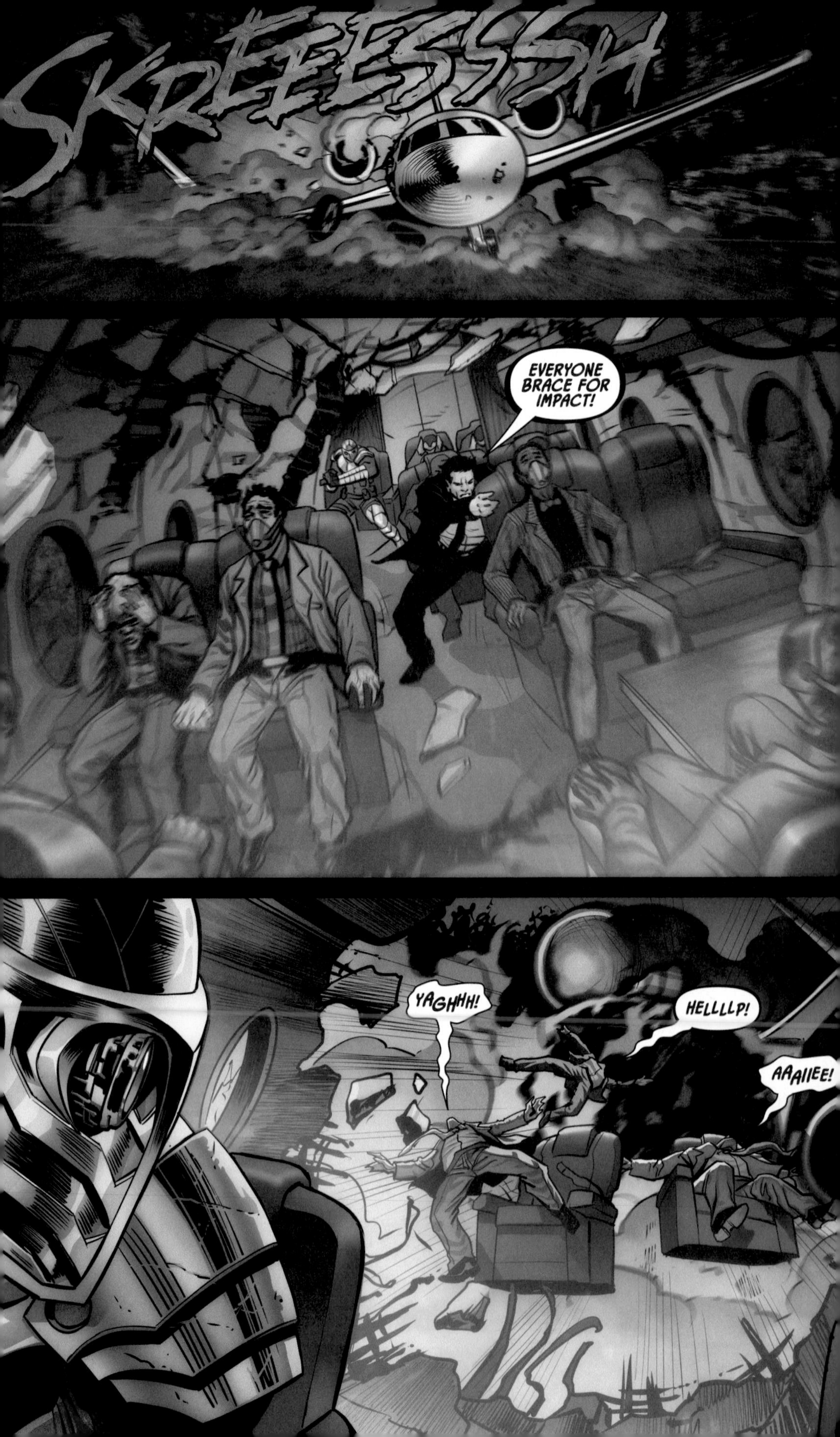
SKREEESSSH
EVERYONE BRACE FOR IMPACT!
YAGHHH!
HELLLLLP!
AAAIIEE!

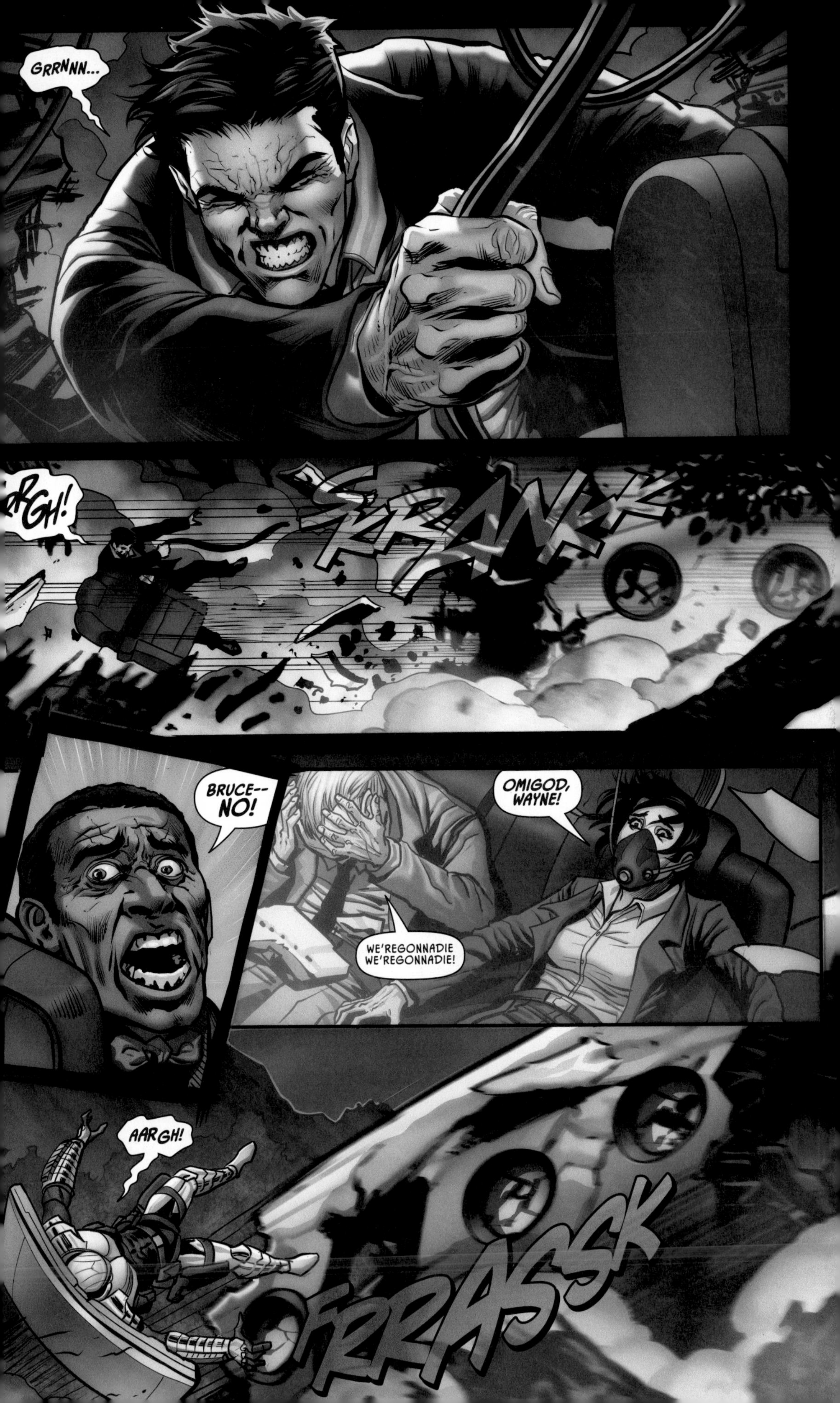
GRRNNN...
RGH!
SKRANK
BRUCE--
NO!
OMIGOD, WAYNE!
WE'REGONNADIE
WE'REGONNADIE!
AARGH!
FRRASSK

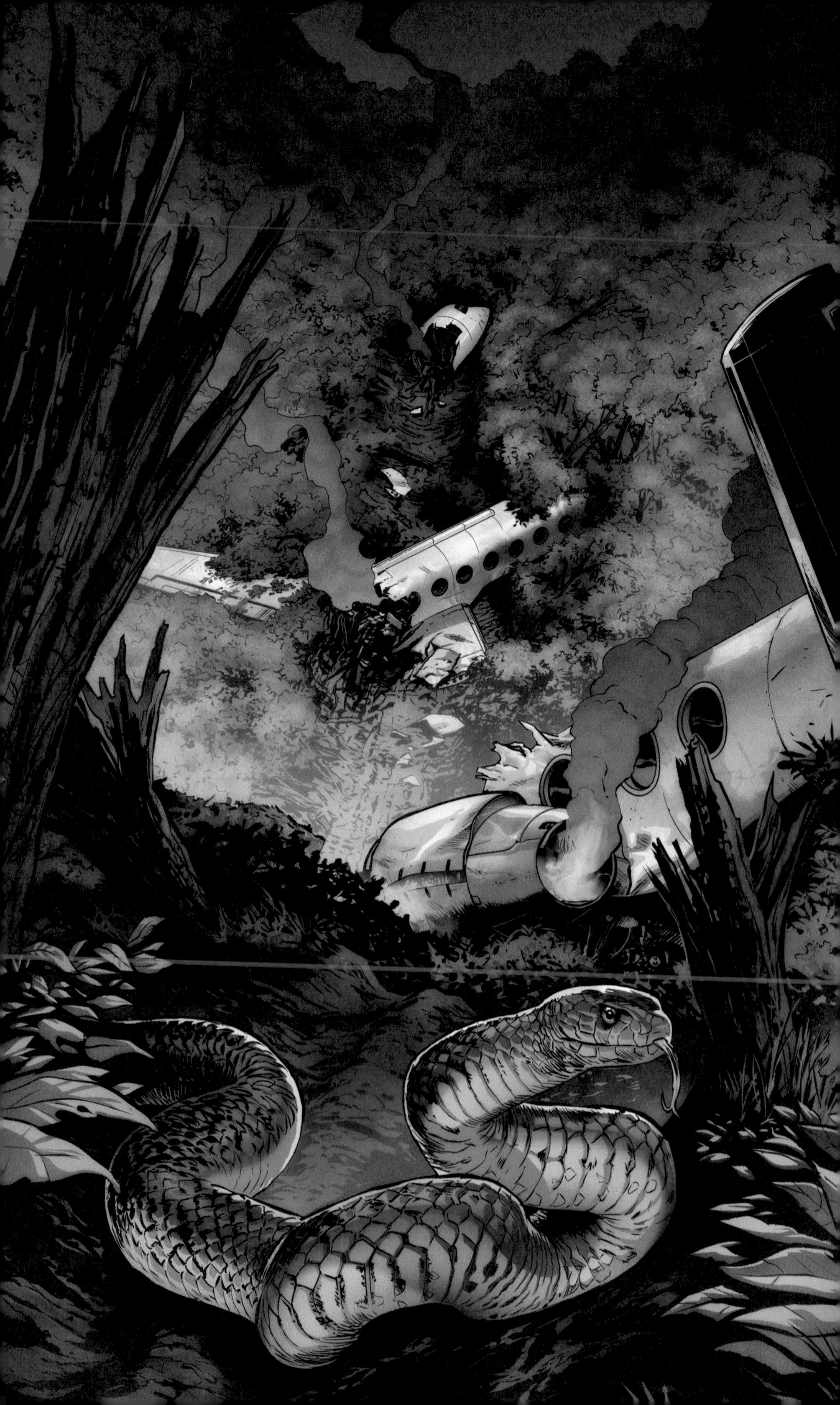

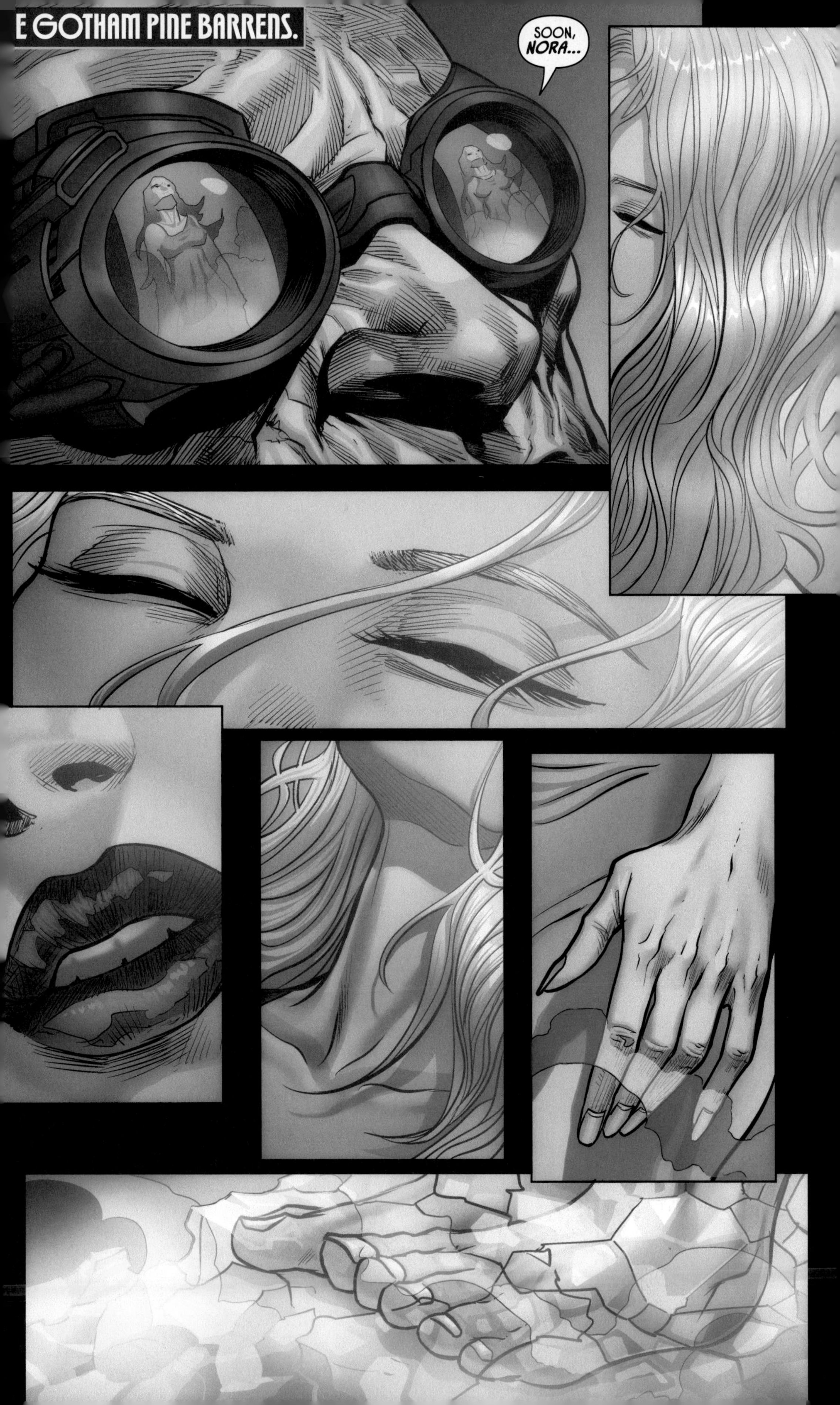
E GOTHAM PINE BARRENS.
SOON, NORA...

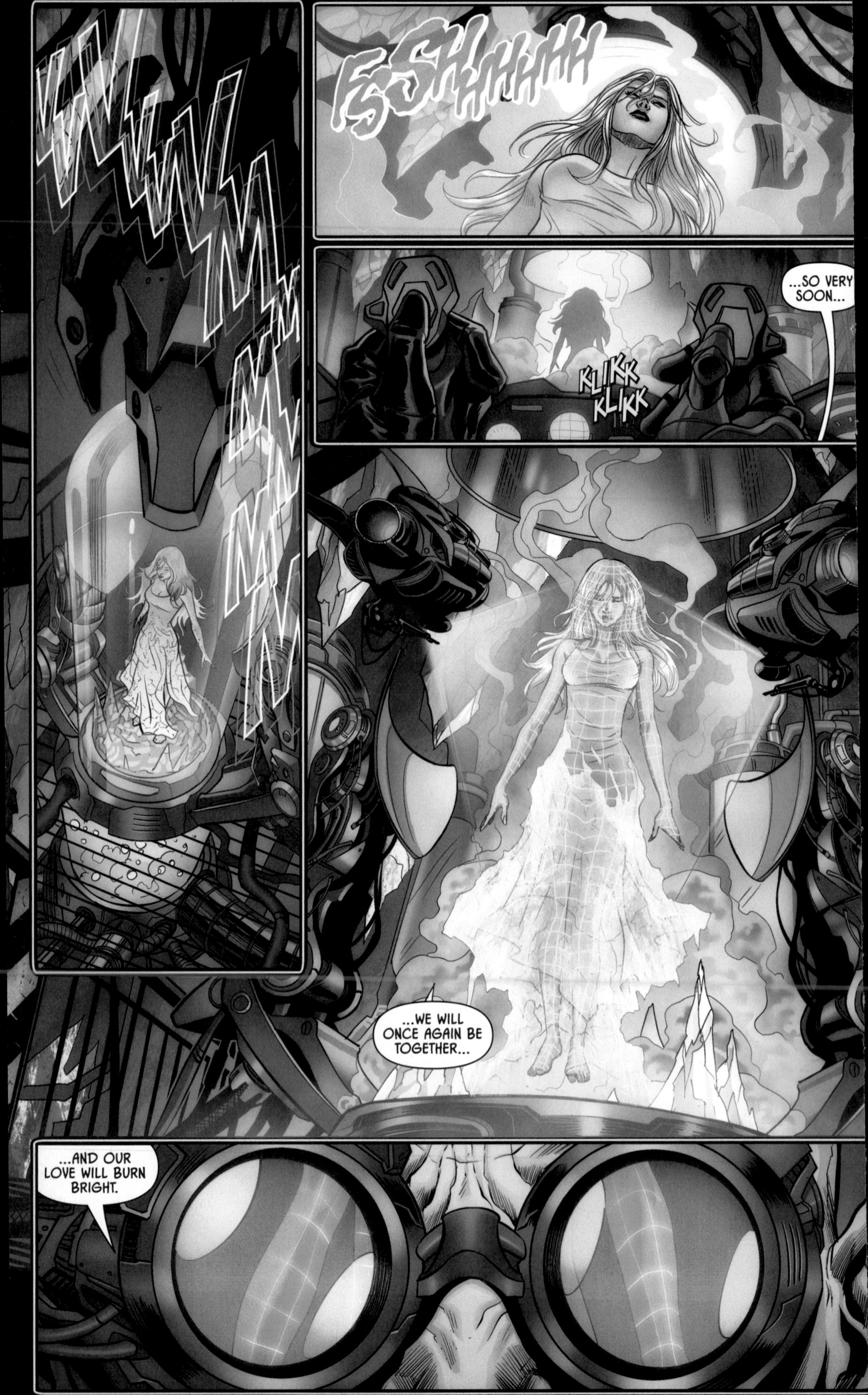
VWWWMMMMMMM
FSHHHHHH
...SO VERY SOON...
KLIKK KLIKK
...WE WILL ONCE AGAIN BE TOGETHER...
...AND OUR LOVE WILL BURN BRIGHT.

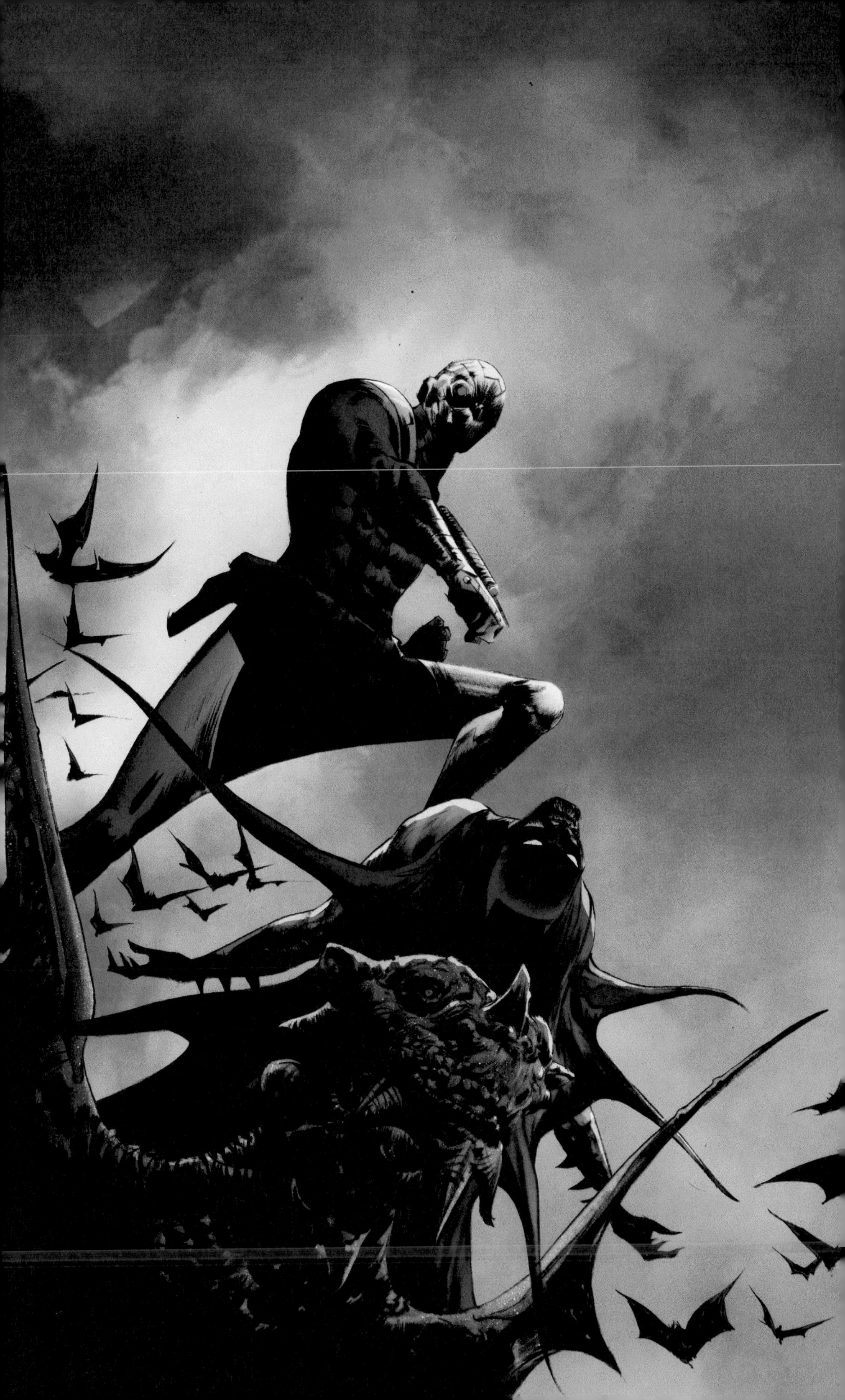

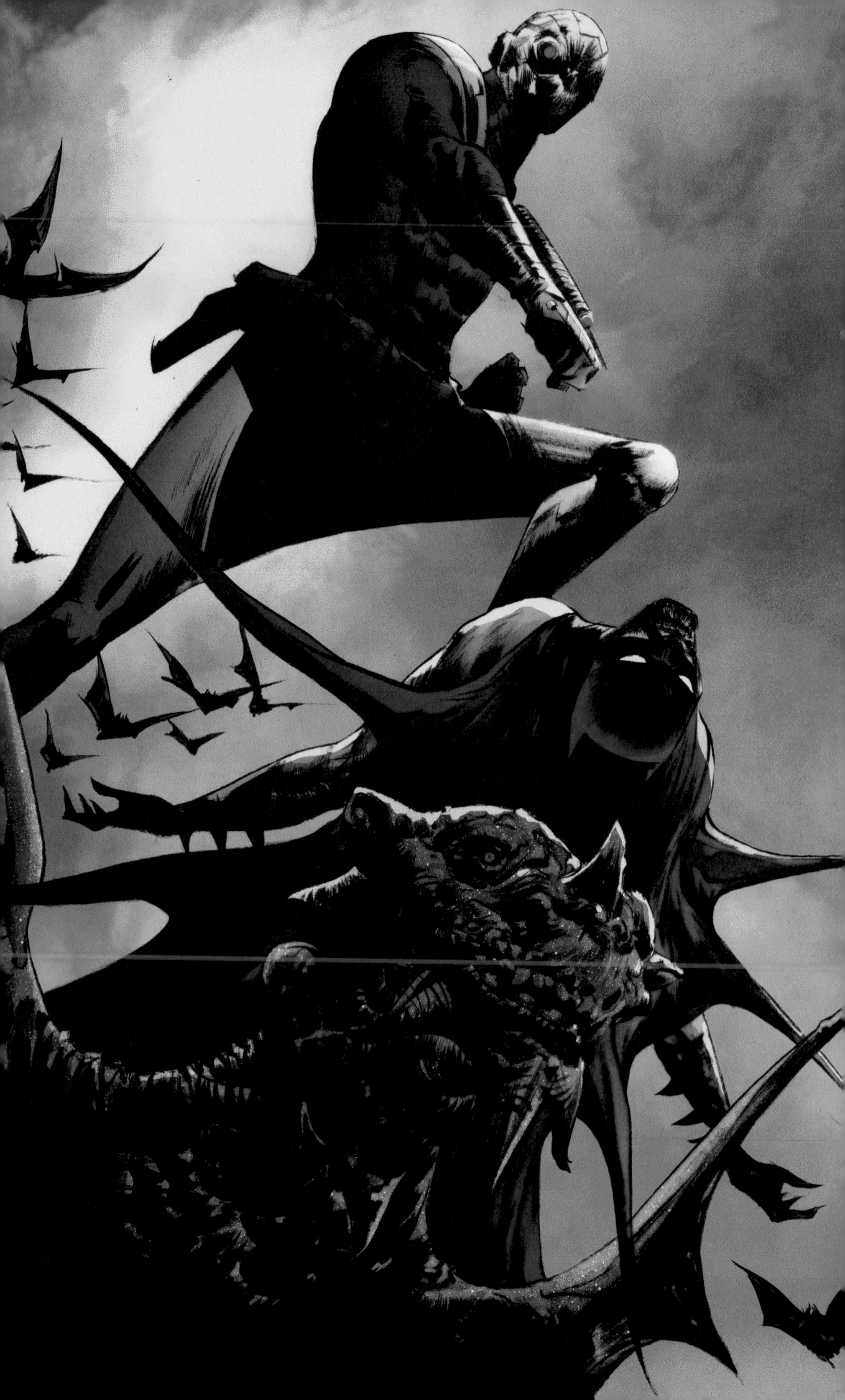

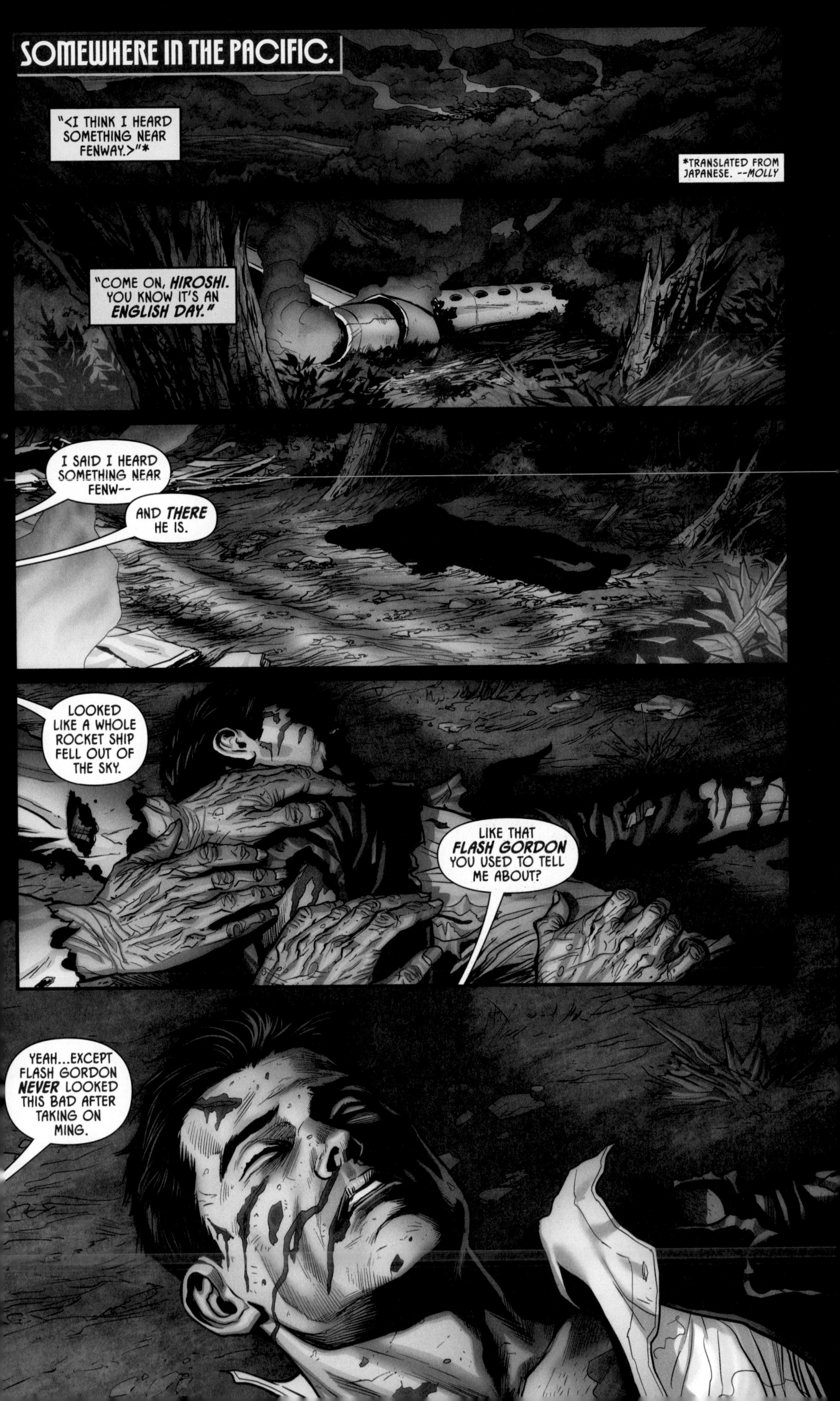
SOMEWHERE IN THE PACIFIC.
"<I THINK I HEARD SOMETHING NEAR FENWAY.>"*
*TRANSLATED FROM JAPANESE. --MOLLY
"COME ON, HIROSHI. YOU KNOW IT'S AN ENGLISH DAY."
I SAID I HEARD SOMETHING NEAR FENW--
AND THERE HE IS.
LOOKED LIKE A WHOLE ROCKET SHIP FELL OUT OF THE SKY.
LIKE THAT FLASH GORDON YOU USED TO TELL ME ABOUT?
YEAH...EXCEPT FLASH GORDON NEVER LOOKED THIS BAD AFTER TAKING ON MING.

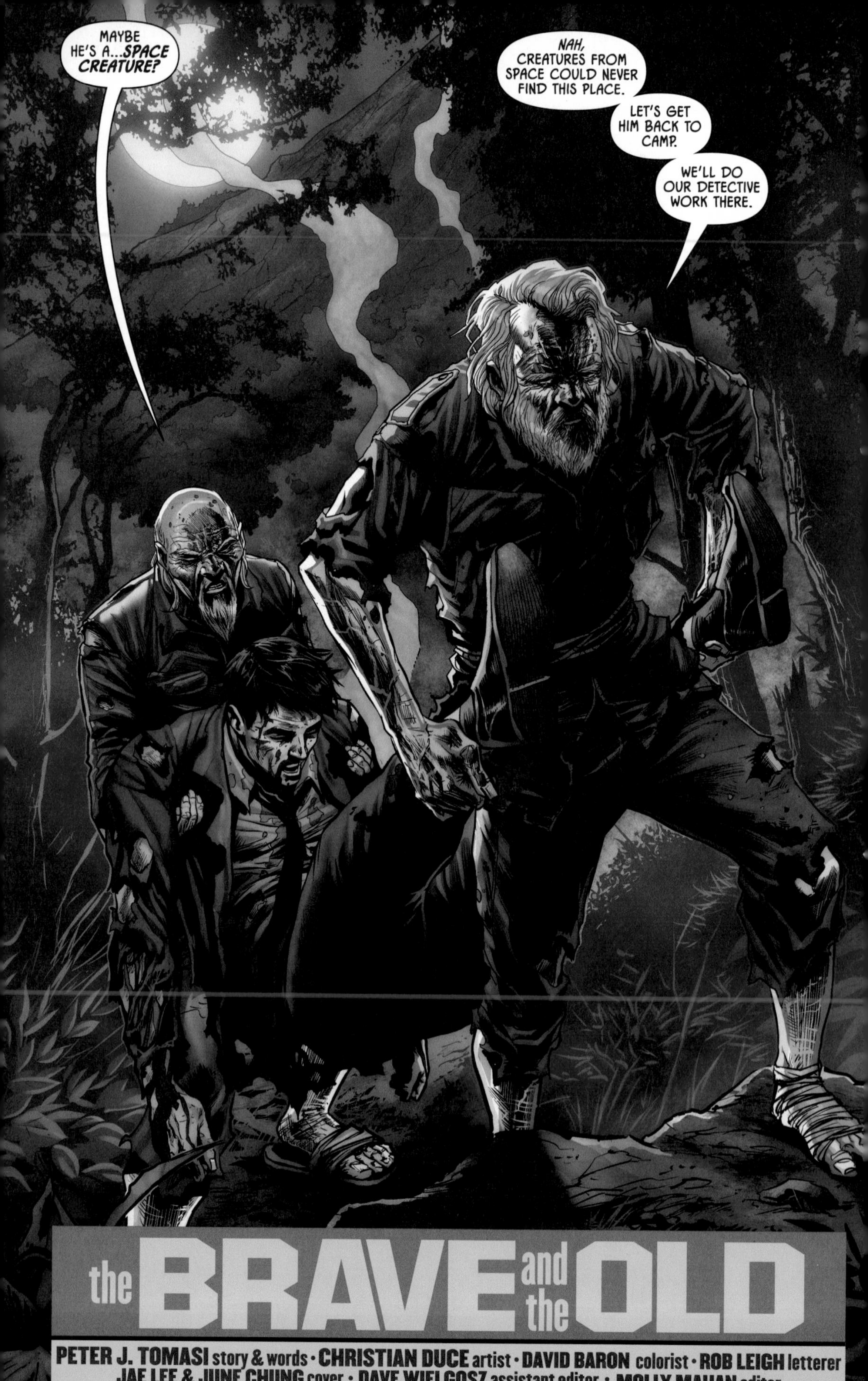
MAYBE HE'S A...SPACE CREATURE?
NAH, CREATURES FROM SPACE COULD NEVER FIND THIS PLACE.
LET'S GET HIM BACK TO CAMP.
WE'LL DO OUR DETECTIVE WORK THERE.

the BRAVE and the OLD

PETER J. TOMASI story & words · **CHRISTIAN DUCE** artist · **DAVID BARON** colorist · **ROB LEIGH** letterer
JAE LEE & JUNE CHUNG cover · **DAVE WIELGOSZ** assistant editor · **MOLLY MAHAN** editor
JAMIE S. RICH group editor

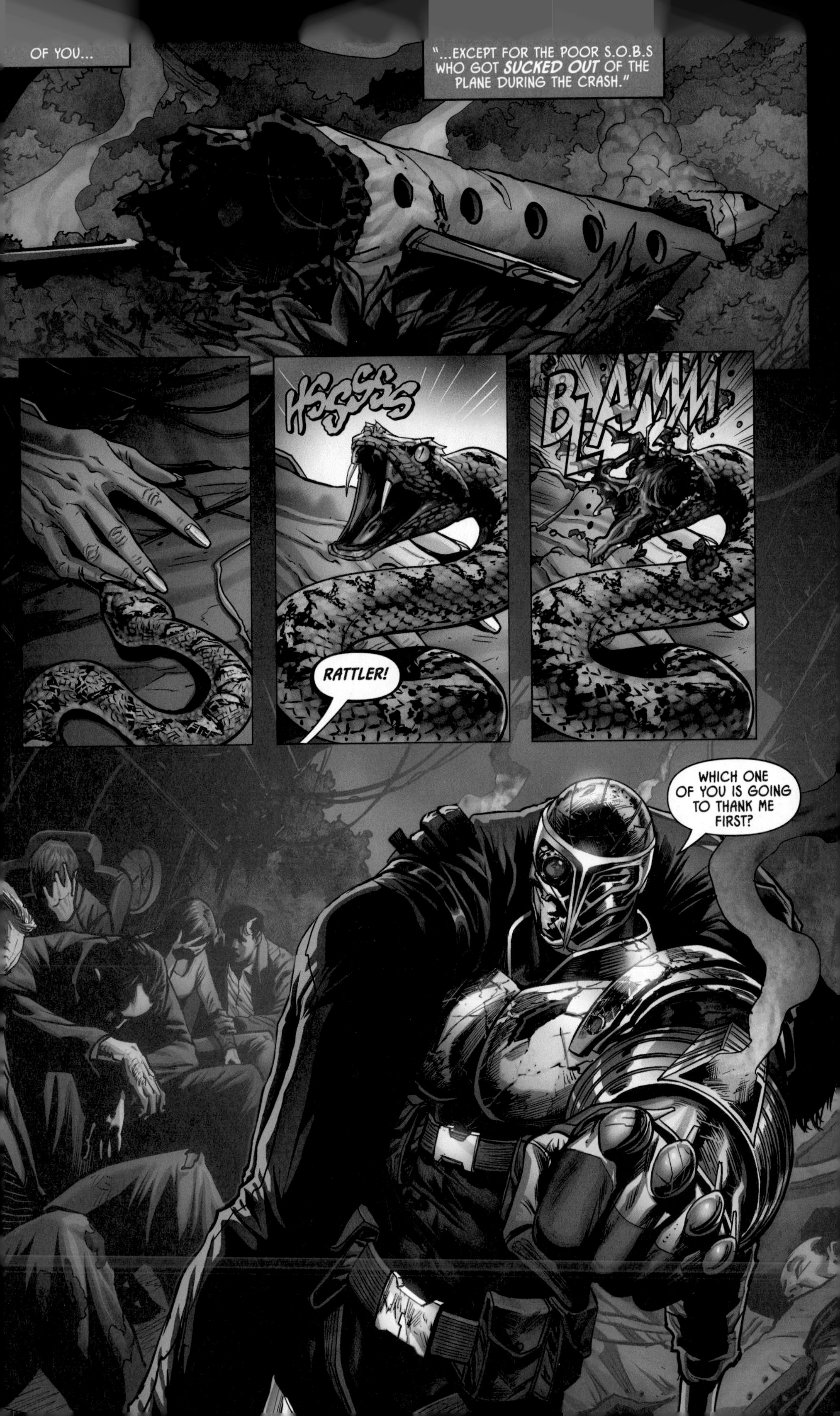

OF YOU...
"...EXCEPT FOR THE POOR S.O.B.S WHO GOT SUCKED OUT OF THE PLANE DURING THE CRASH."
HSSSSS
RATTLER!
BLAMM
WHICH ONE OF YOU IS GOING TO THANK ME FIRST?

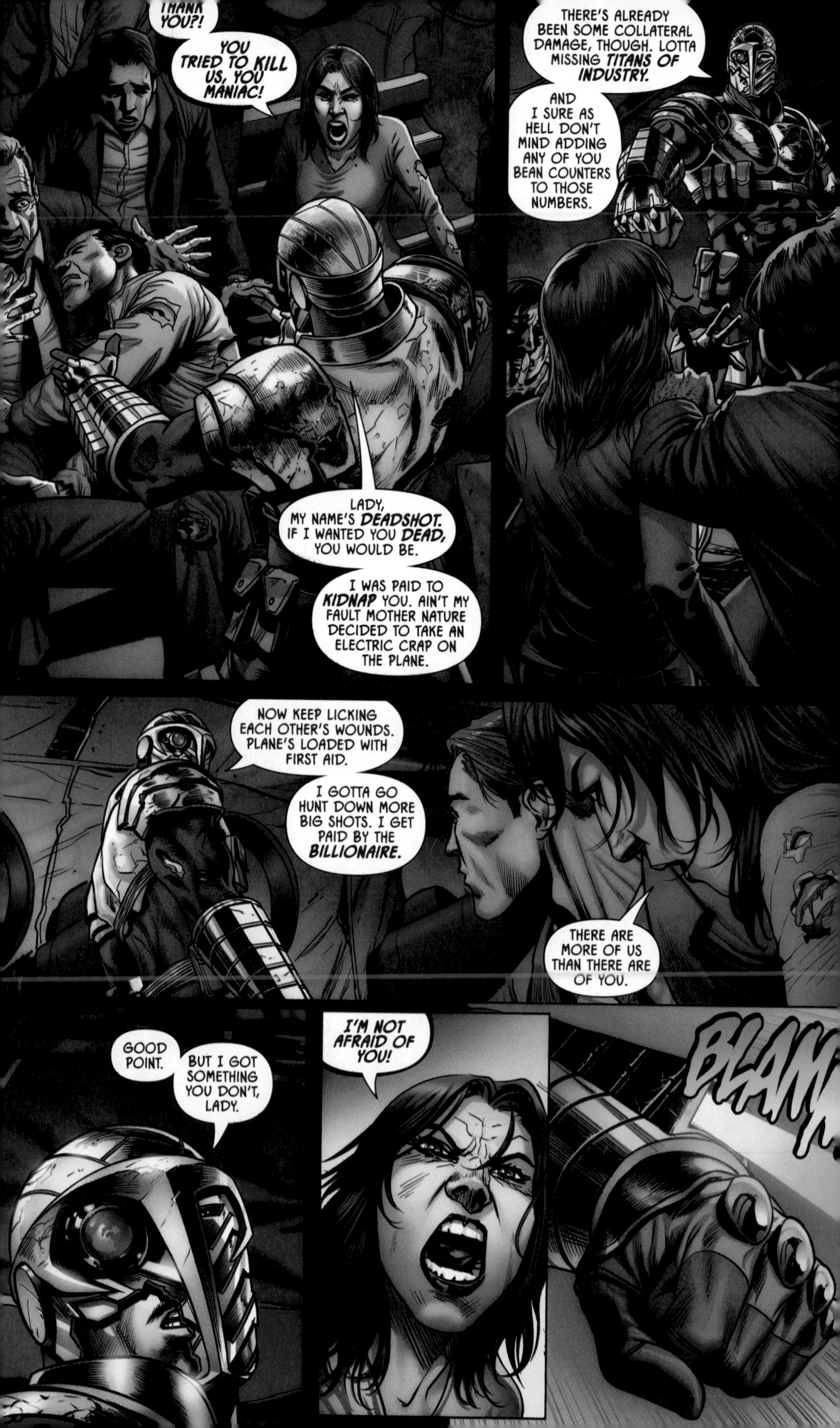
THANK YOU?!
YOU TRIED TO KILL US, YOU MANIAC!
LADY, MY NAME'S DEADSHOT. IF I WANTED YOU DEAD, YOU WOULD BE.
I WAS PAID TO KIDNAP YOU. AIN'T MY FAULT MOTHER NATURE DECIDED TO TAKE AN ELECTRIC CRAP ON THE PLANE.
THERE'S ALREADY BEEN SOME COLLATERAL DAMAGE, THOUGH. LOTTA MISSING TITANS OF INDUSTRY.
AND I SURE AS HELL DON'T MIND ADDING ANY OF YOU BEAN COUNTERS TO THOSE NUMBERS.
NOW KEEP LICKING EACH OTHER'S WOUNDS. PLANE'S LOADED WITH FIRST AID.
I GOTTA GO HUNT DOWN MORE BIG SHOTS. I GET PAID BY THE BILLIONAIRE.
THERE ARE MORE OF US THAN THERE ARE OF YOU.
GOOD POINT.
BUT I GOT SOMETHING YOU DON'T, LADY.
I'M NOT AFRAID OF YOU!
BLAM

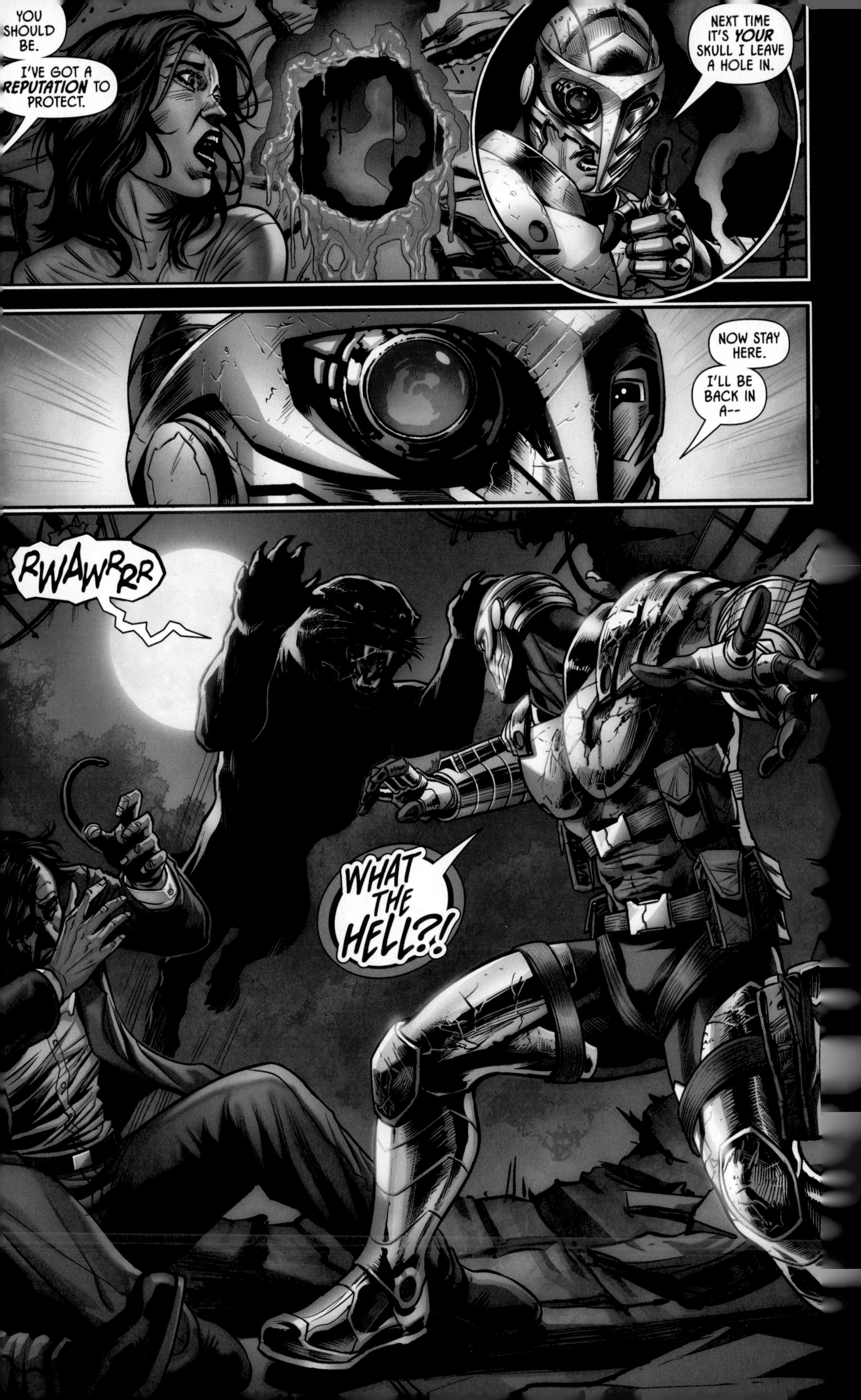
YOU SHOULD BE.
I'VE GOT A REPUTATION TO PROTECT.
NEXT TIME IT'S YOUR SKULL I LEAVE A HOLE IN.
NOW STAY HERE.
I'LL BE BACK IN A--
RWAWRRR
WHAT THE HELL?!

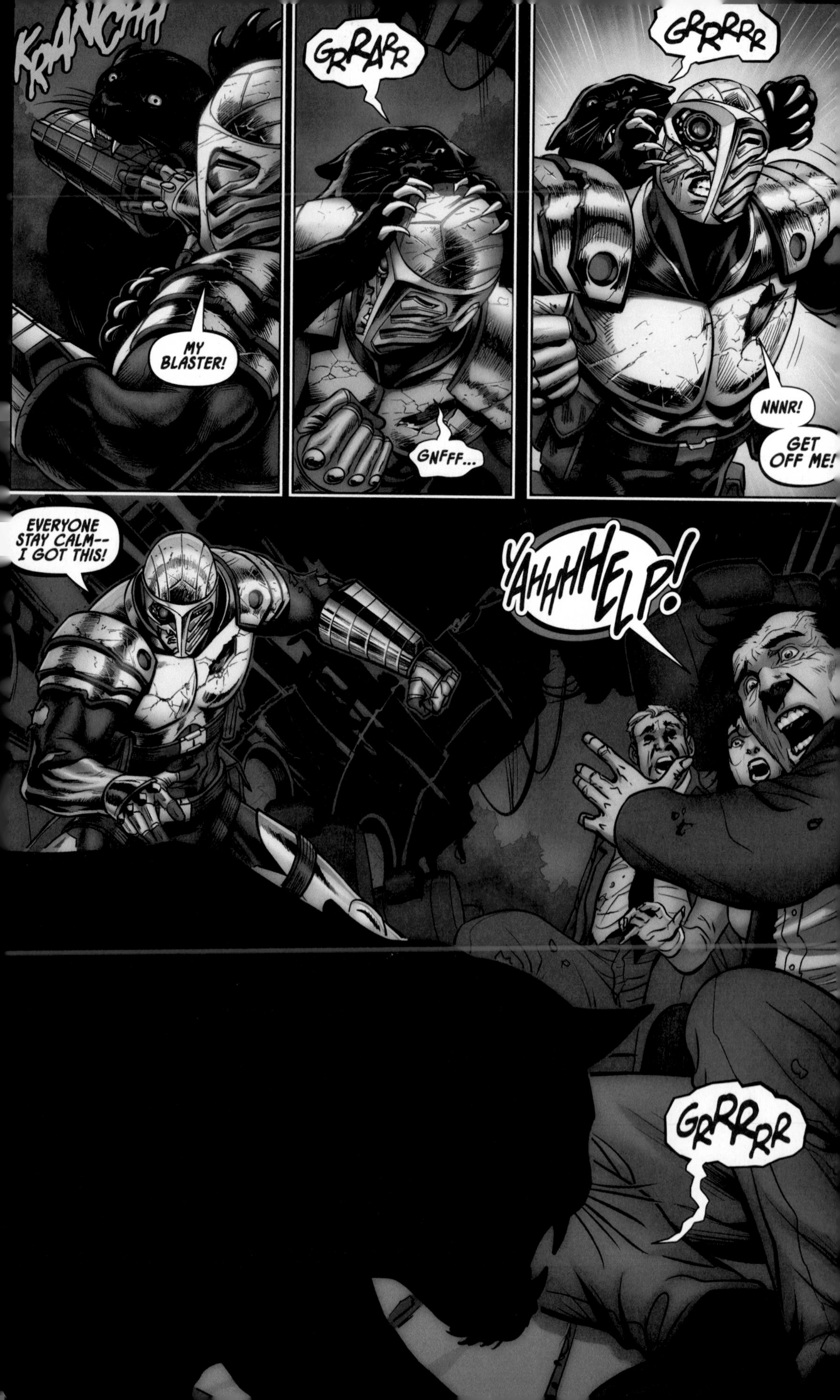
KRANCHH
MY BLASTER!
GRRARR
GNFFF...
GRRRRR
NNNR!
GET OFF ME!
EVERYONE STAY CALM-- I GOT THIS!
YAHHHHELP!
GRRRRR

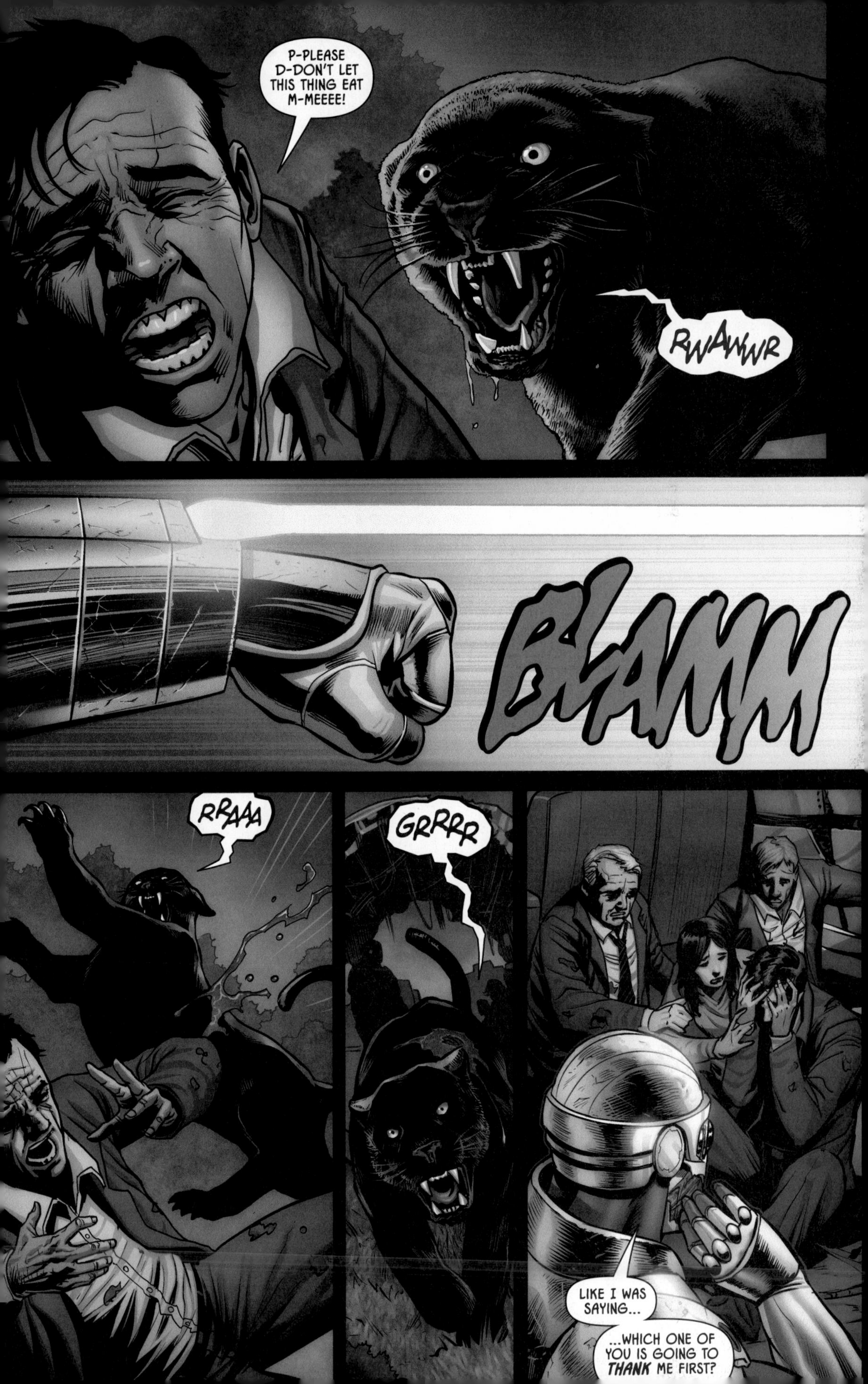
P-PLEASE D-DON'T LET THIS THING EAT M-MEEEE!
RWAWWR
BLAMM
RRAAA
GRRRR
LIKE I WAS SAYING...
...WHICH ONE OF YOU IS GOING TO THANK ME FIRST?

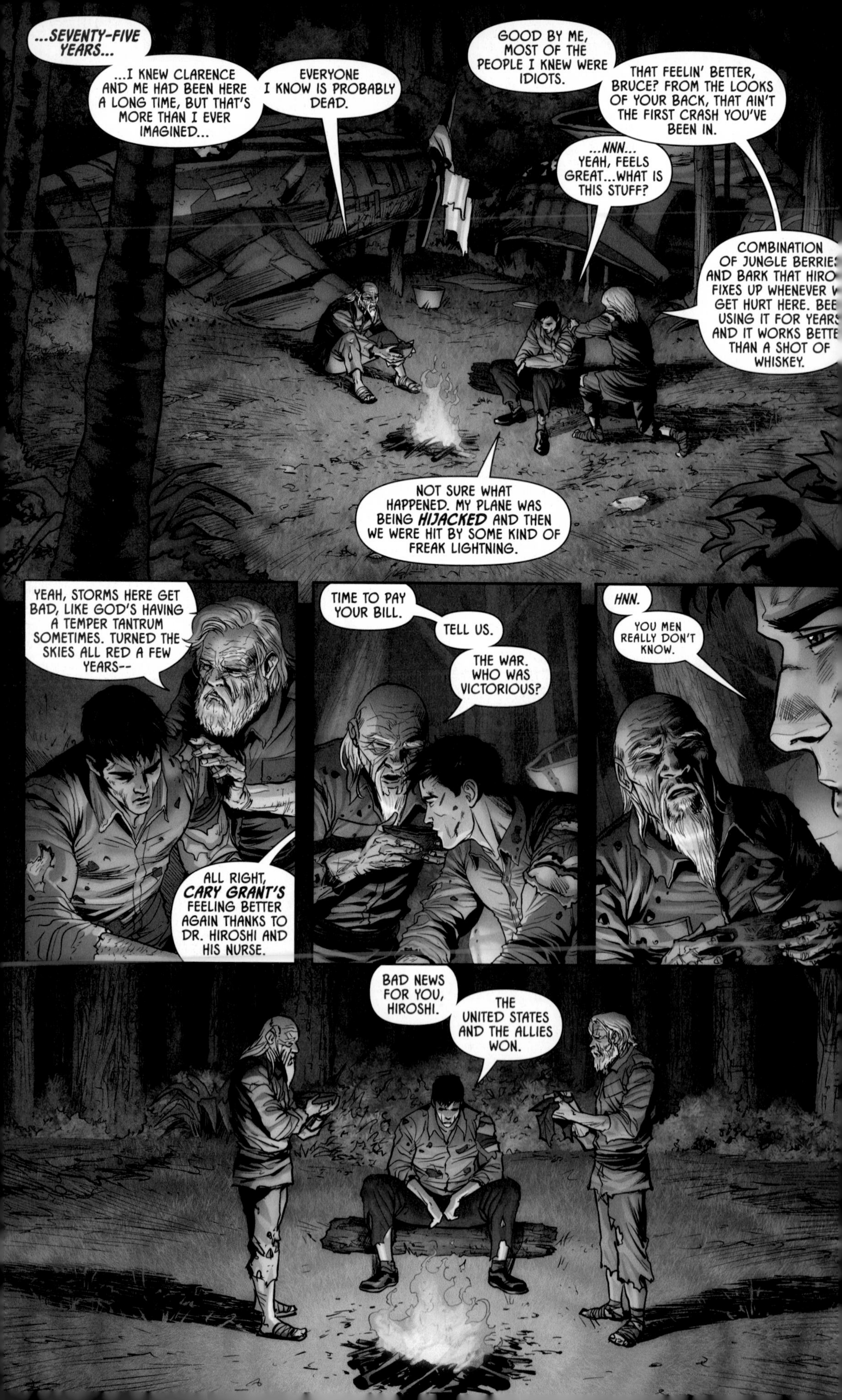
...SEVENTY-FIVE YEARS...
...I KNEW CLARENCE AND ME HAD BEEN HERE A LONG TIME, BUT THAT'S MORE THAN I EVER IMAGINED...
EVERYONE I KNOW IS PROBABLY DEAD.
GOOD BY ME, MOST OF THE PEOPLE I KNEW WERE IDIOTS.
THAT FEELIN' BETTER, BRUCE? FROM THE LOOKS OF YOUR BACK, THAT AIN'T THE FIRST CRASH YOU'VE BEEN IN.
...NNN... YEAH, FEELS GREAT...WHAT IS THIS STUFF?
COMBINATION OF JUNGLE BERRIES AND BARK THAT HIRO FIXES UP WHENEVER W GET HURT HERE. BEE USING IT FOR YEARS AND IT WORKS BETTE THAN A SHOT OF WHISKEY.
NOT SURE WHAT HAPPENED. MY PLANE WAS BEING HIJACKED AND THEN WE WERE HIT BY SOME KIND OF FREAK LIGHTNING.
YEAH, STORMS HERE GET BAD, LIKE GOD'S HAVING A TEMPER TANTRUM SOMETIMES. TURNED THE SKIES ALL RED A FEW YEARS--
ALL RIGHT, CARY GRANT'S FEELING BETTER AGAIN THANKS TO DR. HIROSHI AND HIS NURSE.
TIME TO PAY YOUR BILL.
TELL US.
THE WAR. WHO WAS VICTORIOUS?
HNN.
YOU MEN REALLY DON'T KNOW.
BAD NEWS FOR YOU, HIROSHI.
THE UNITED STATES AND THE ALLIES WON.

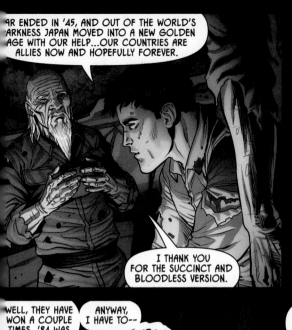

AR ENDED IN '45, AND OUT OF THE WORLD'S ARKNESS JAPAN MOVED INTO A NEW GOLDEN AGE WITH OUR HELP...OUR COUNTRIES ARE ALLIES NOW AND HOPEFULLY FOREVER.

I THANK YOU FOR THE SUCCINCT AND BLOODLESS VERSION.

FAH, WHO CARES ABOUT WAR? THAT WAS LIFETIMES AGO.

TELL US SOMETHING IMPORTANT, *FUTURE-MAN.*

I NEED 75 YEARS OF *WORLD SERIES* SCORES.

WELL, THE YANKEES HAVE WON QUITE A FEW TIMES.

AND GOTHAM HAS A TEAM NOW, TOO. SINCE '46.

WHAT ABOUT MY DETROIT TIGERS? THEY MUST HAVE WON THE MOST, RIGHT?

WELL, THEY HAVE WON A COUPLE TIMES. '84 WAS THE LAST...

ANYWAY, I HAVE TO--

HRNN!

WHY ARE YOU STANDING? YOU MUST REST, CARY GRANT.

HIROSHI'S RIGHT, KID, FALLING OUT OF THE SKY AIN'T JUST SOMETHING YOU WALK AWAY FROM.

...I'VE GOT PEOPLE WHO NEED HELP...

...LIKE I TOLD YOU, I WASN'T ON THAT PLANE ALONE...

RRN... DAMN IT...

COME ON. YOU'RE NOT GONNA DO ANYONE ANY GOOD IF YOU CAN'T EVEN WALK.

...OKAY... I'LL REST A FEW MORE MINUTES.

MY TURN FOR QUESTIONS, THOUGH.

GIVE ME *YOUR* STORY.

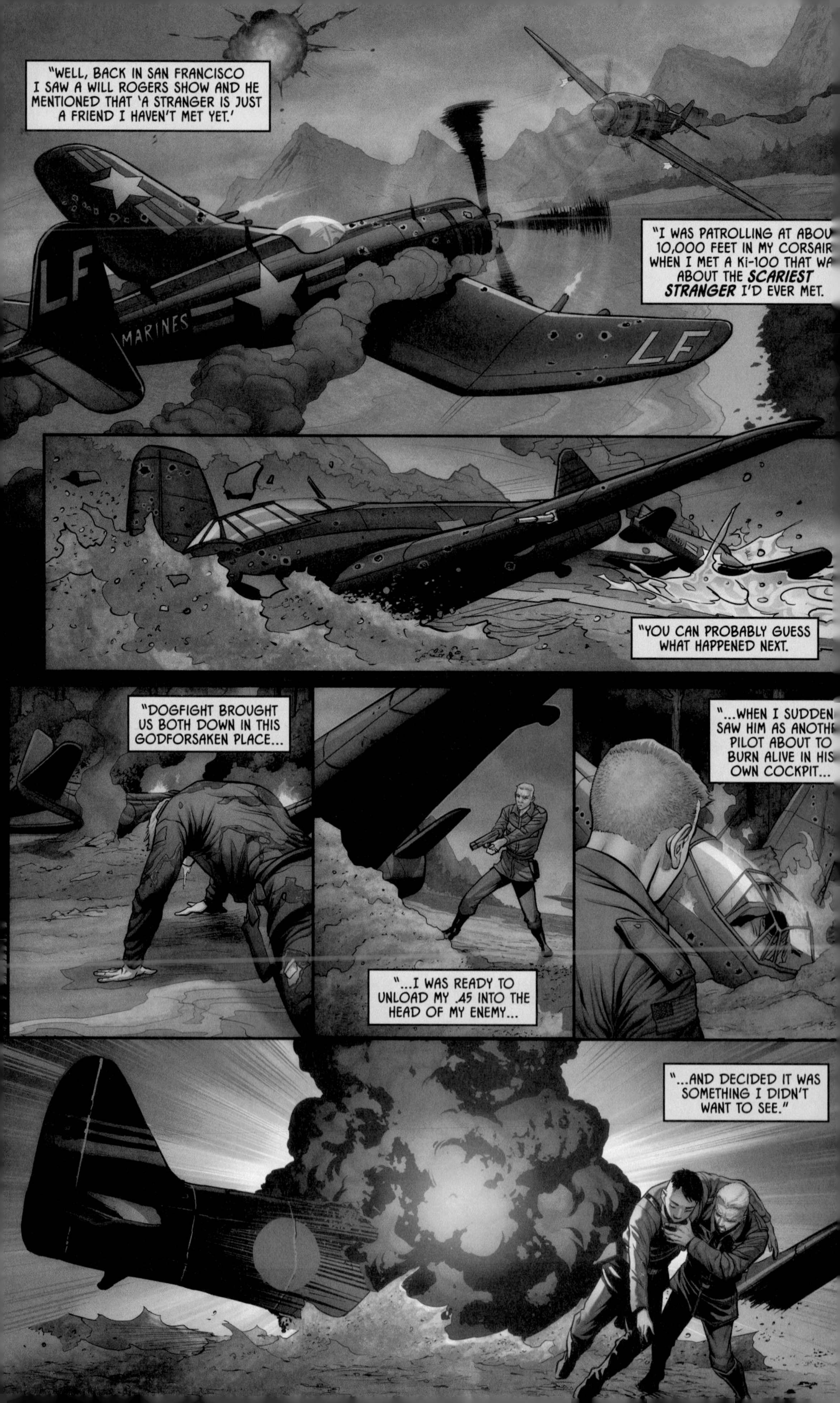
"WELL, BACK IN SAN FRANCISCO I SAW A WILL ROGERS SHOW AND HE MENTIONED THAT 'A STRANGER IS JUST A FRIEND I HAVEN'T MET YET.'
LF
MARINES
LF
"I WAS PATROLLING AT ABOU 10,000 FEET IN MY CORSAIR WHEN I MET A Ki-100 THAT WA ABOUT THE SCARIEST STRANGER I'D EVER MET.
"YOU CAN PROBABLY GUESS WHAT HAPPENED NEXT.
"DOGFIGHT BROUGHT US BOTH DOWN IN THIS GODFORSAKEN PLACE...
"...I WAS READY TO UNLOAD MY .45 INTO THE HEAD OF MY ENEMY...
"...WHEN I SUDDEN SAW HIM AS ANOTH PILOT ABOUT TO BURN ALIVE IN HIS OWN COCKPIT...
"...AND DECIDED IT WAS SOMETHING I DIDN'T WANT TO SEE."

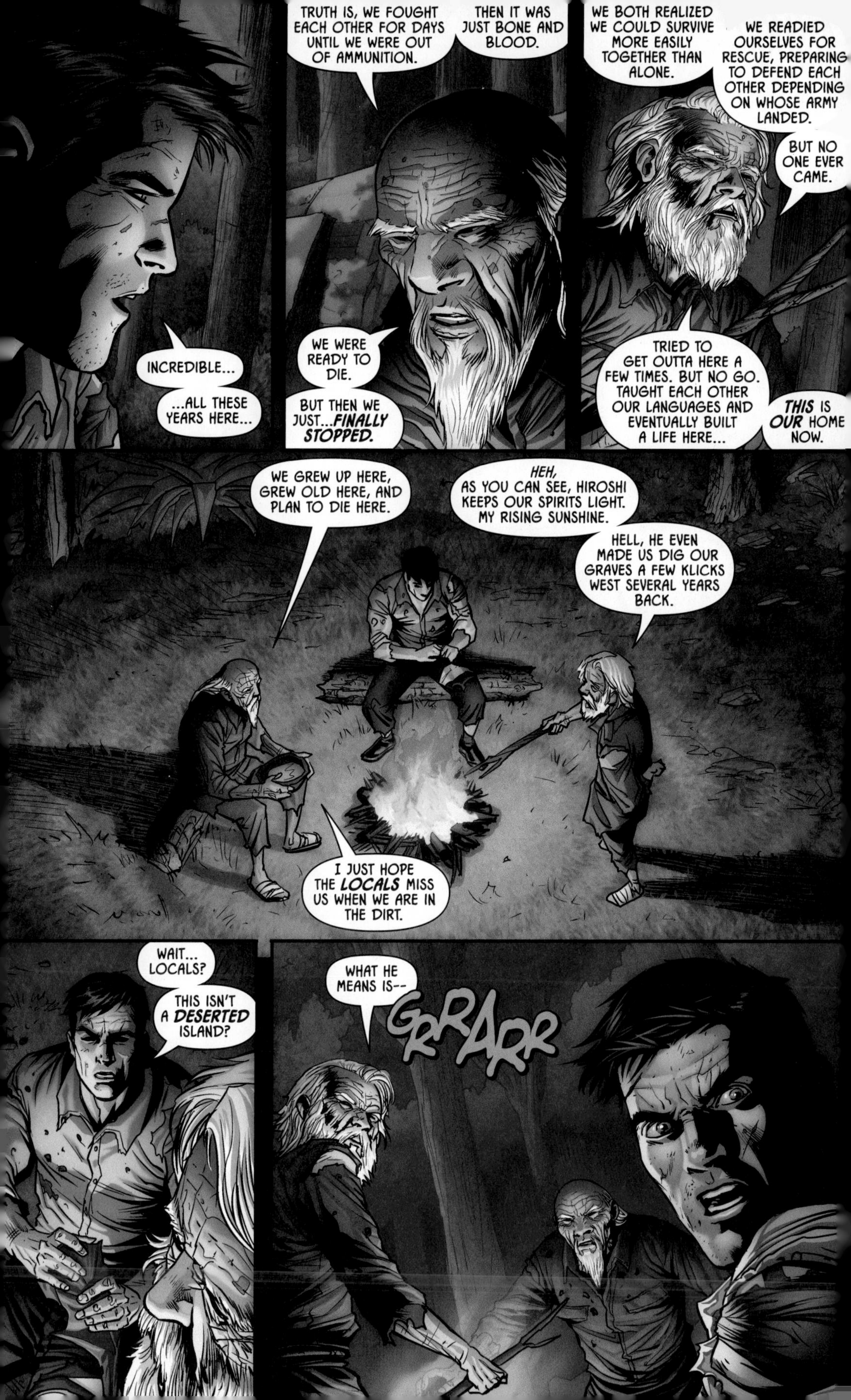
INCREDIBLE...
...ALL THESE YEARS HERE...
TRUTH IS, WE FOUGHT EACH OTHER FOR DAYS UNTIL WE WERE OUT OF AMMUNITION.
THEN IT WAS JUST BONE AND BLOOD.
WE WERE READY TO DIE.
BUT THEN WE JUST...FINALLY STOPPED.
WE BOTH REALIZED WE COULD SURVIVE MORE EASILY TOGETHER THAN ALONE.
WE READIED OURSELVES FOR RESCUE, PREPARING TO DEFEND EACH OTHER DEPENDING ON WHOSE ARMY LANDED.
BUT NO ONE EVER CAME.
TRIED TO GET OUTTA HERE A FEW TIMES. BUT NO GO. TAUGHT EACH OTHER OUR LANGUAGES AND EVENTUALLY BUILT A LIFE HERE...
THIS IS OUR HOME NOW.
WE GREW UP HERE, GREW OLD HERE, AND PLAN TO DIE HERE.
HEH, AS YOU CAN SEE, HIROSHI KEEPS OUR SPIRITS LIGHT. MY RISING SUNSHINE.
HELL, HE EVEN MADE US DIG OUR GRAVES A FEW KLICKS WEST SEVERAL YEARS BACK.
I JUST HOPE THE LOCALS MISS US WHEN WE ARE IN THE DIRT.
WAIT... LOCALS?
THIS ISN'T A DESERTED ISLAND?
WHAT HE MEANS IS--
GRRARR

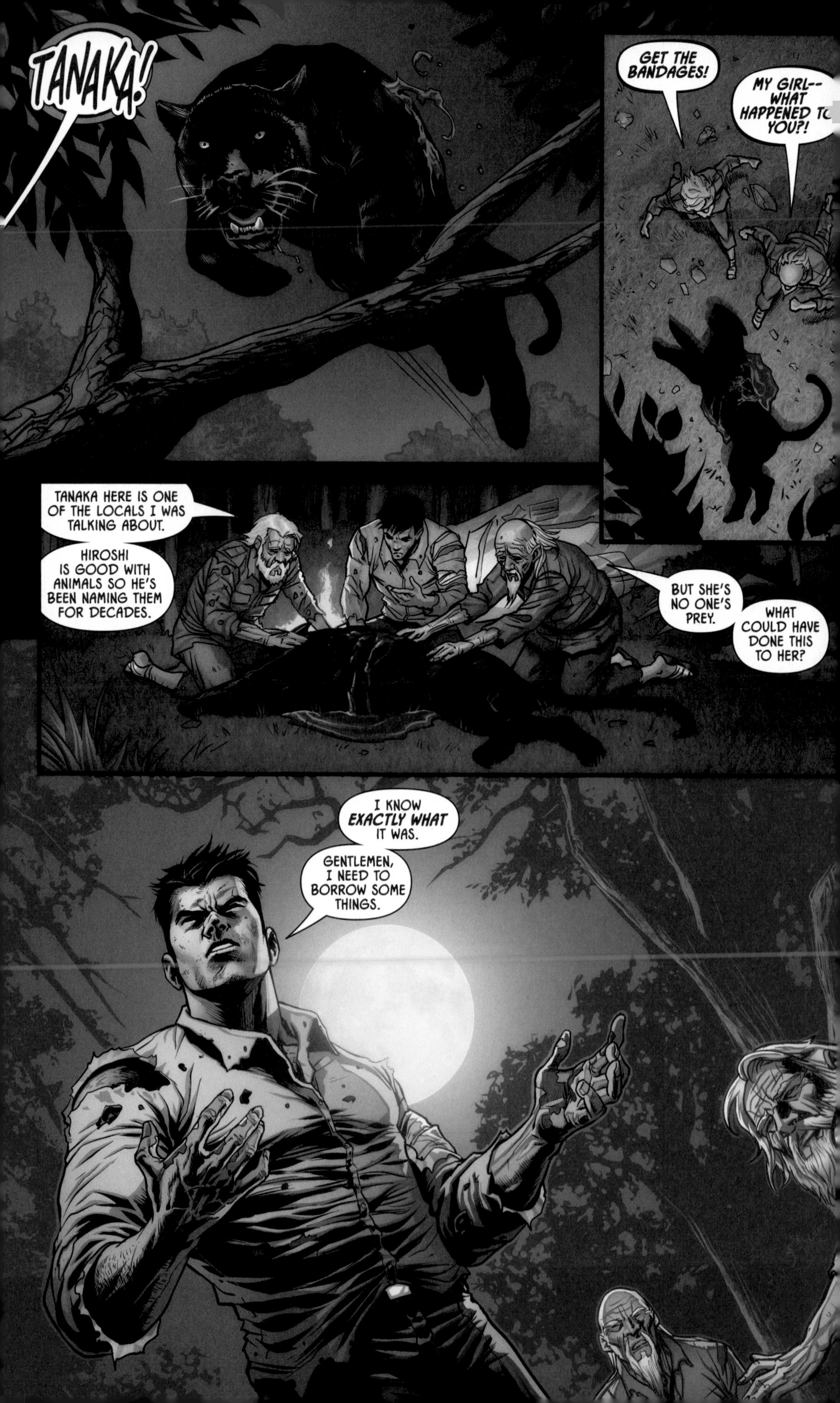
TANAKA!
GET THE BANDAGES!
MY GIRL-- WHAT HAPPENED TO YOU?!
TANAKA HERE IS ONE OF THE LOCALS I WAS TALKING ABOUT.
HIROSHI IS GOOD WITH ANIMALS SO HE'S BEEN NAMING THEM FOR DECADES.
BUT SHE'S NO ONE'S PREY.
WHAT COULD HAVE DONE THIS TO HER?
I KNOW **EXACTLY WHAT** IT WAS.
GENTLEMEN, I NEED TO BORROW SOME THINGS.

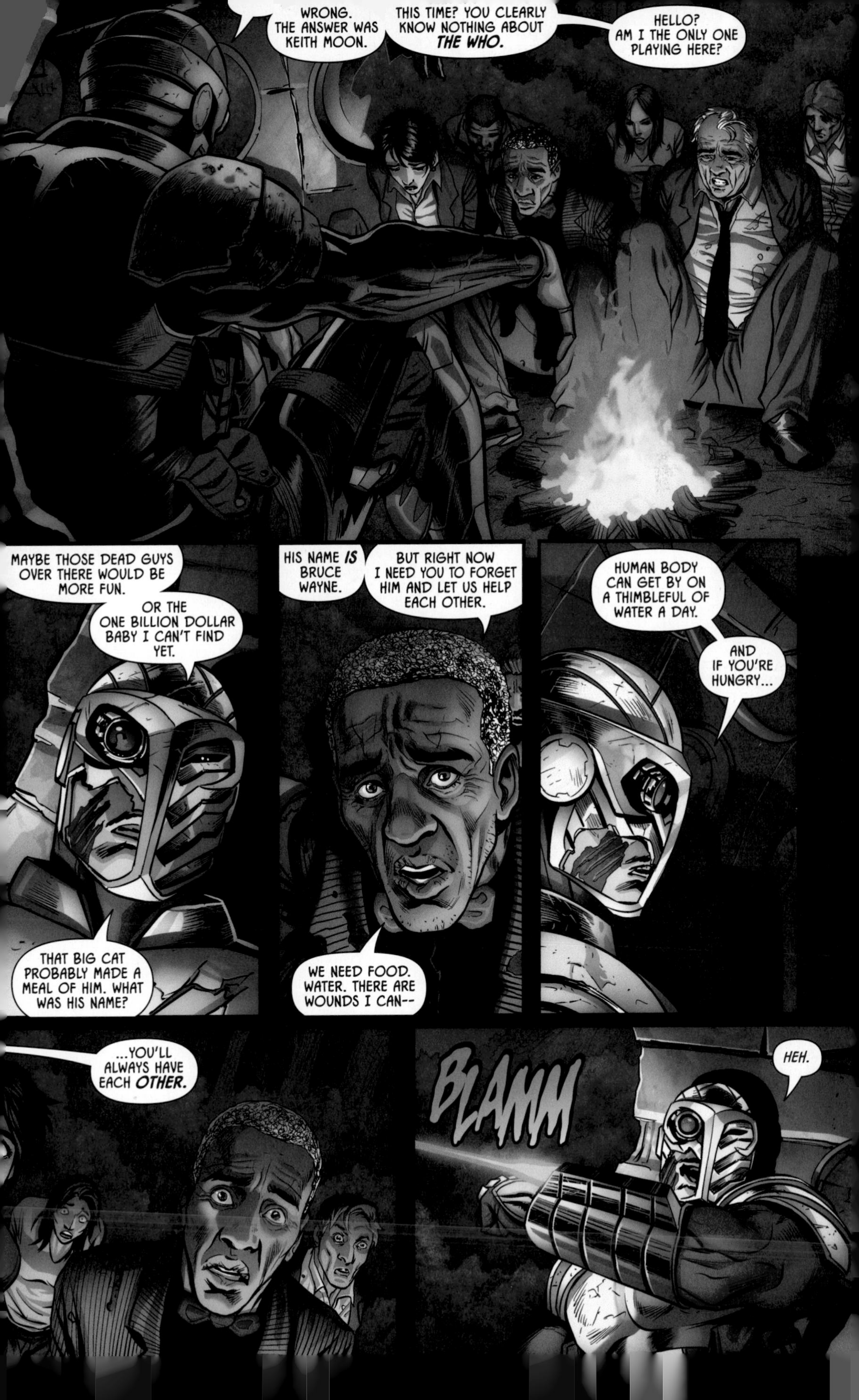
WRONG. THE ANSWER WAS KEITH MOON.
THIS TIME? YOU CLEARLY KNOW NOTHING ABOUT *THE WHO.*
HELLO? AM I THE ONLY ONE PLAYING HERE?
MAYBE THOSE DEAD GUYS OVER THERE WOULD BE MORE FUN.
OR THE ONE BILLION DOLLAR BABY I CAN'T FIND YET.
THAT BIG CAT PROBABLY MADE A MEAL OF HIM. WHAT WAS HIS NAME?
HIS NAME *IS* BRUCE WAYNE.
BUT RIGHT NOW I NEED YOU TO FORGET HIM AND LET US HELP EACH OTHER.
WE NEED FOOD. WATER. THERE ARE WOUNDS I CAN--
HUMAN BODY CAN GET BY ON A THIMBLEFUL OF WATER A DAY.
AND IF YOU'RE HUNGRY...
...YOU'LL ALWAYS HAVE EACH *OTHER.*
BLAMM
HEH.

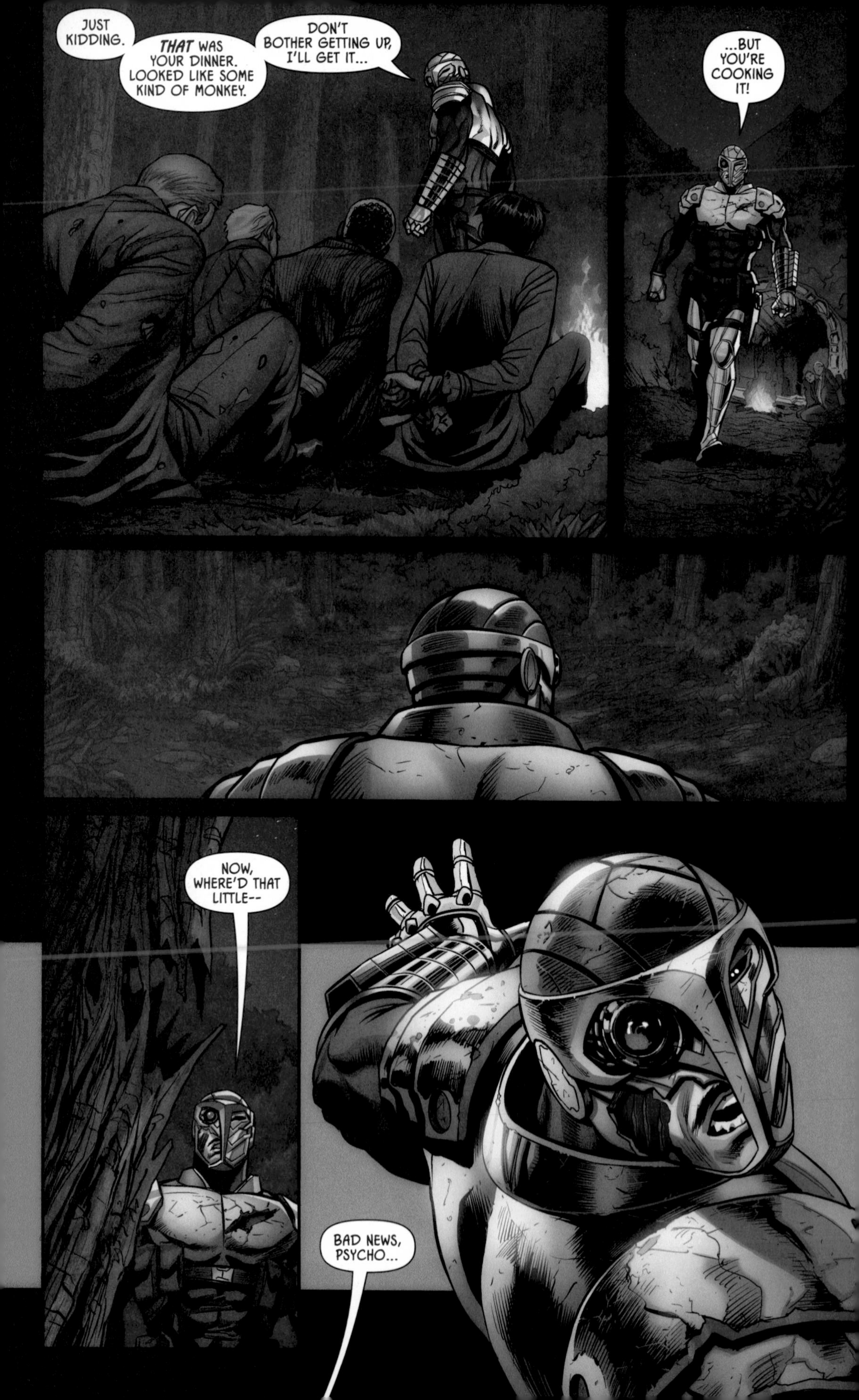
JUST KIDDING.
THAT WAS YOUR DINNER. LOOKED LIKE SOME KIND OF MONKEY.
DON'T BOTHER GETTING UP, I'LL GET IT...
...BUT YOU'RE COOKING IT!
NOW, WHERE'D THAT LITTLE--
BAD NEWS, PSYCHO...

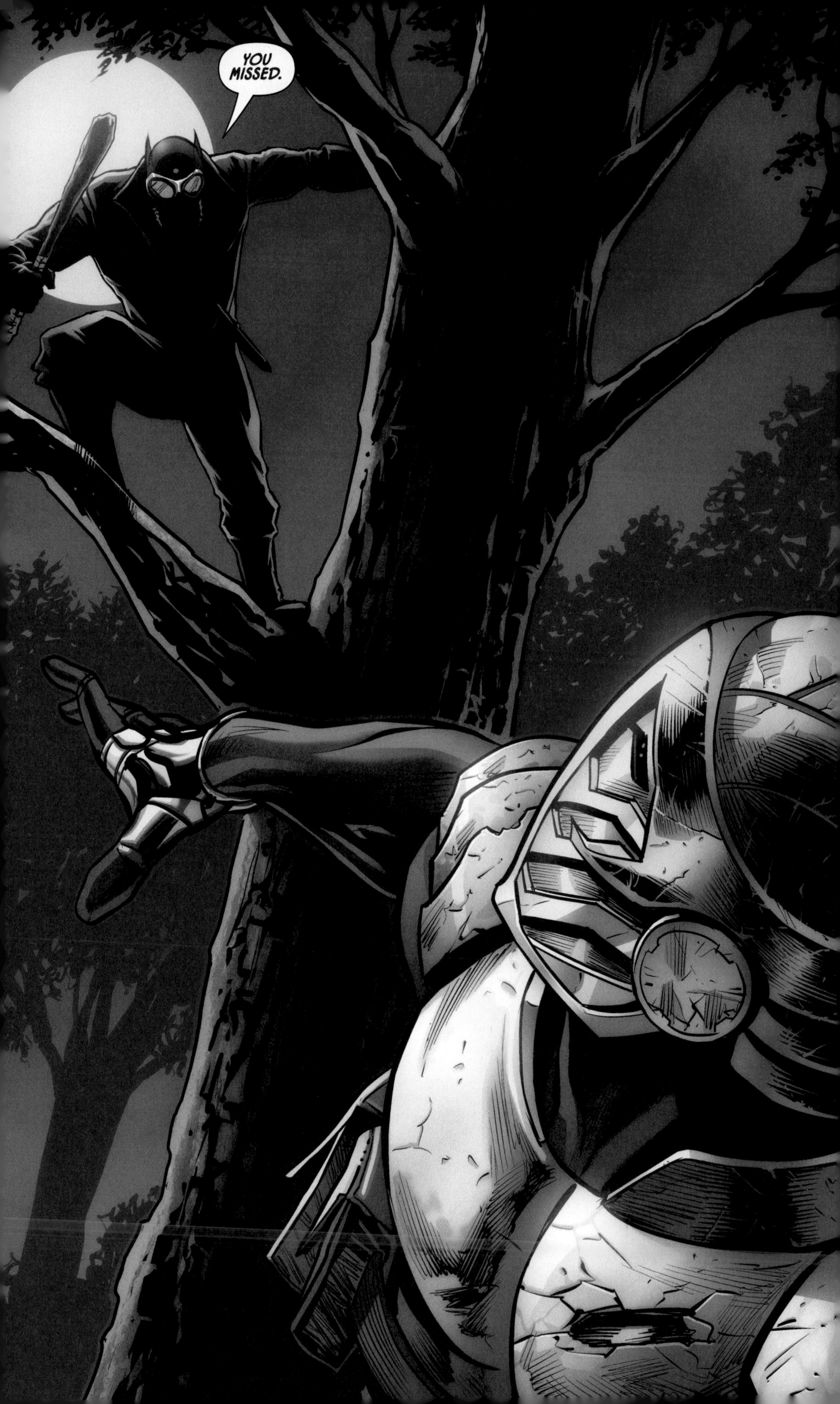
YOU MISSED.

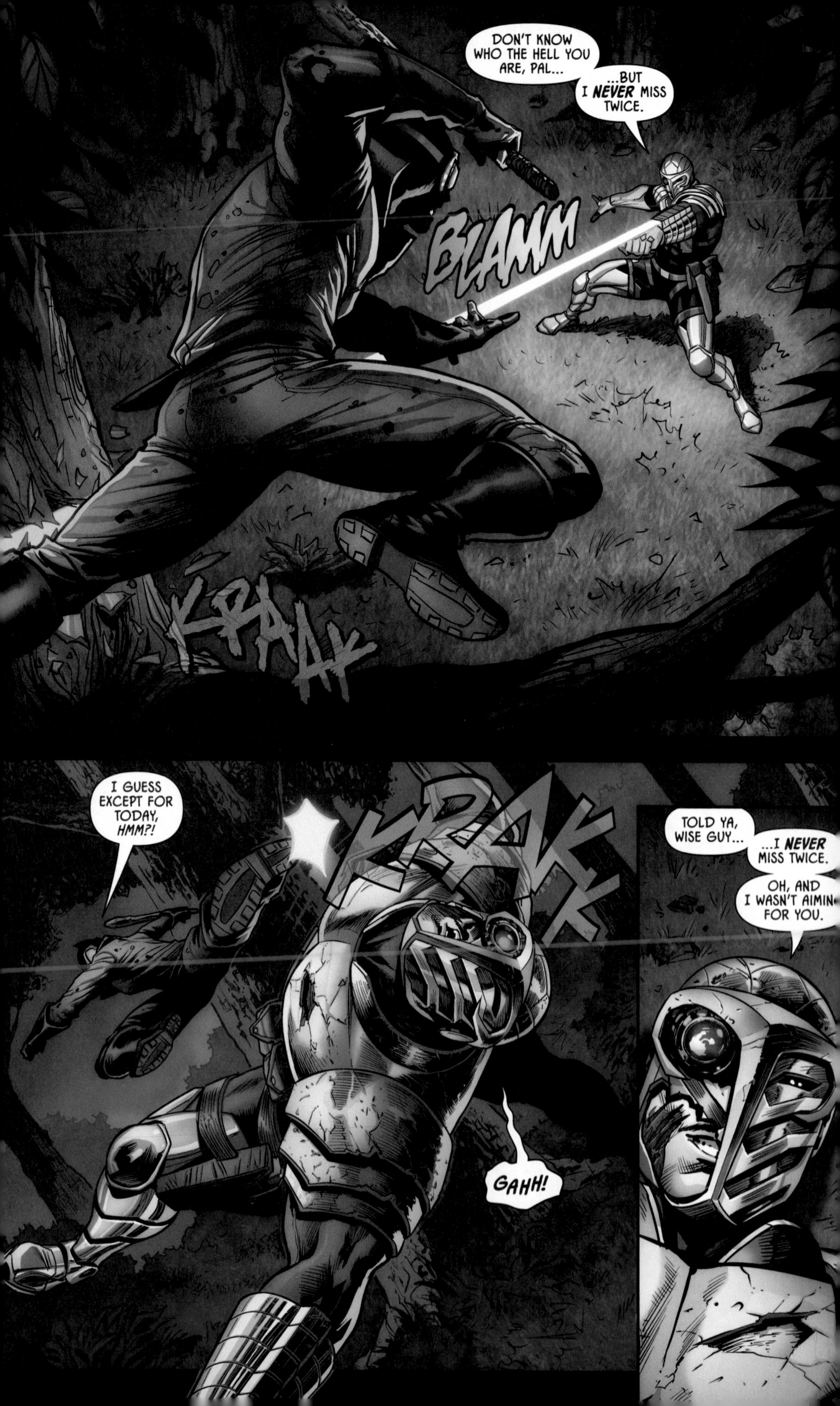
DON'T KNOW WHO THE HELL YOU ARE, PAL...
...BUT I NEVER MISS TWICE.
BLAMM
KRAAK
I GUESS EXCEPT FOR TODAY, HMM?!
KRAK
GAHH!
TOLD YA, WISE GUY...
...I NEVER MISS TWICE.
OH, AND I WASN'T AIMIN' FOR YOU.

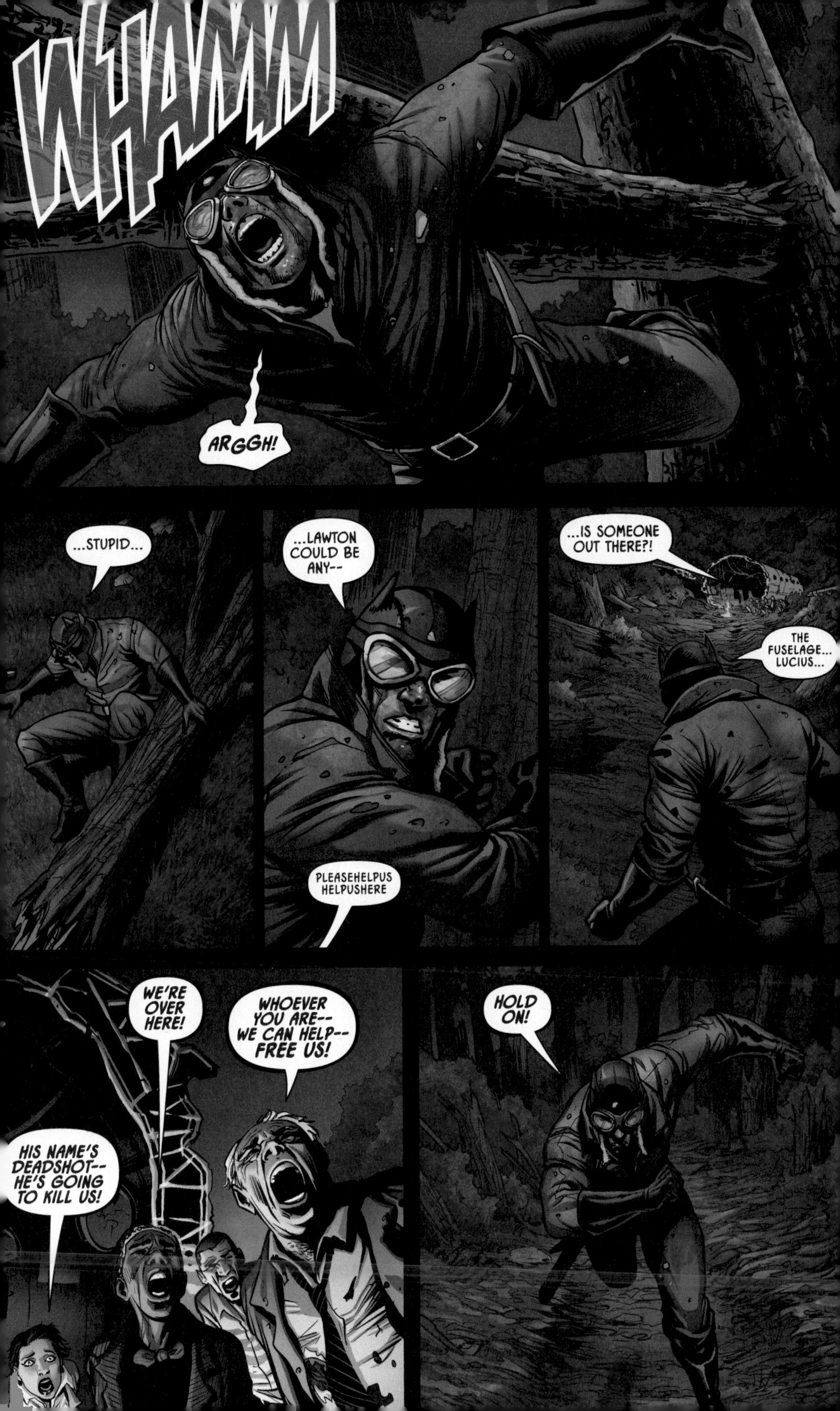
WHAMM
ARGGH!
...STUPID...
...LAWTON COULD BE ANY--
PLEASEHELPUS HELPUSHERE
...IS SOMEONE OUT THERE?!
THE FUSELAGE... LUCIUS...
WE'RE OVER HERE!
WHOEVER YOU ARE-- WE CAN HELP-- FREE US!
HIS NAME'S DEADSHOT-- HE'S GOING TO KILL US!
HOLD ON!

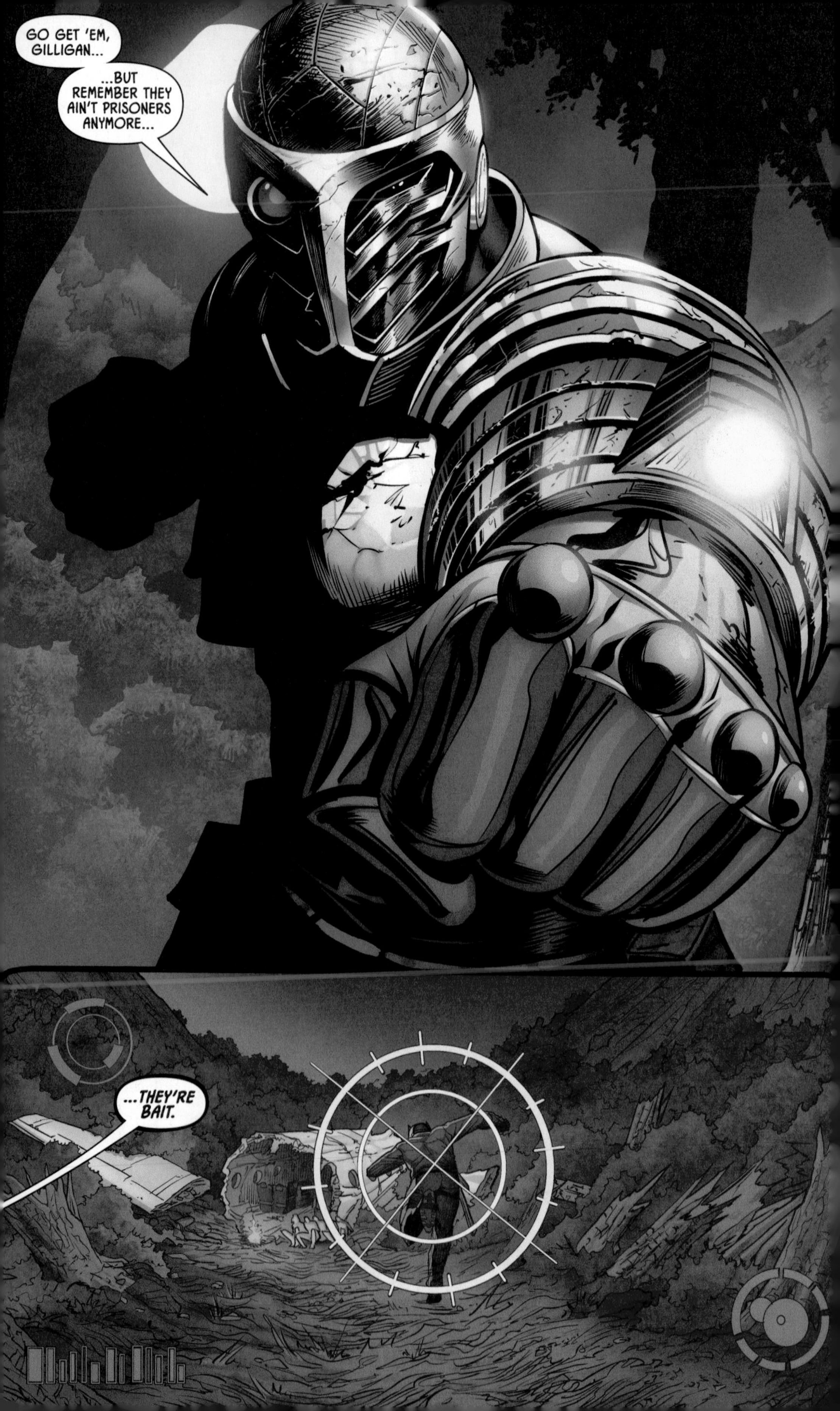
GO GET 'EM, GILLIGAN...
...BUT REMEMBER THEY AIN'T PRISONERS ANYMORE...
...THEY'RE BAIT.

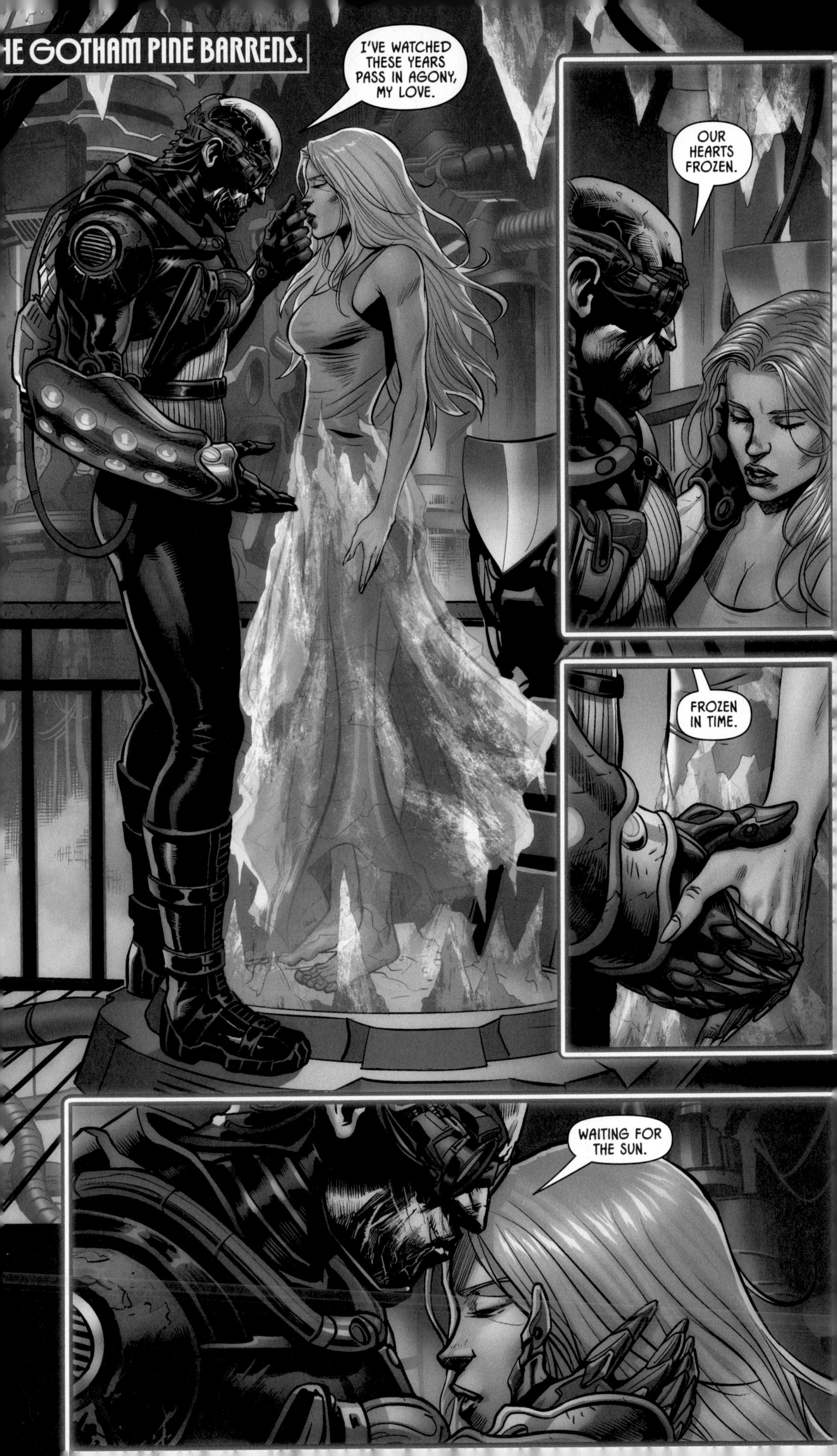

HE GOTHAM PINE BARRENS.
I'VE WATCHED THESE YEARS PASS IN AGONY, MY LOVE.
OUR HEARTS FROZEN.
FROZEN IN TIME.
WAITING FOR THE SUN.

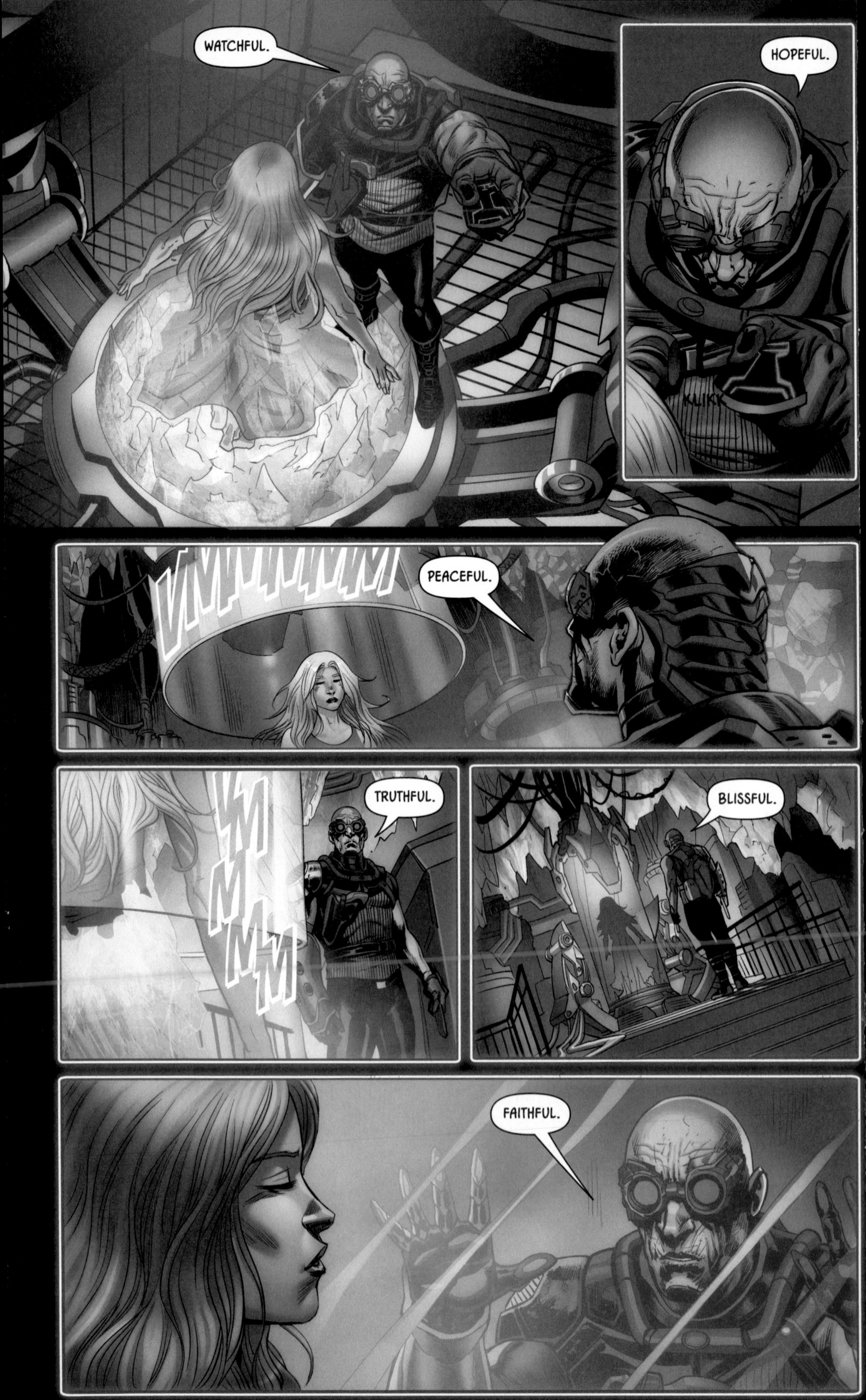
WATCHFUL.
HOPEFUL.
KLIKK
VMMMMMMM
PEACEFUL.
VMMMMM
TRUTHFUL.
BLISSFUL.
FAITHFUL.

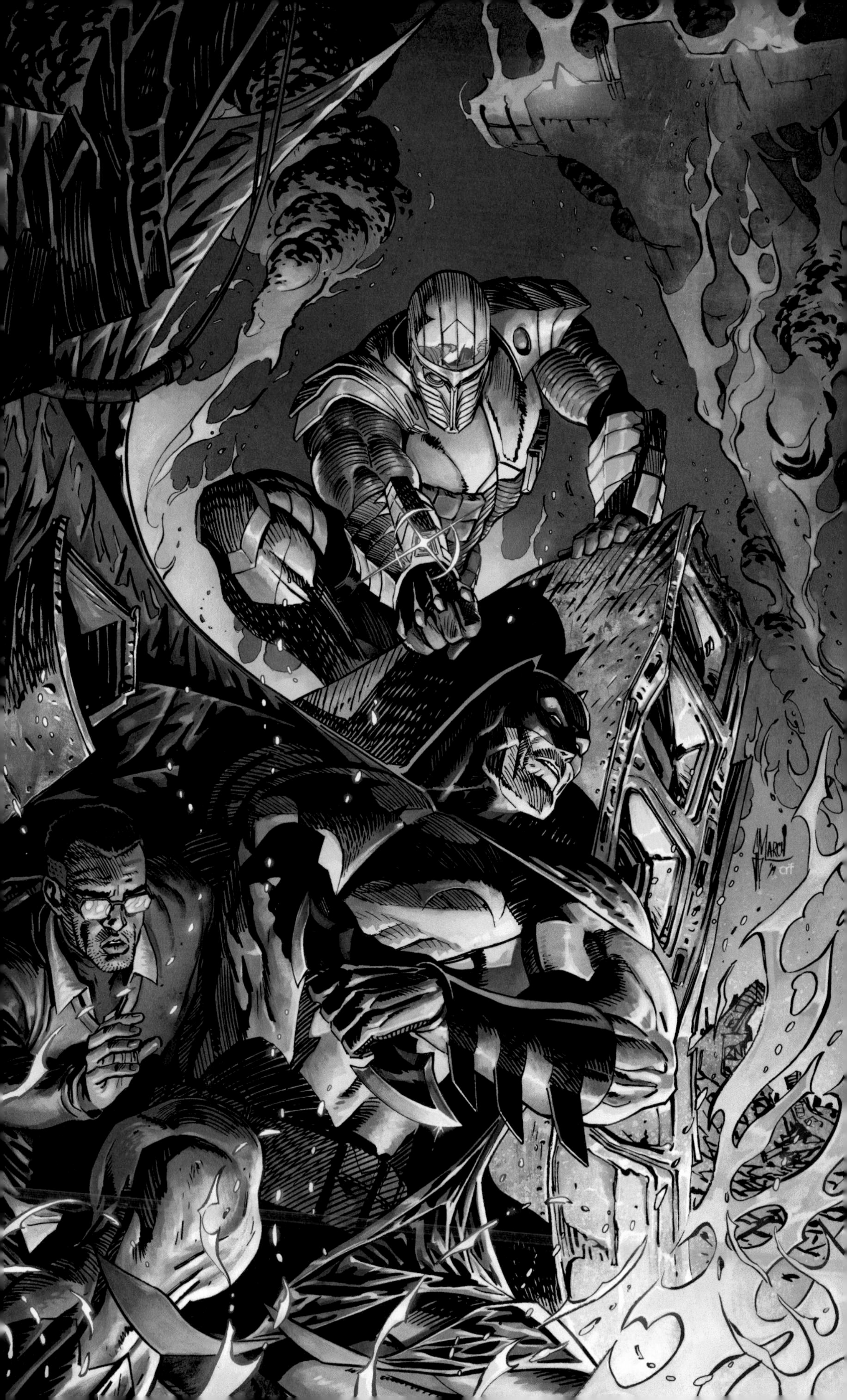

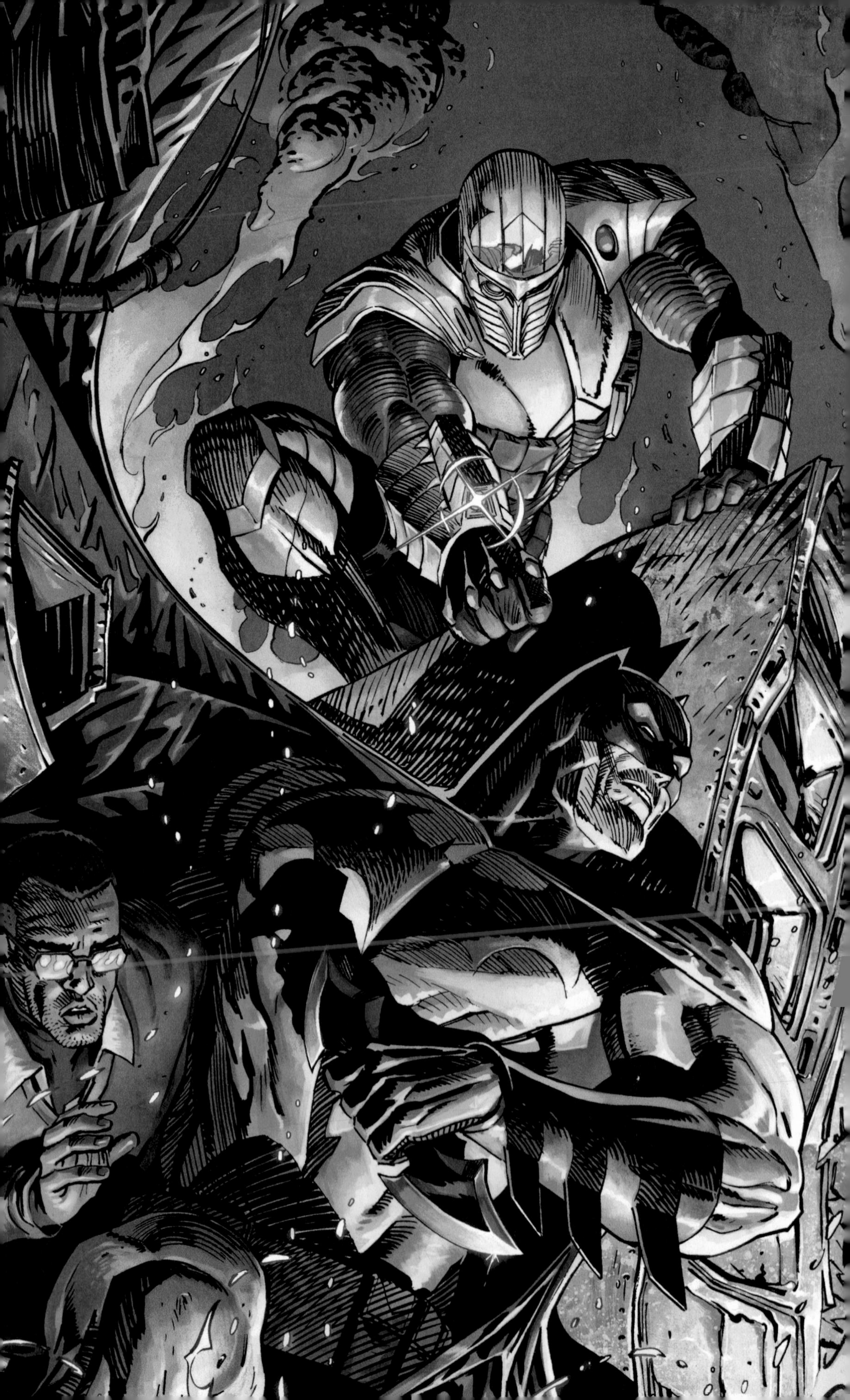

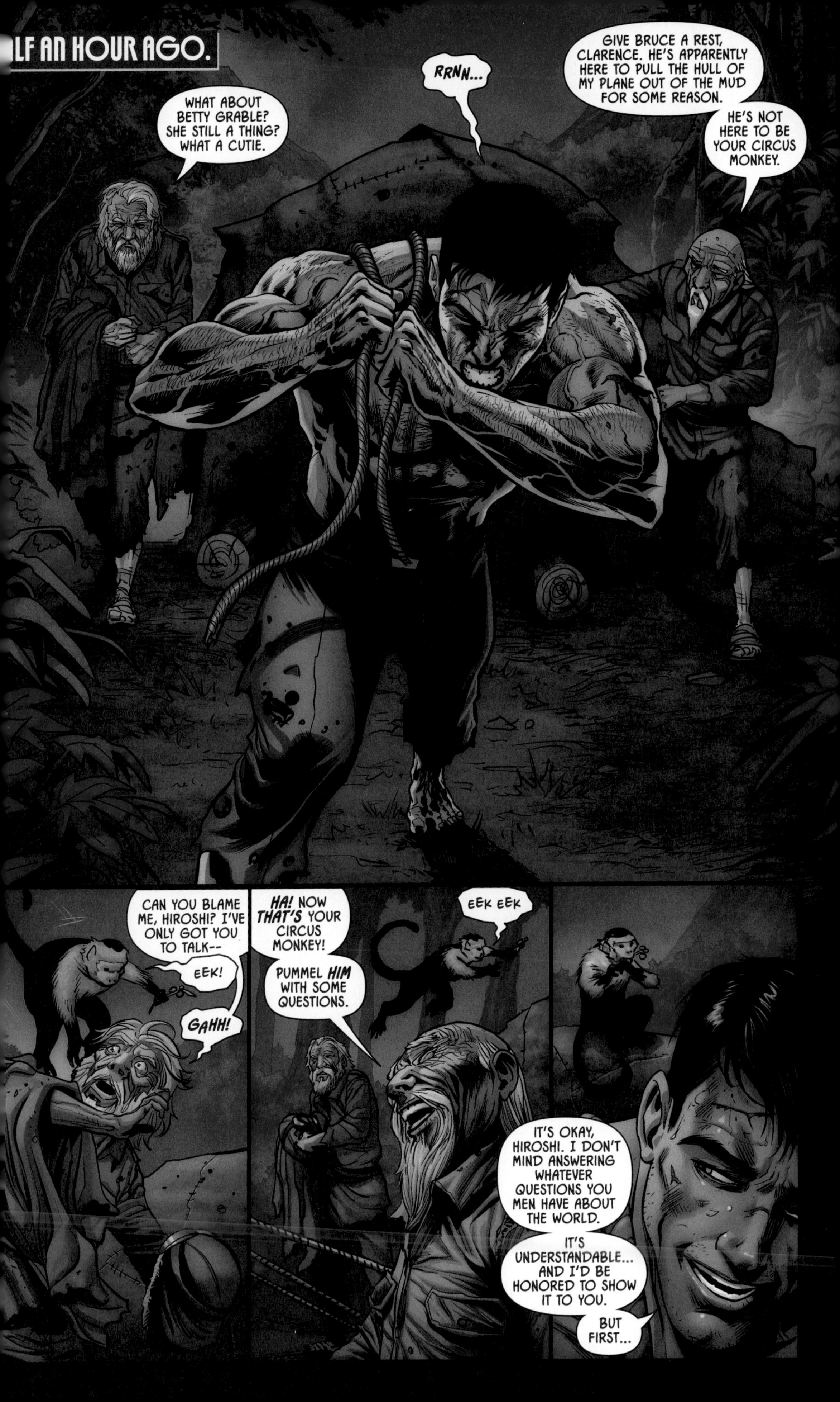
LF AN HOUR AGO.
WHAT ABOUT BETTY GRABLE? SHE STILL A THING? WHAT A CUTIE.
RRNN...
GIVE BRUCE A REST, CLARENCE. HE'S APPARENTLY HERE TO PULL THE HULL OF MY PLANE OUT OF THE MUD FOR SOME REASON.
HE'S NOT HERE TO BE YOUR CIRCUS MONKEY.
CAN YOU BLAME ME, HIROSHI? I'VE ONLY GOT YOU TO TALK--
EEK!
GAHH!
HA! NOW THAT'S YOUR CIRCUS MONKEY!
PUMMEL HIM WITH SOME QUESTIONS.
EEK EEK
IT'S OKAY, HIROSHI. I DON'T MIND ANSWERING WHATEVER QUESTIONS YOU MEN HAVE ABOUT THE WORLD.
IT'S UNDERSTANDABLE... AND I'D BE HONORED TO SHOW IT TO YOU.
BUT FIRST...

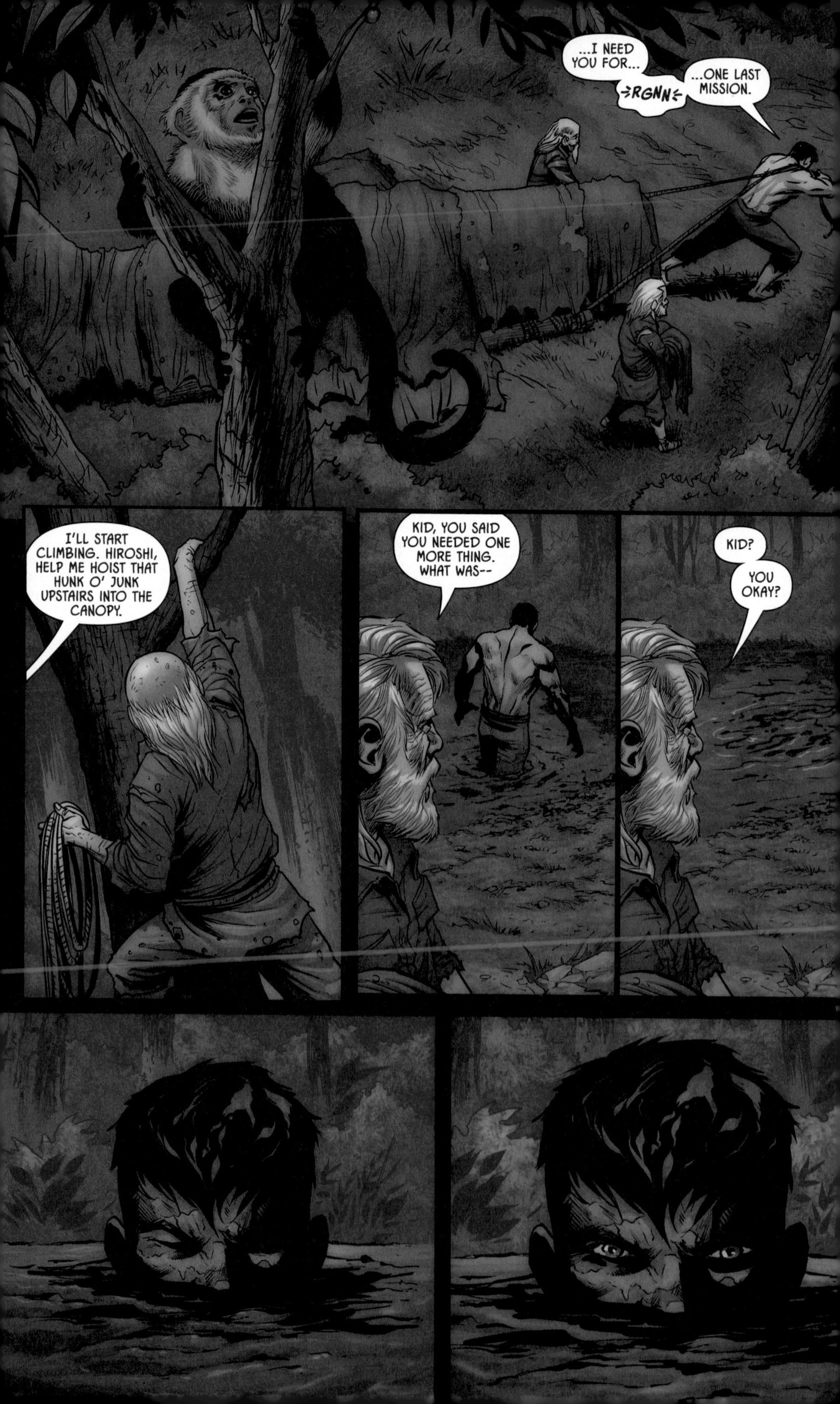
...I NEED YOU FOR...
RGNN
...ONE LAST MISSION.
I'LL START CLIMBING. HIROSHI, HELP ME HOIST THAT HUNK O' JUNK UPSTAIRS INTO THE CANOPY.
KID, YOU SAID YOU NEEDED ONE MORE THING. WHAT WAS--
KID?
YOU OKAY?

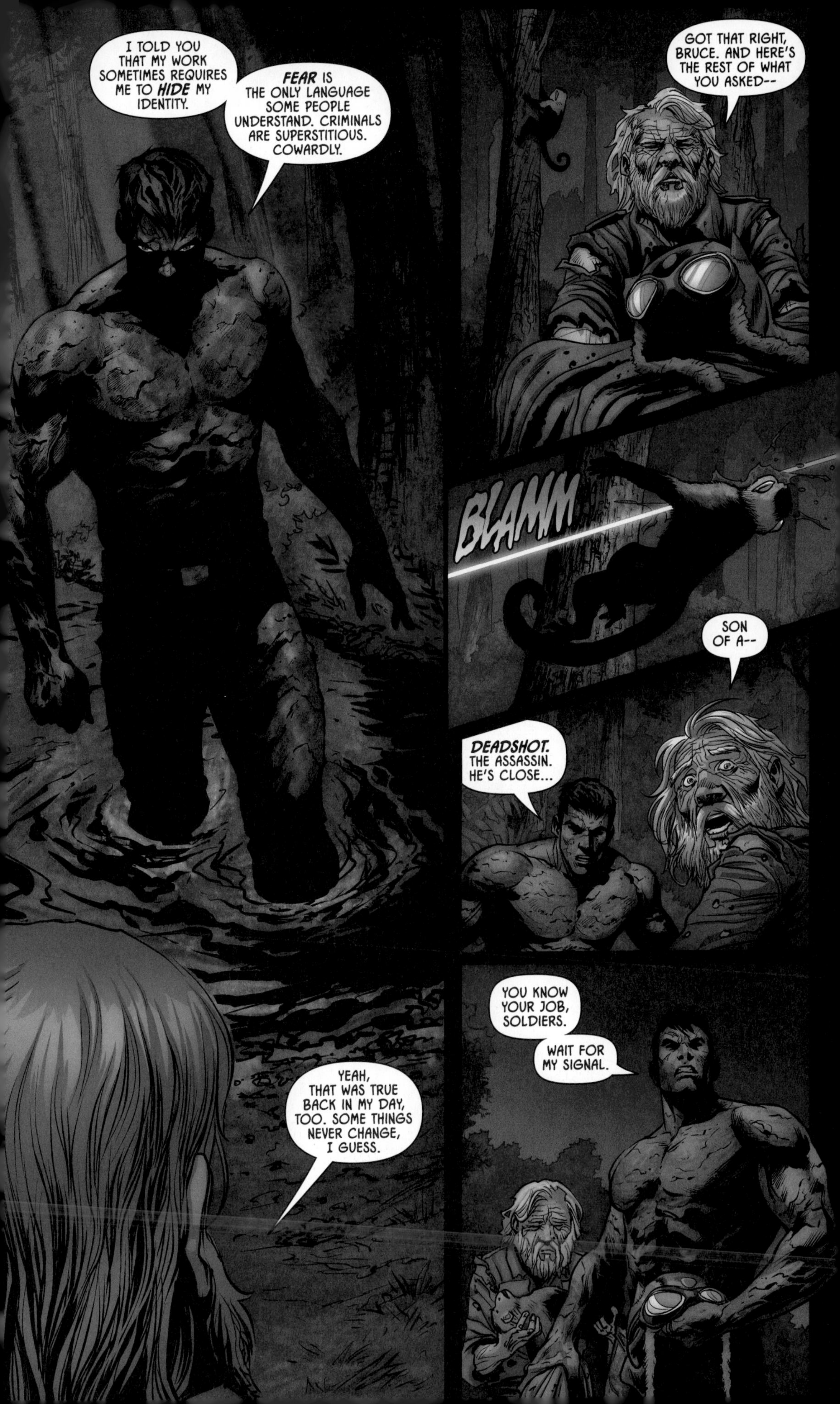
I TOLD YOU THAT MY WORK SOMETIMES REQUIRES ME TO **HIDE** MY IDENTITY.
FEAR IS THE ONLY LANGUAGE SOME PEOPLE UNDERSTAND. CRIMINALS ARE SUPERSTITIOUS. COWARDLY.
YEAH, THAT WAS TRUE BACK IN MY DAY, TOO. SOME THINGS NEVER CHANGE, I GUESS.
GOT THAT RIGHT, BRUCE. AND HERE'S THE REST OF WHAT YOU ASKED--
BLAMM
SON OF A--
DEADSHOT. THE ASSASSIN. HE'S CLOSE...
YOU KNOW YOUR JOB, SOLDIERS.
WAIT FOR MY SIGNAL.

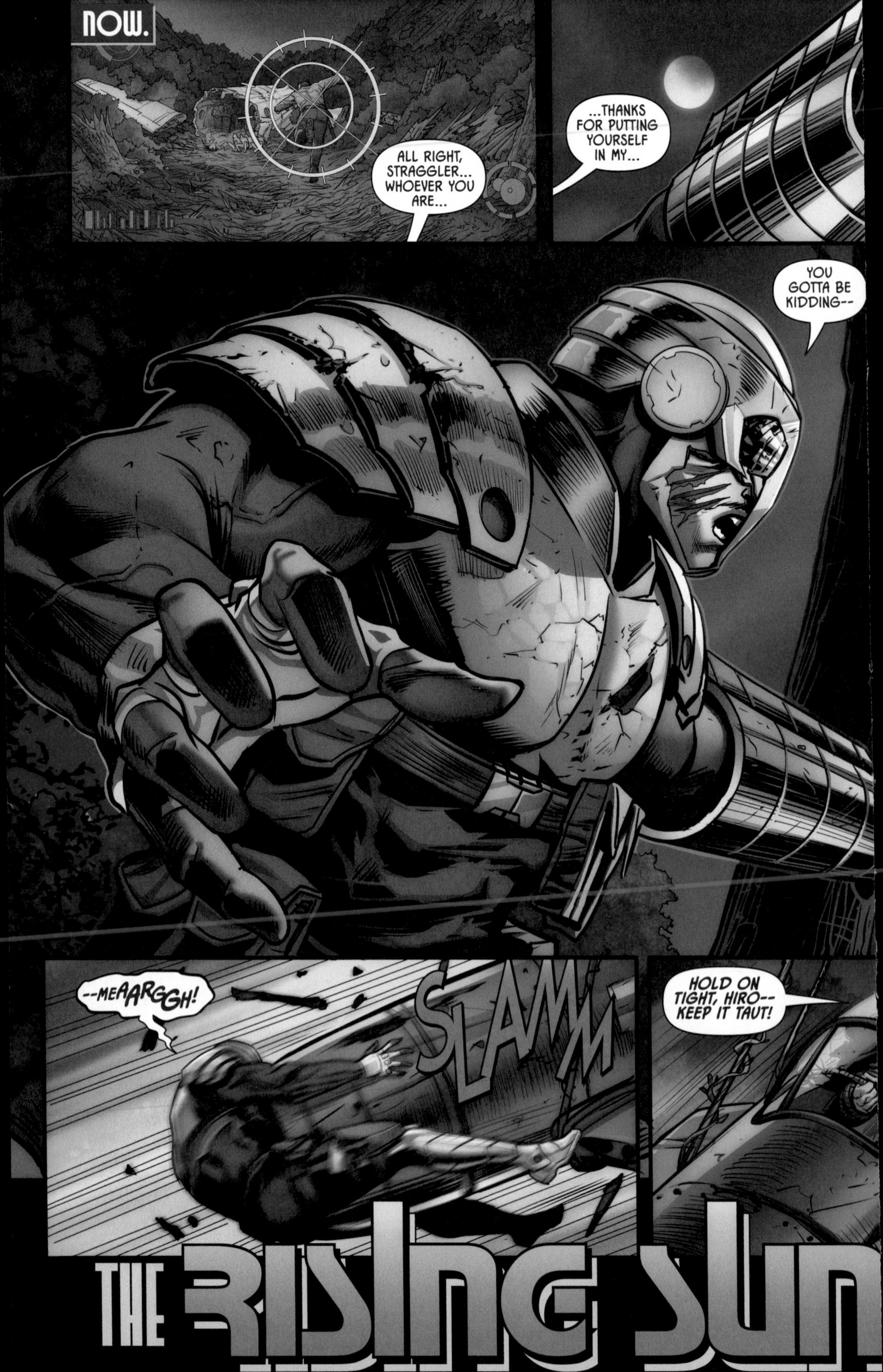
NOW.
ALL RIGHT, STRAGGLER... WHOEVER YOU ARE...
...THANKS FOR PUTTING YOURSELF IN MY...
YOU GOTTA BE KIDDING--
--MEAARGGH!
SLAMM
HOLD ON TIGHT, HIRO-- KEEP IT TAUT!
THE RISING SUN

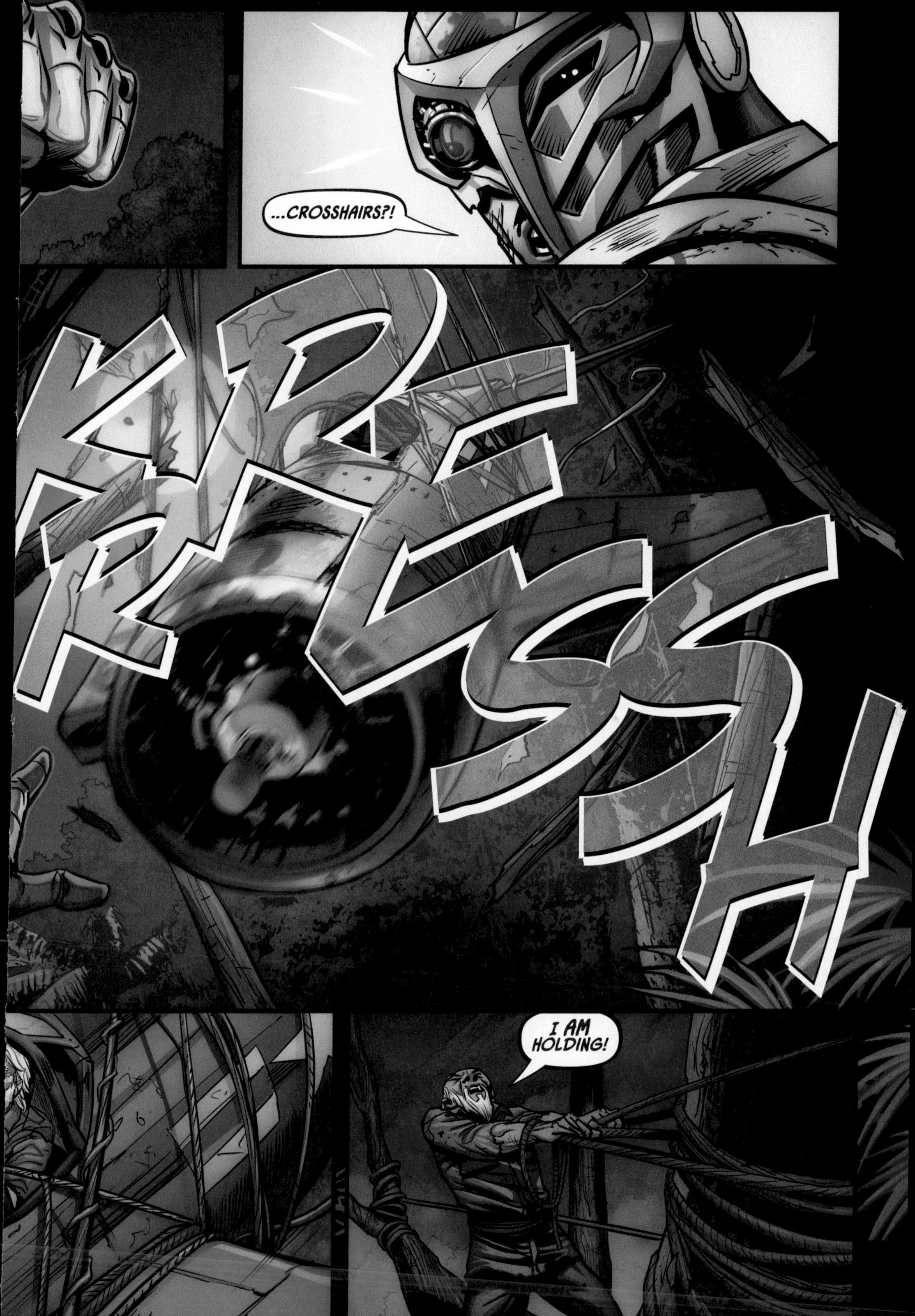
...CROSSHAIRS?!
I AM HOLDING!

ETER J. TOMASI story & words • CHRISTIAN DUCE artist • LUIS GUERRERO colorist • ROB LEIGH letterer
UILLEM MARCH & ARIF PRIANTO cover • DAVE WIELGOSZ assistant editor • MOLLY MAHAN editor
AMIE S. RICH group editor

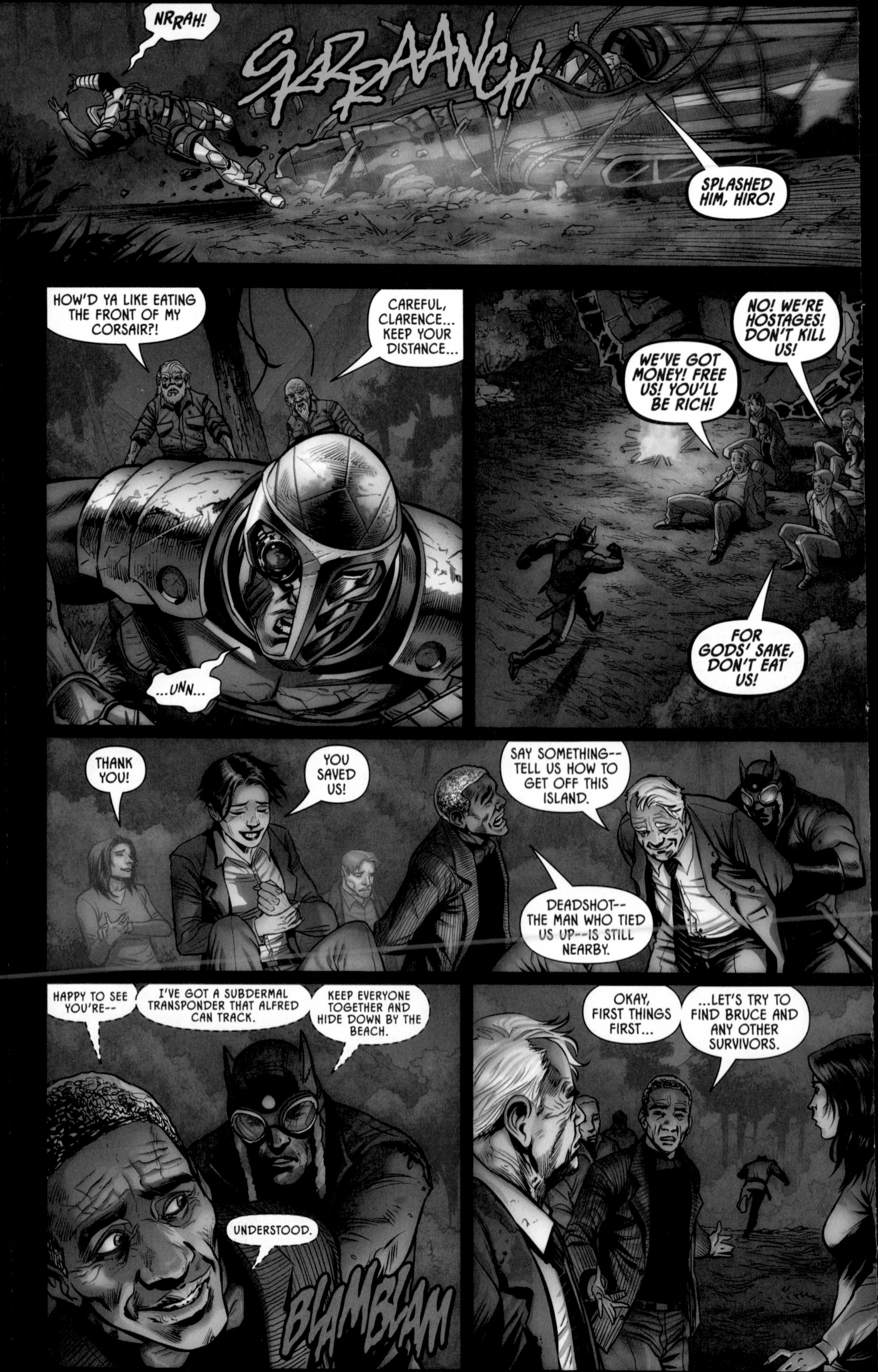
NRRAH!
SKRRAANCH
SPLASHED HIM, HIRO!
HOW'D YA LIKE EATING THE FRONT OF MY CORSAIR?!
CAREFUL, CLARENCE... KEEP YOUR DISTANCE...
...UNN...
NO! WE'RE HOSTAGES! DON'T KILL US!
WE'VE GOT MONEY! FREE US! YOU'LL BE RICH!
FOR GODS' SAKE, DON'T EAT US!
THANK YOU!
YOU SAVED US!
SAY SOMETHING-- TELL US HOW TO GET OFF THIS ISLAND.
DEADSHOT-- THE MAN WHO TIED US UP--IS STILL NEARBY.
HAPPY TO SEE YOU'RE--
I'VE GOT A SUBDERMAL TRANSPONDER THAT ALFRED CAN TRACK.
KEEP EVERYONE TOGETHER AND HIDE DOWN BY THE BEACH.
UNDERSTOOD.
BLAMBLAM
OKAY, FIRST THINGS FIRST...
...LET'S TRY TO FIND BRUCE AND ANY OTHER SURVIVORS.

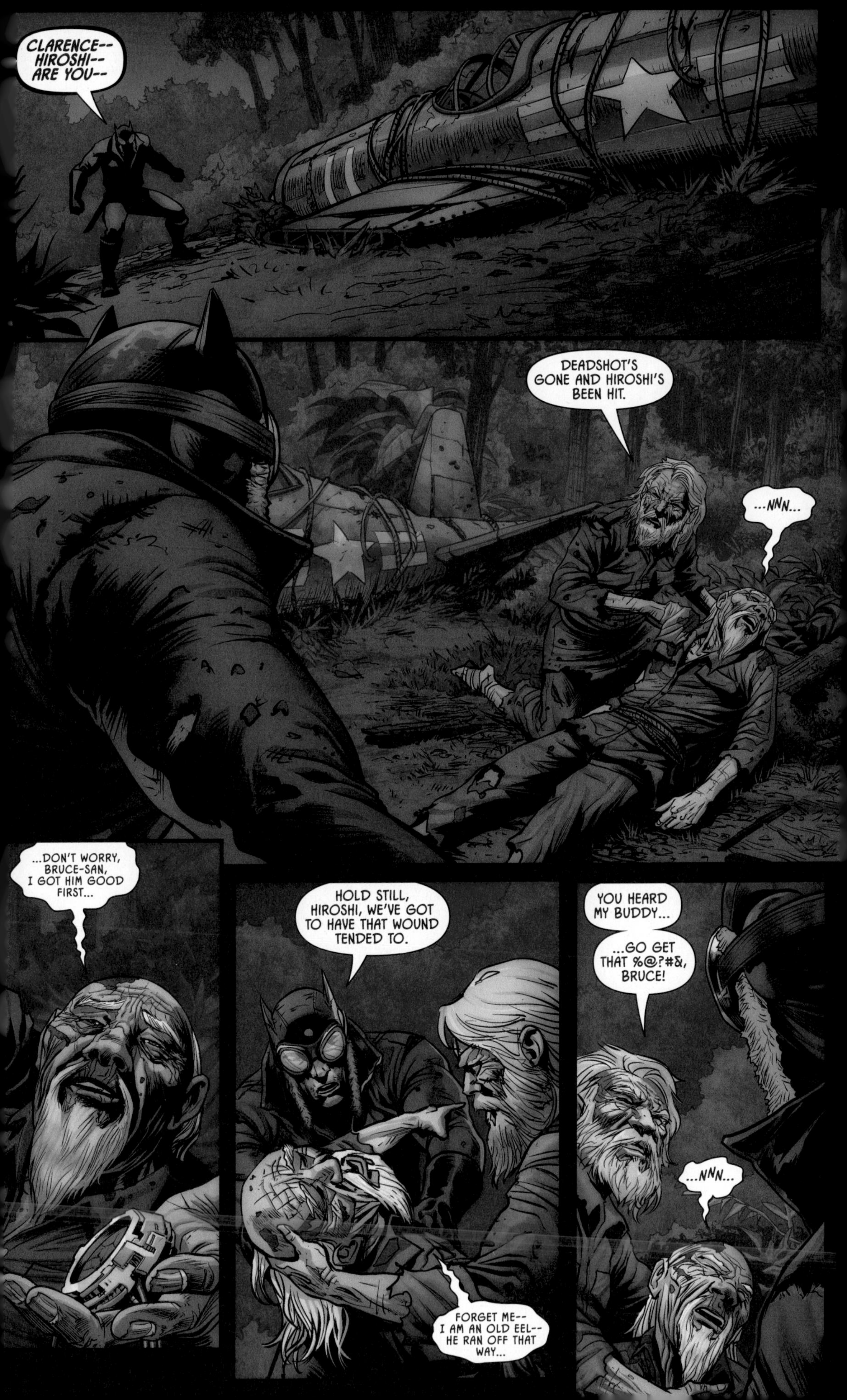
CLARENCE-- HIROSHI-- ARE YOU--
DEADSHOT'S GONE AND HIROSHI'S BEEN HIT.
...NNN...
...DON'T WORRY, BRUCE-SAN, I GOT HIM GOOD FIRST...
HOLD STILL, HIROSHI, WE'VE GOT TO HAVE THAT WOUND TENDED TO.
FORGET ME-- I AM AN OLD EEL-- HE RAN OFF THAT WAY...
YOU HEARD MY BUDDY...
...GO GET THAT %@?#&, BRUCE!
...NNN...

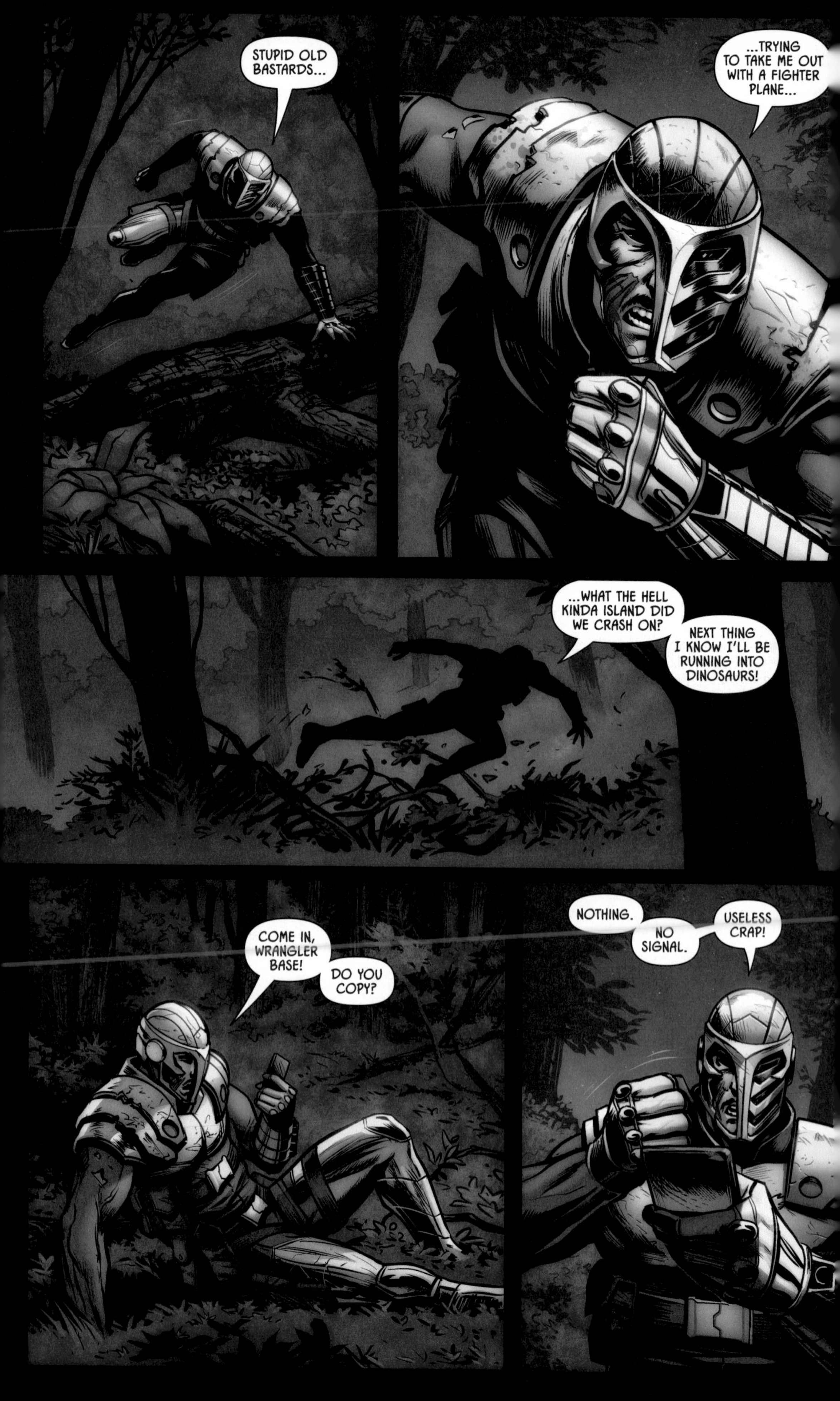
STUPID OLD BASTARDS...
...TRYING TO TAKE ME OUT WITH A FIGHTER PLANE...
...WHAT THE HELL KINDA ISLAND DID WE CRASH ON?
NEXT THING I KNOW I'LL BE RUNNING INTO DINOSAURS!
COME IN, WRANGLER BASE!
DO YOU COPY?
NOTHING.
NO SIGNAL.
USELESS CRAP!

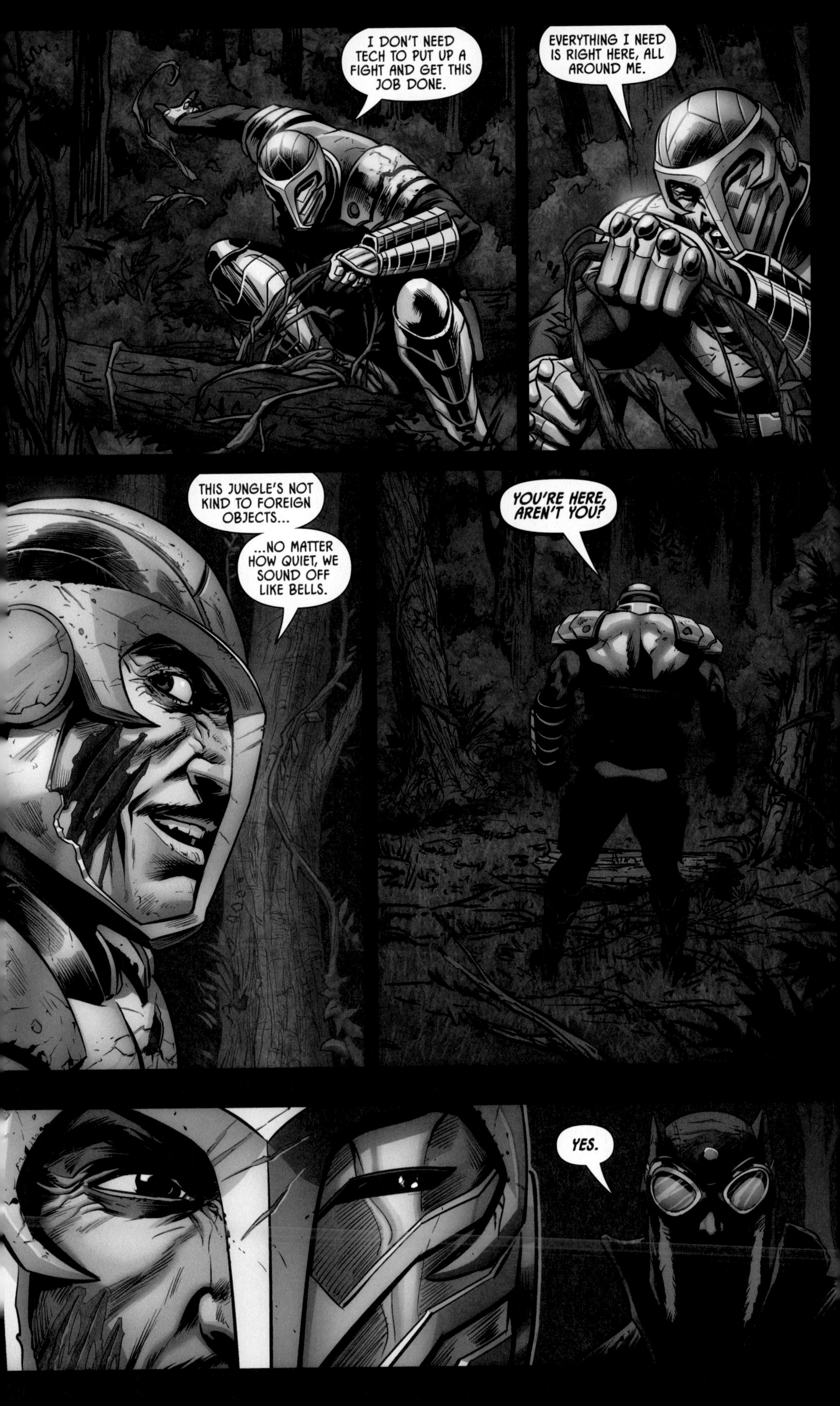
I DON'T NEED TECH TO PUT UP A FIGHT AND GET THIS JOB DONE.
EVERYTHING I NEED IS RIGHT HERE, ALL AROUND ME.
THIS JUNGLE'S NOT KIND TO FOREIGN OBJECTS...
...NO MATTER HOW QUIET, WE SOUND OFF LIKE BELLS.
YOU'RE HERE, AREN'T YOU?
YES.

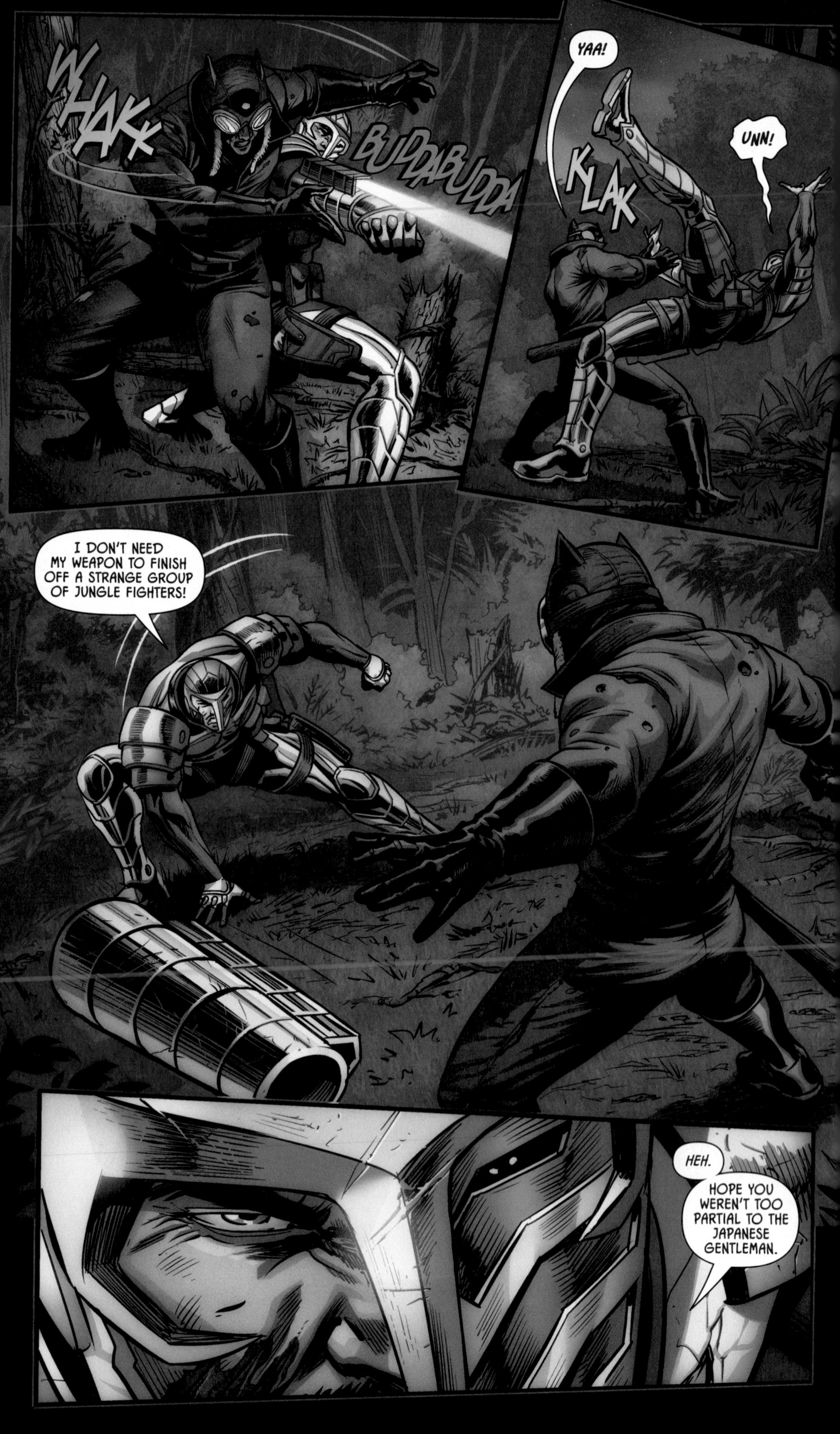

WHAKK
BUDDABUDDA
YAA!
KLAK
UNN!
I DON'T NEED MY WEAPON TO FINISH OFF A STRANGE GROUP OF JUNGLE FIGHTERS!
HEH.
HOPE YOU WEREN'T TOO PARTIAL TO THE JAPANESE GENTLEMAN.

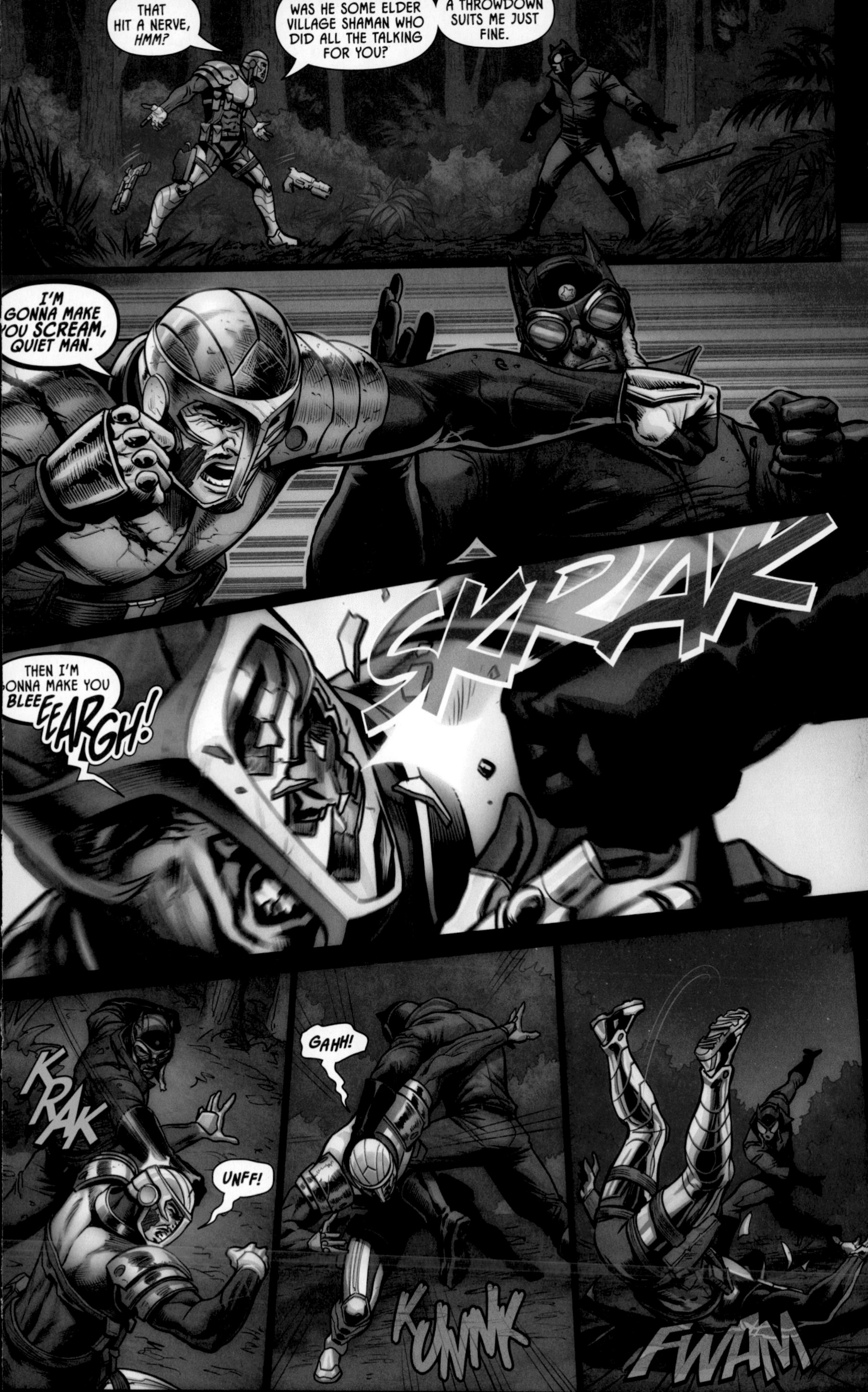
THAT HIT A NERVE, HMM?
WAS HE SOME ELDER VILLAGE SHAMAN WHO DID ALL THE TALKING FOR YOU?
A THROWDOWN SUITS ME JUST FINE.
I'M GONNA MAKE YOU SCREAM, QUIET MAN.
SKRAK
THEN I'M GONNA MAKE YOU BLEEEEARGH!
KRAK
UNFF!
GAHH!
KUNNK
FWAM

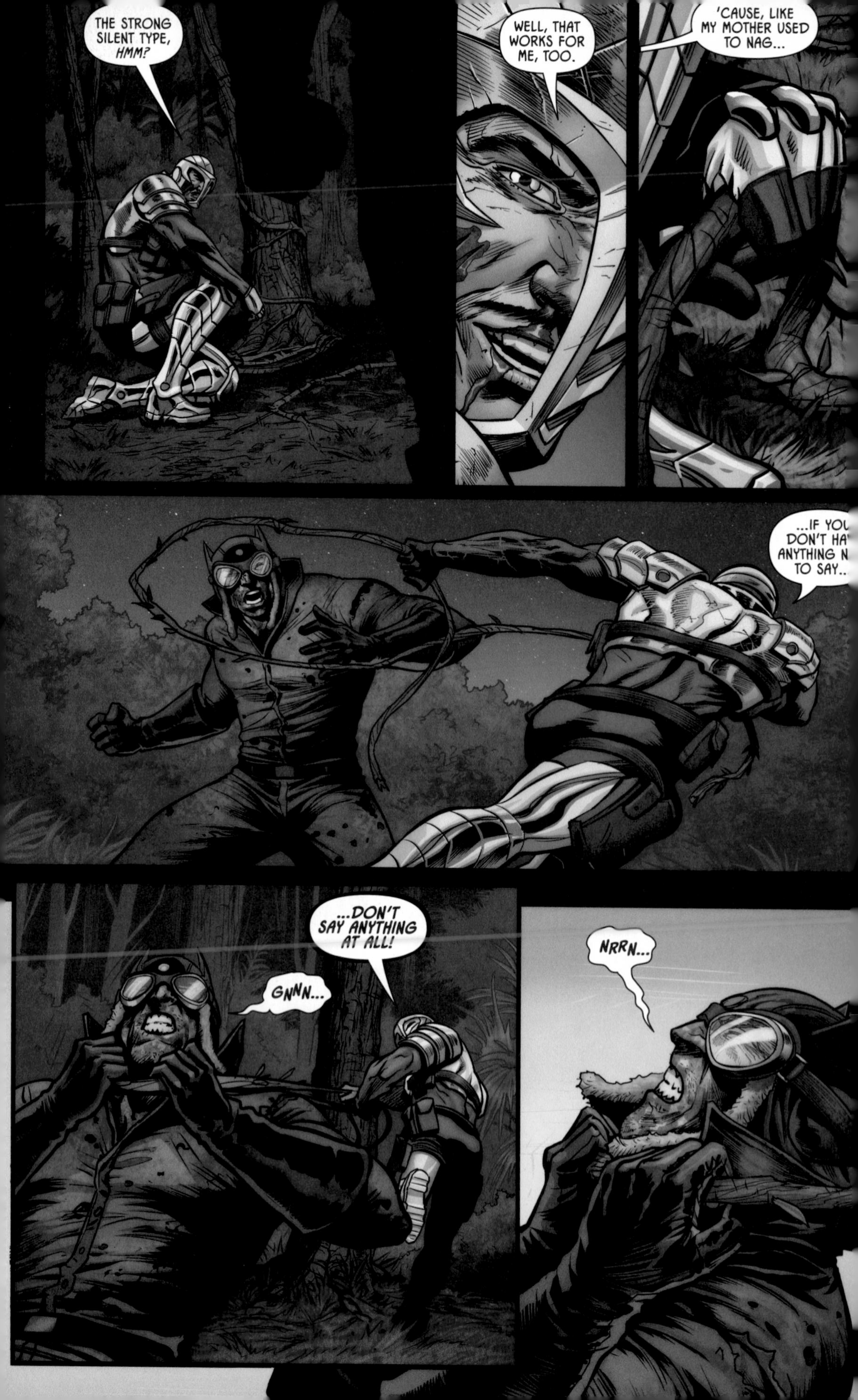
THE STRONG SILENT TYPE, HMM?
WELL, THAT WORKS FOR ME, TOO.
'CAUSE, LIKE MY MOTHER USED TO NAG...
...IF YOU DON'T HA ANYTHING N TO SAY...
...DON'T SAY ANYTHING AT ALL!
GNNN...
NRRN...

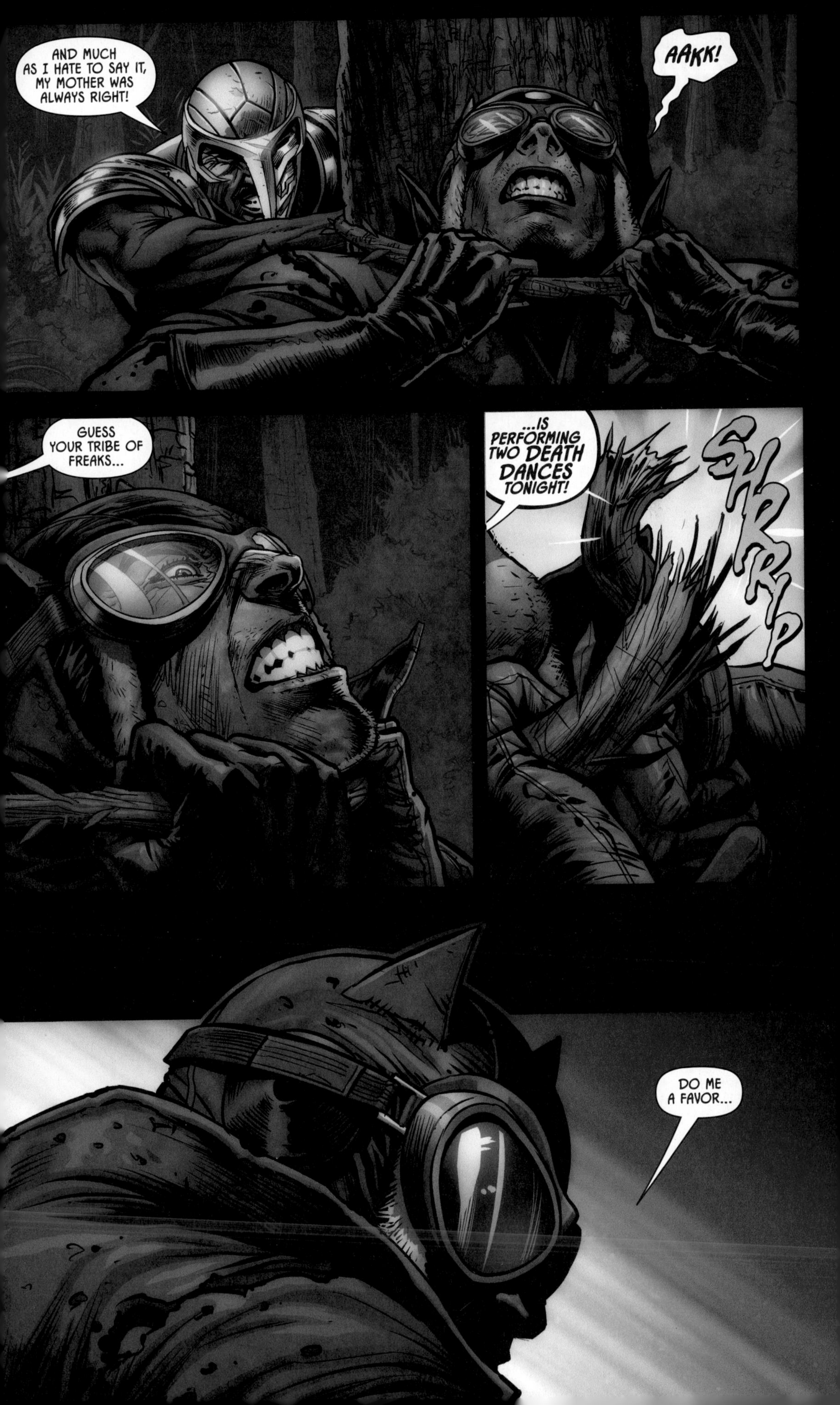
AND MUCH AS I HATE TO SAY IT, MY MOTHER WAS ALWAYS RIGHT!
AAKK!
GUESS YOUR TRIBE OF FREAKS...
...IS PERFORMING TWO DEATH DANCES TONIGHT!
SHRIP
DO ME A FAVOR...

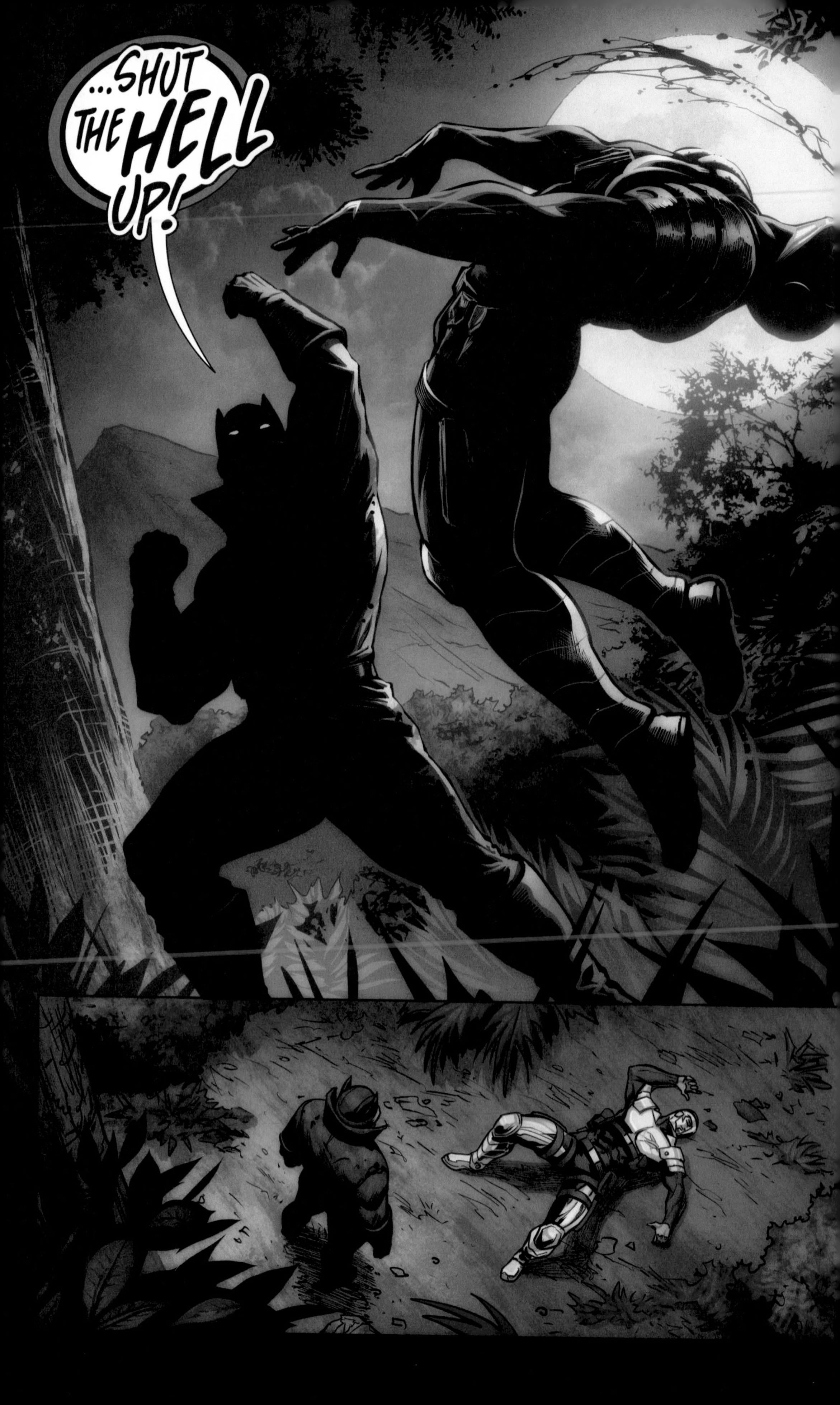
...SHUT THE HELL UP!

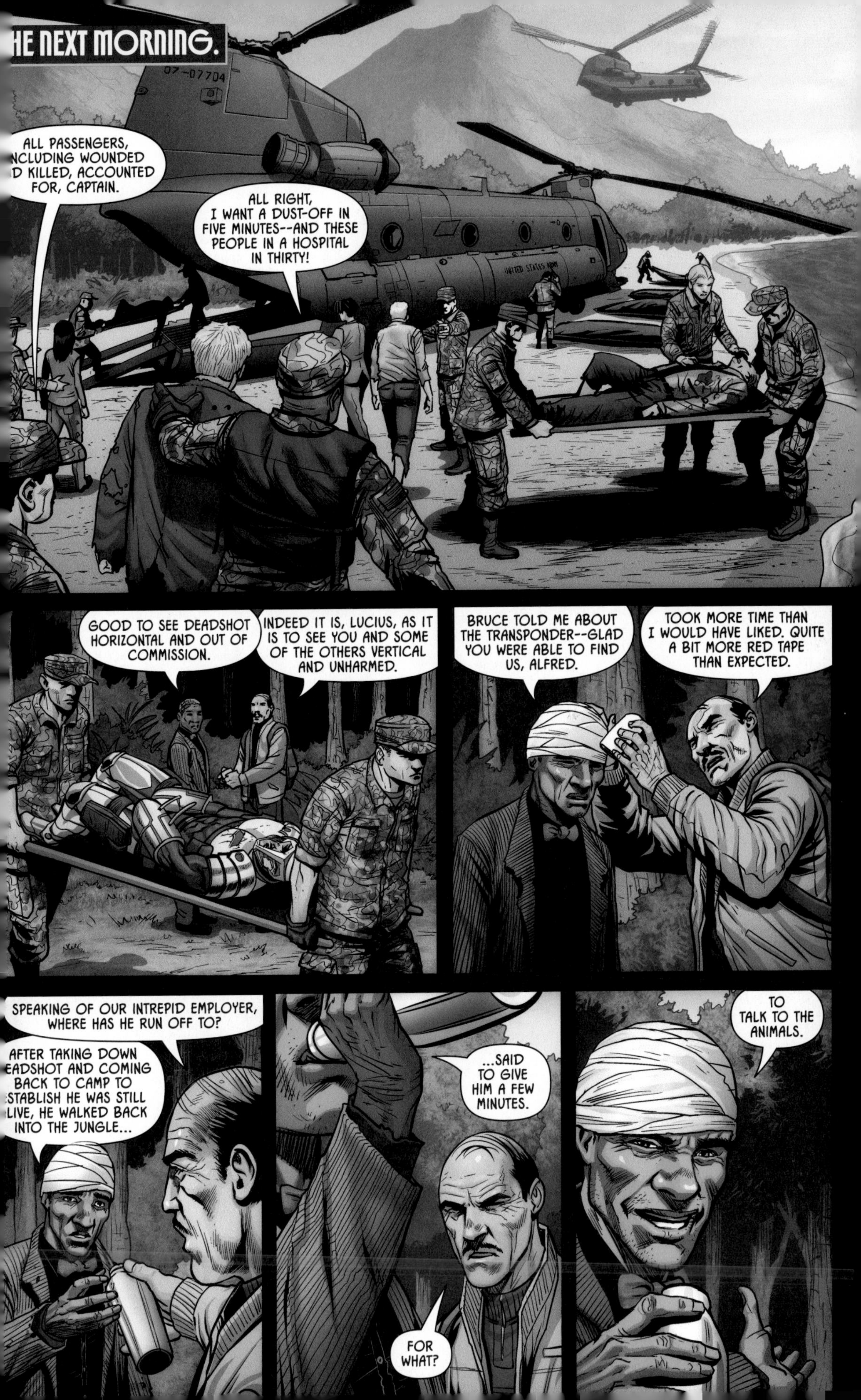
HE NEXT MORNING.
07-07704
ALL PASSENGERS, NCLUDING WOUNDED D KILLED, ACCOUNTED FOR, CAPTAIN.
ALL RIGHT, I WANT A DUST-OFF IN FIVE MINUTES--AND THESE PEOPLE IN A HOSPITAL IN THIRTY!
UNITED STATES ARMY
GOOD TO SEE DEADSHOT HORIZONTAL AND OUT OF COMMISSION.
INDEED IT IS, LUCIUS, AS IT IS TO SEE YOU AND SOME OF THE OTHERS VERTICAL AND UNHARMED.
BRUCE TOLD ME ABOUT THE TRANSPONDER--GLAD YOU WERE ABLE TO FIND US, ALFRED.
TOOK MORE TIME THAN I WOULD HAVE LIKED. QUITE A BIT MORE RED TAPE THAN EXPECTED.
SPEAKING OF OUR INTREPID EMPLOYER, WHERE HAS HE RUN OFF TO?
AFTER TAKING DOWN EADSHOT AND COMING BACK TO CAMP TO STABLISH HE WAS STILL LIVE, HE WALKED BACK INTO THE JUNGLE...
...SAID TO GIVE HIM A FEW MINUTES.
FOR WHAT?
TO TALK TO THE ANIMALS.

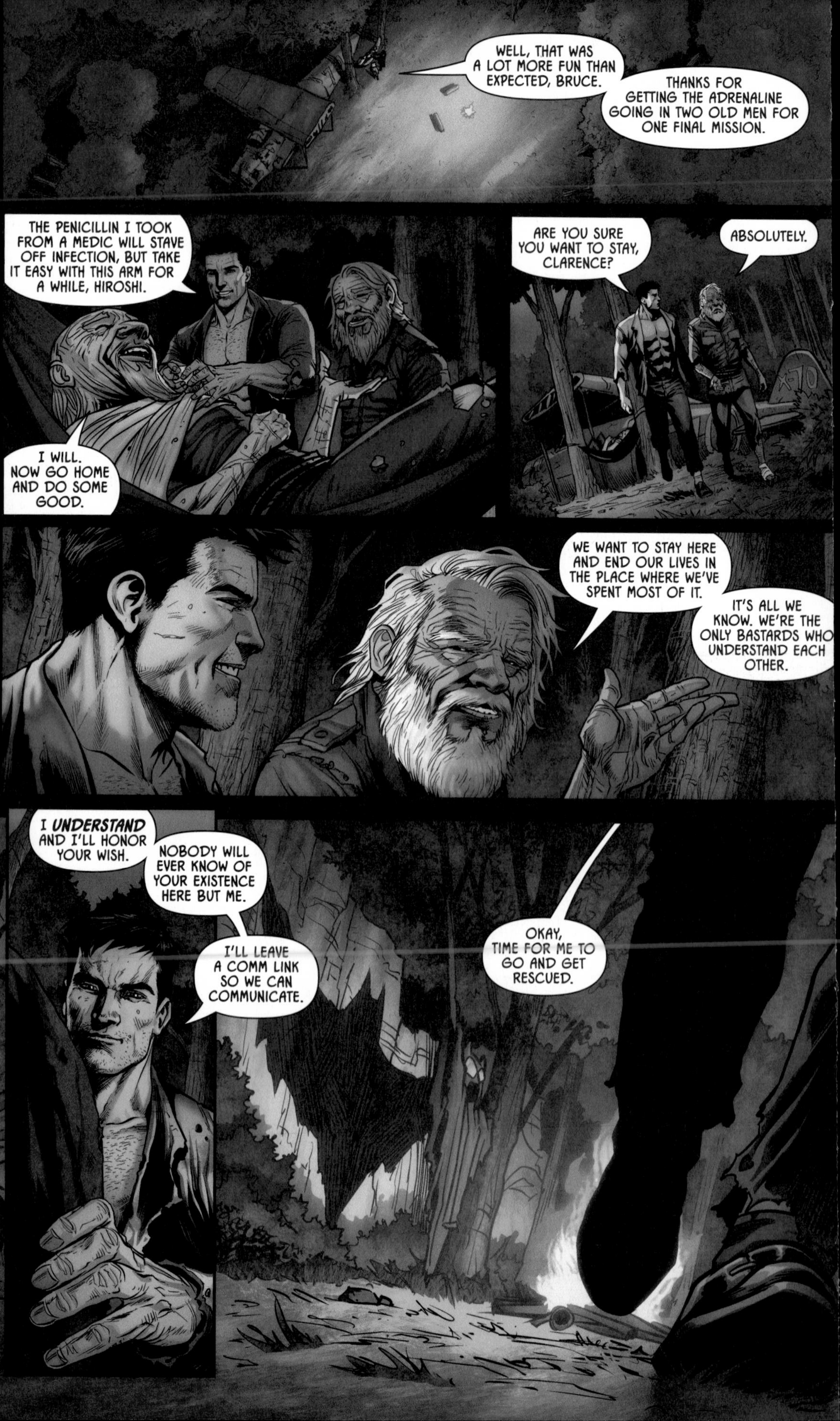
WELL, THAT WAS A LOT MORE FUN THAN EXPECTED, BRUCE.
THANKS FOR GETTING THE ADRENALINE GOING IN TWO OLD MEN FOR ONE FINAL MISSION.
THE PENICILLIN I TOOK FROM A MEDIC WILL STAVE OFF INFECTION, BUT TAKE IT EASY WITH THIS ARM FOR A WHILE, HIROSHI.
I WILL. NOW GO HOME AND DO SOME GOOD.
ARE YOU SURE YOU WANT TO STAY, CLARENCE?
ABSOLUTELY.
X-70
WE WANT TO STAY HERE AND END OUR LIVES IN THE PLACE WHERE WE'VE SPENT MOST OF IT.
IT'S ALL WE KNOW. WE'RE THE ONLY BASTARDS WHO UNDERSTAND EACH OTHER.
I *UNDERSTAND* AND I'LL HONOR YOUR WISH.
NOBODY WILL EVER KNOW OF YOUR EXISTENCE HERE BUT ME.
I'LL LEAVE A COMM LINK SO WE CAN COMMUNICATE.
OKAY, TIME FOR ME TO GO AND GET RESCUED.

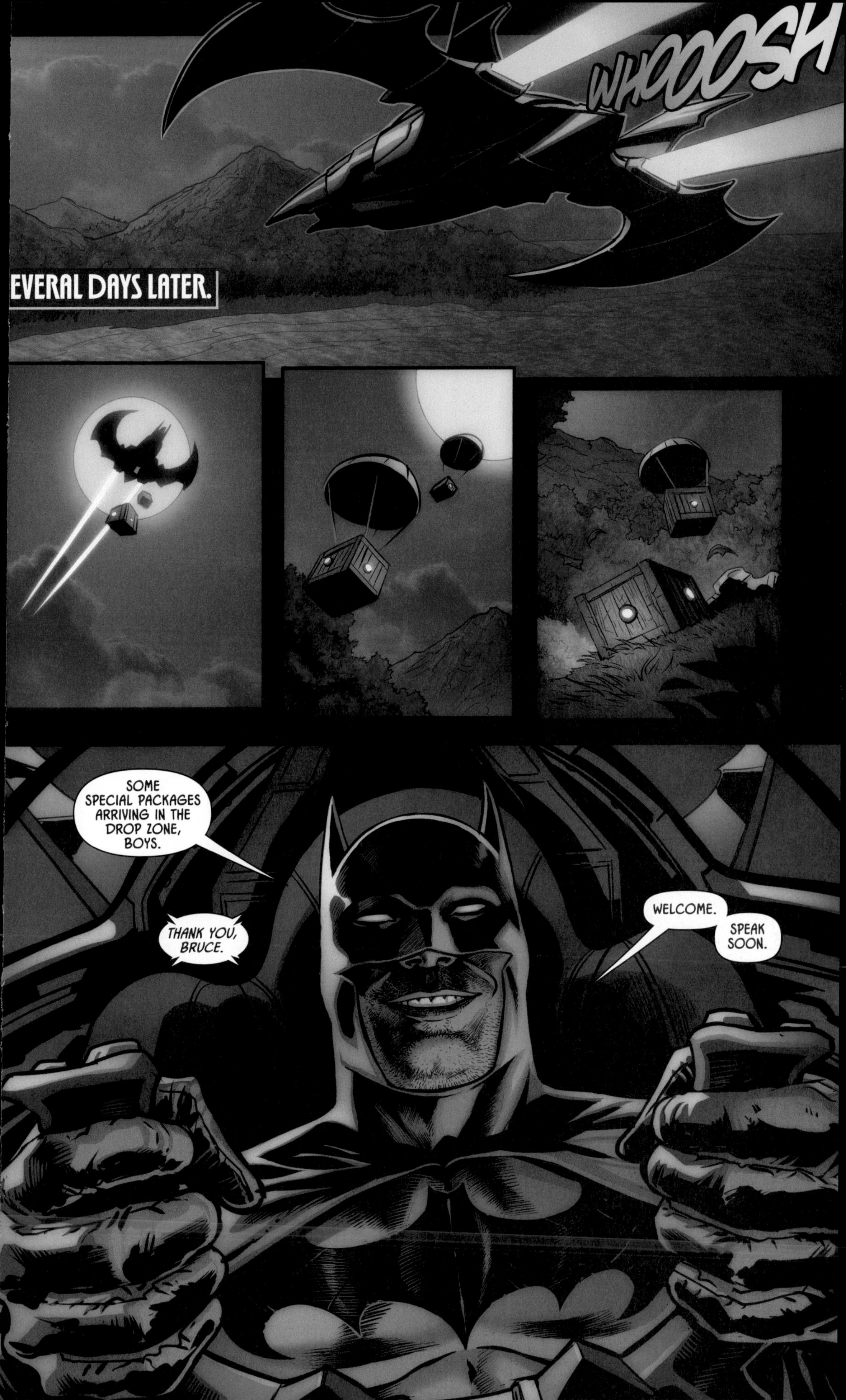
WHOOOOSH
EVERAL DAYS LATER.
SOME SPECIAL PACKAGES ARRIVING IN THE DROP ZONE, BOYS.
THANK YOU, BRUCE.
WELCOME.
SPEAK SOON.

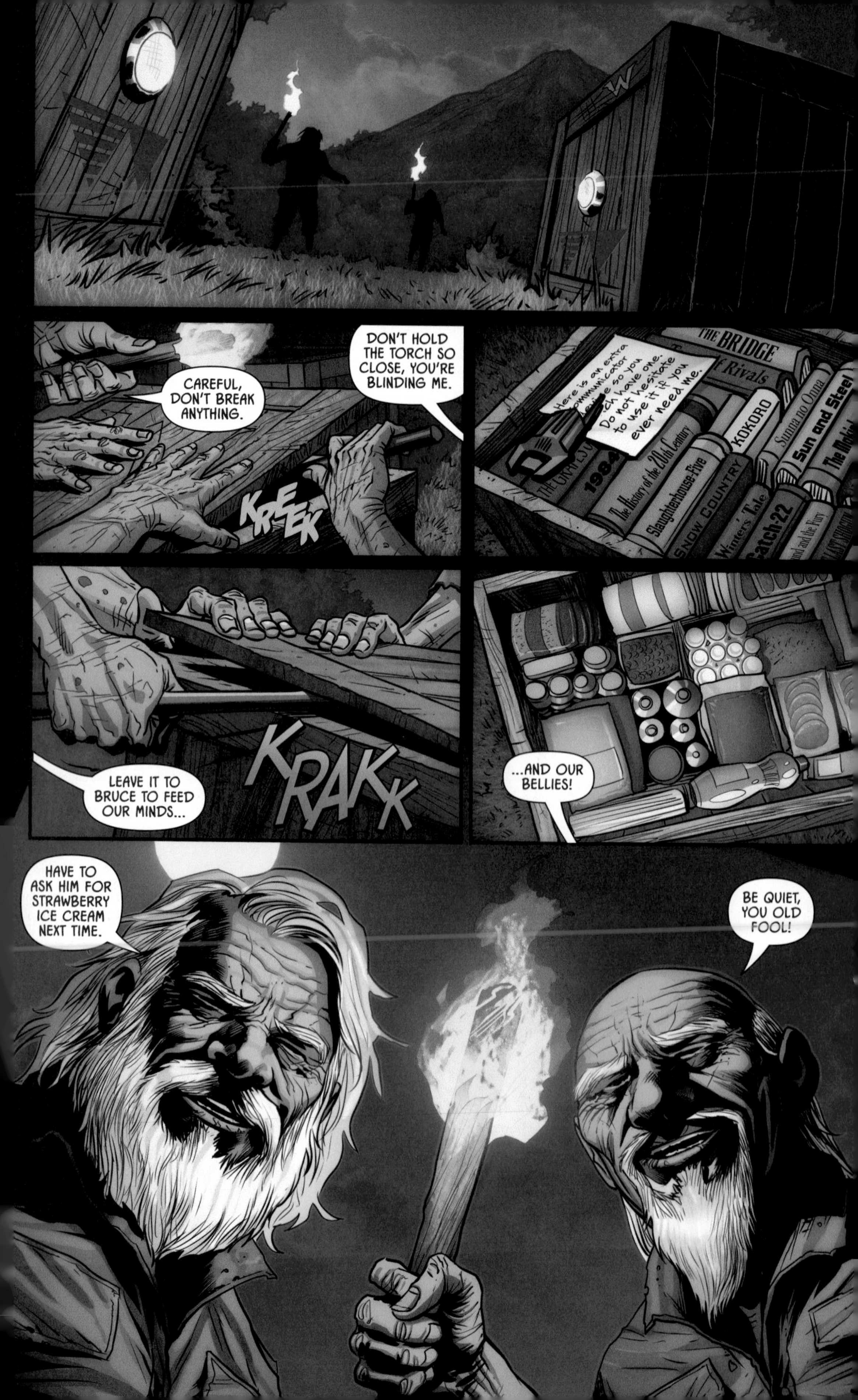
CAREFUL, DON'T BREAK ANYTHING.
DON'T HOLD THE TORCH SO CLOSE, YOU'RE BLINDING ME.
KREEEK
Do not hesitate
to use it if you
ever need me.
THE BRIDGE
KOKORO
Sun and Steel
1984
The History of the 20th Century
Slaughterhouse-Five
SNOW COUNTRY
Catch-22
LEAVE IT TO BRUCE TO FEED OUR MINDS...
KRAKK
...AND OUR BELLIES!
HAVE TO ASK HIM FOR STRAWBERRY ICE CREAM NEXT TIME.
BE QUIET, YOU OLD FOOL!

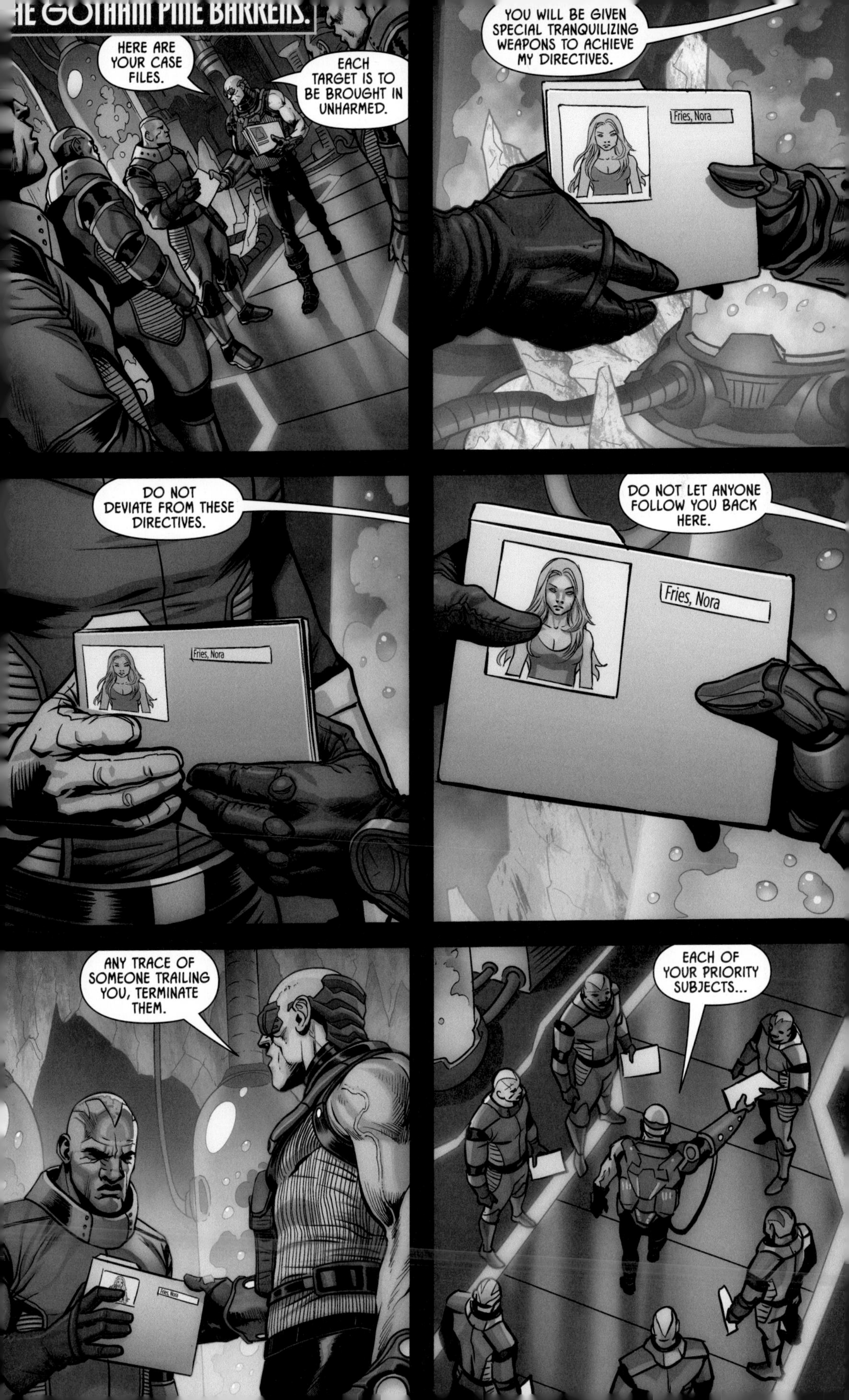
HE GOTHAM PINE BARRENS.
HERE ARE YOUR CASE FILES.
EACH TARGET IS TO BE BROUGHT IN UNHARMED.
YOU WILL BE GIVEN SPECIAL TRANQUILIZING WEAPONS TO ACHIEVE MY DIRECTIVES.
Fries, Nora
DO NOT DEVIATE FROM THESE DIRECTIVES.
Fries, Nora
DO NOT LET ANYONE FOLLOW YOU BACK HERE.
Fries, Nora
ANY TRACE OF SOMEONE TRAILING YOU, TERMINATE THEM.
Fries, Nora
EACH OF YOUR PRIORITY SUBJECTS...

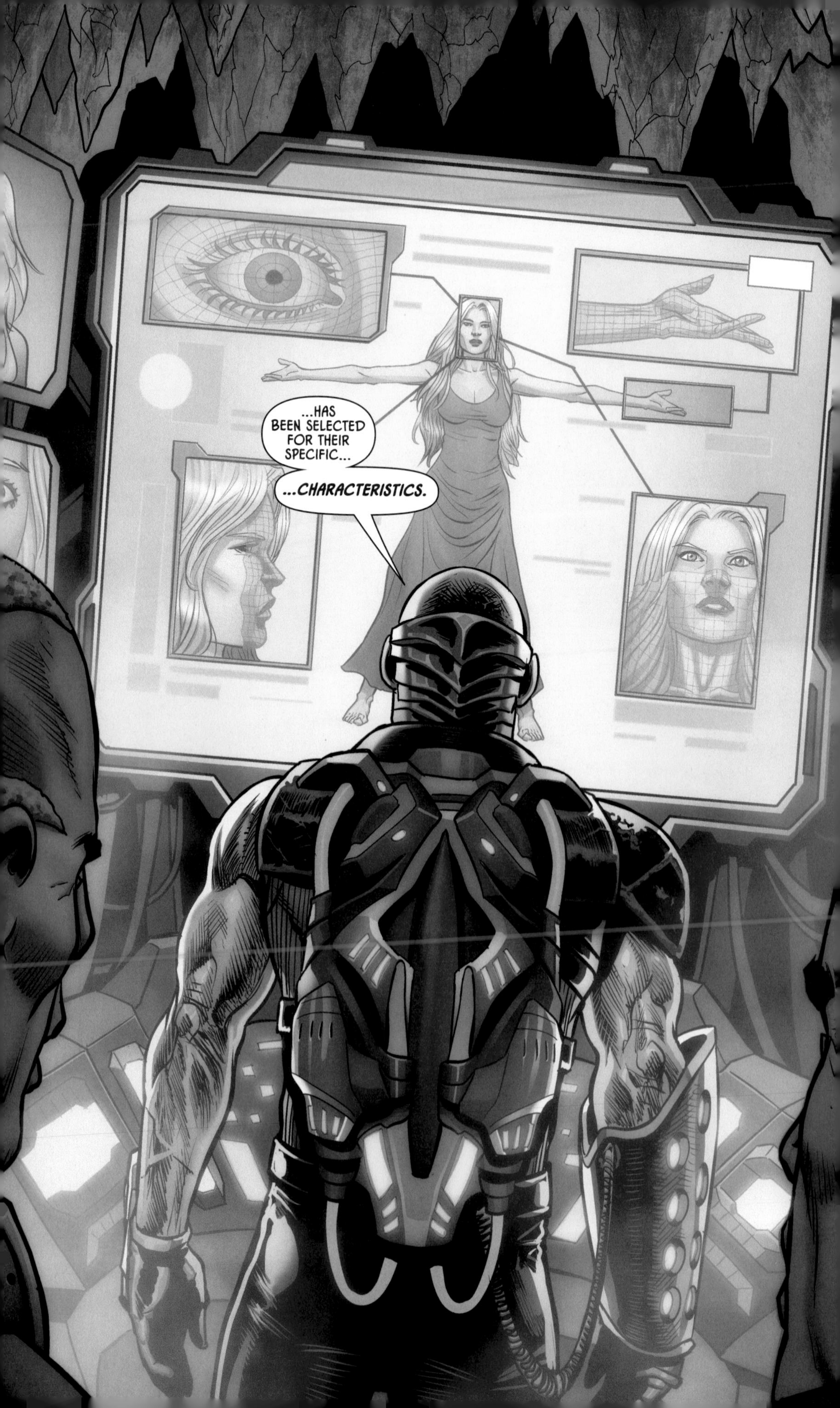
...HAS BEEN SELECTED FOR THEIR SPECIFIC...
...CHARACTERISTICS.

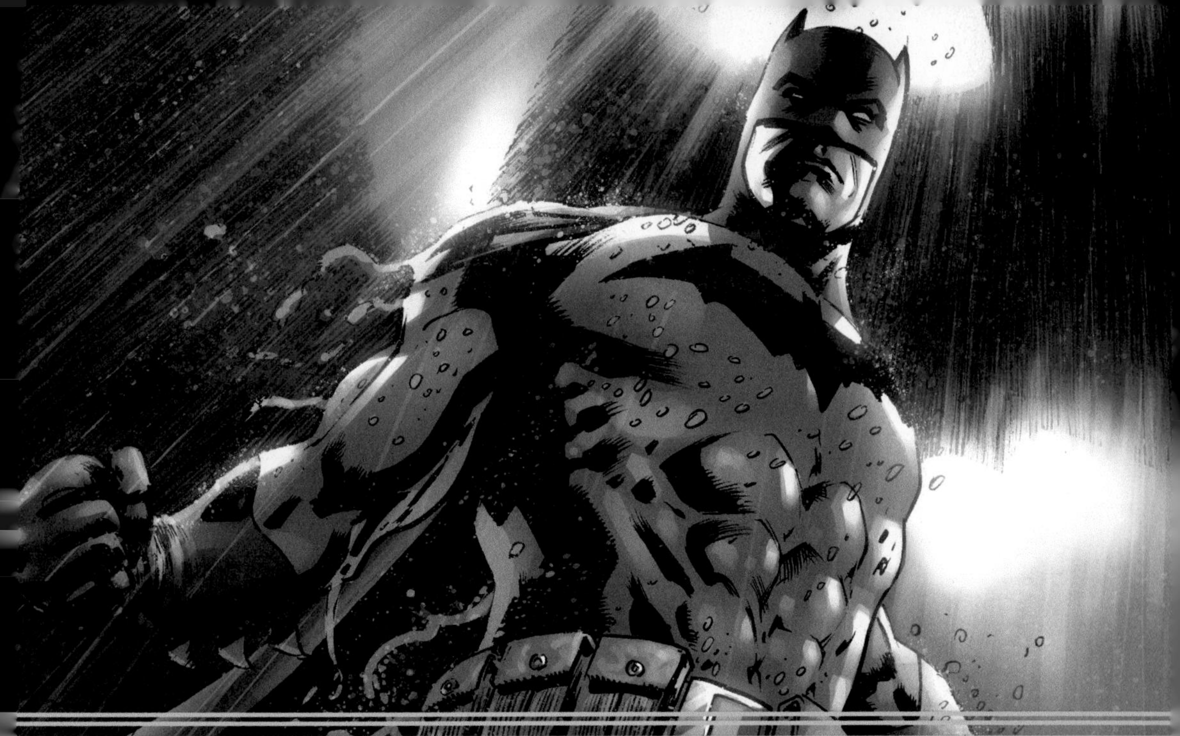

VARIANT COVER GALLERY

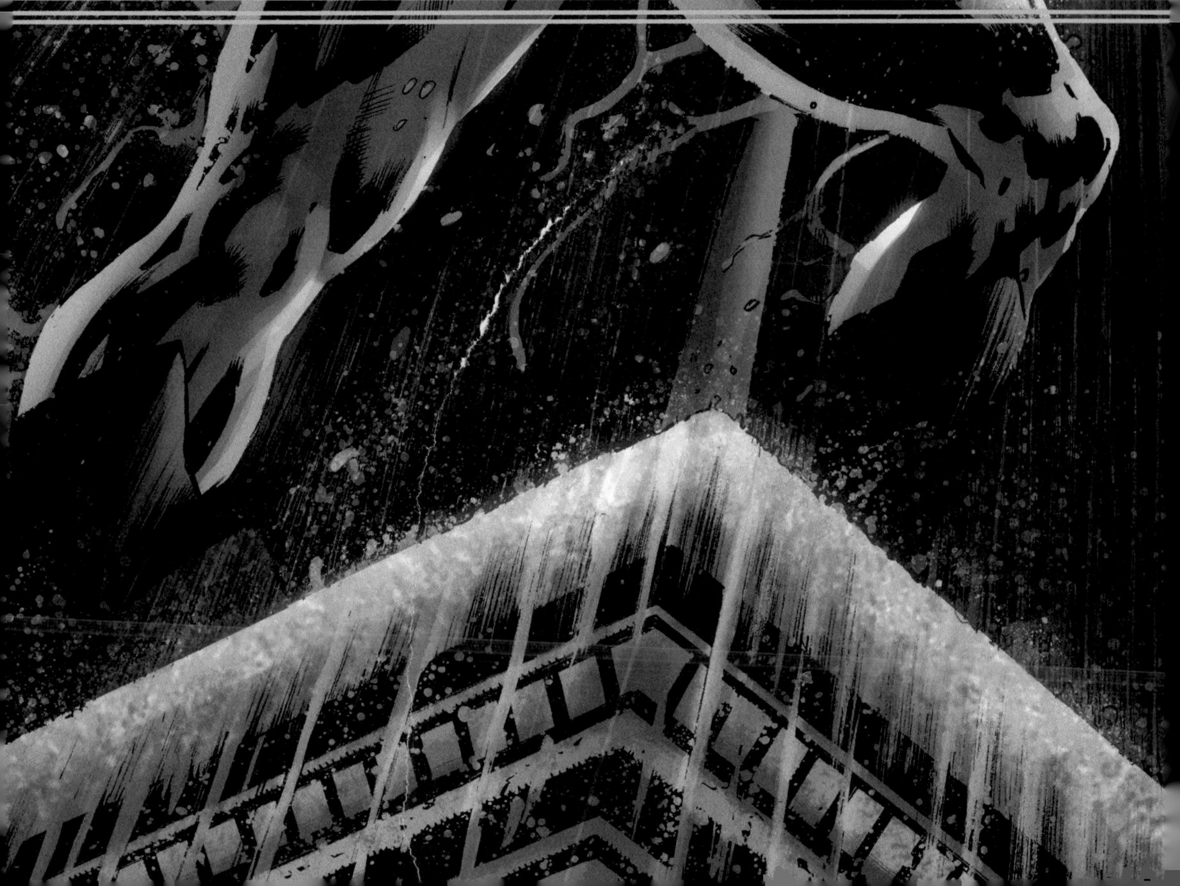

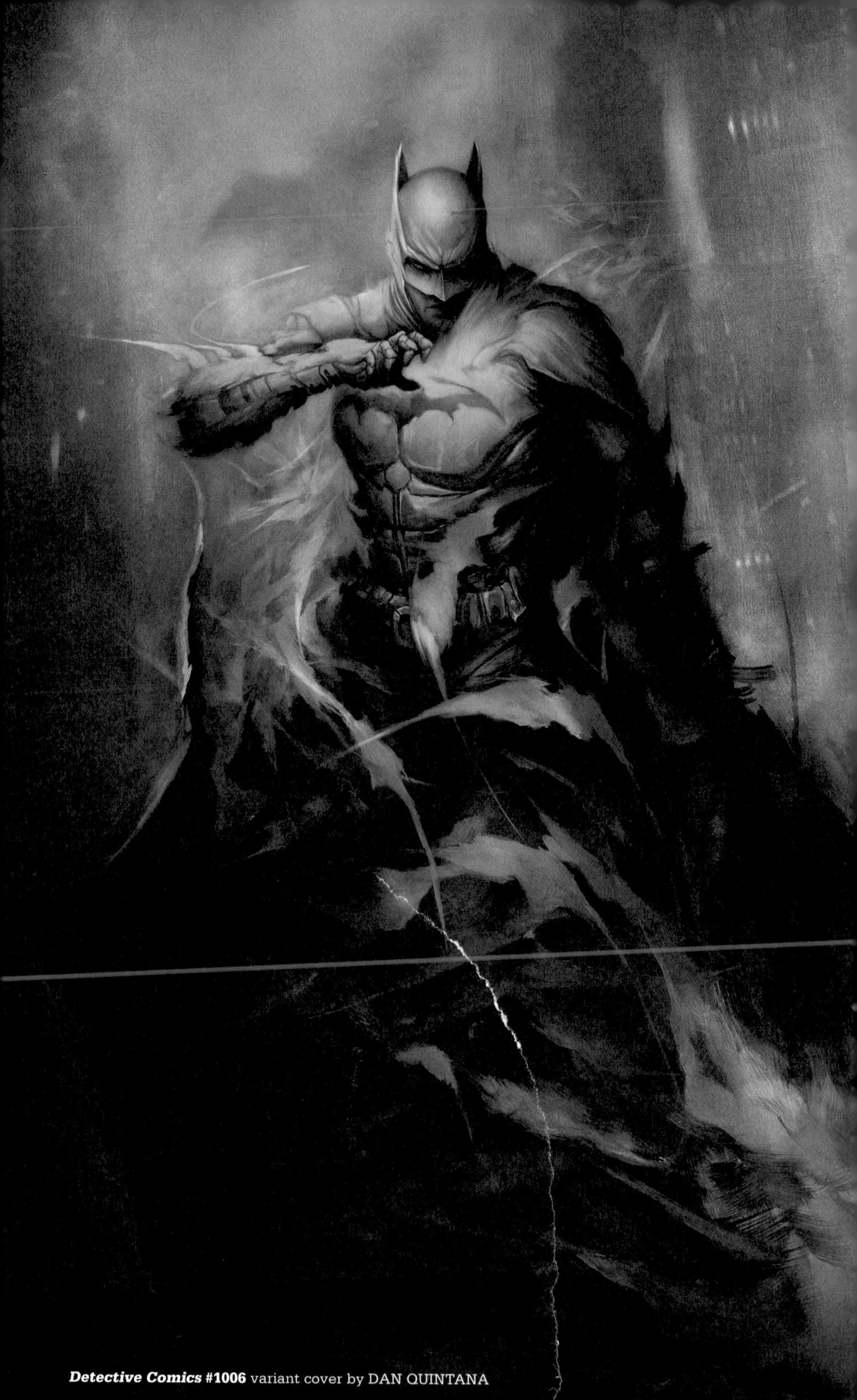

Detective Comics #1006 variant cover by DAN QUINTANA

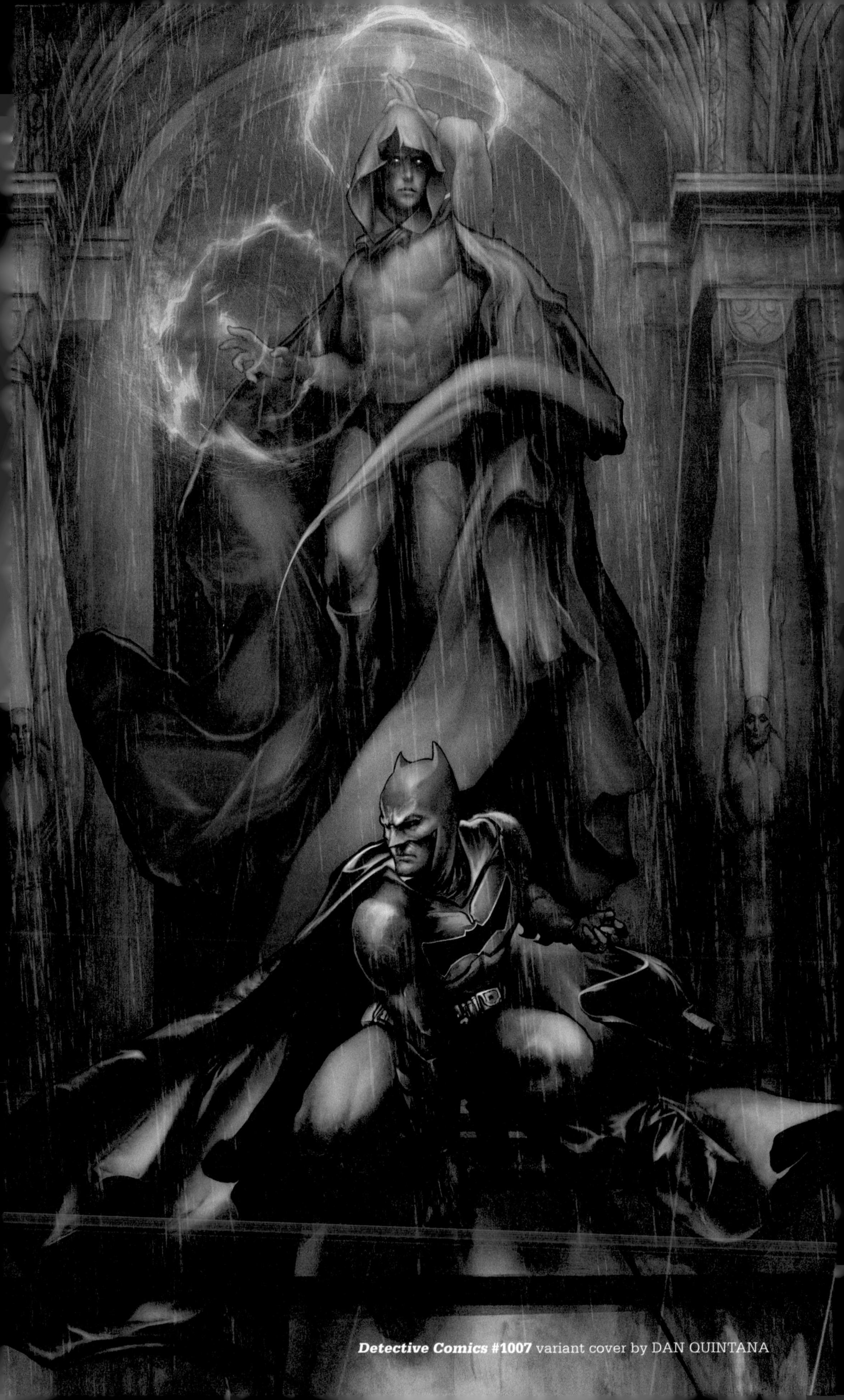

***Detective Comics* #1007** variant cover by DAN QUINTANA

***Detective Comics* #1008** variant cover by BRYAN HITCH and ALEX SINCLAIR

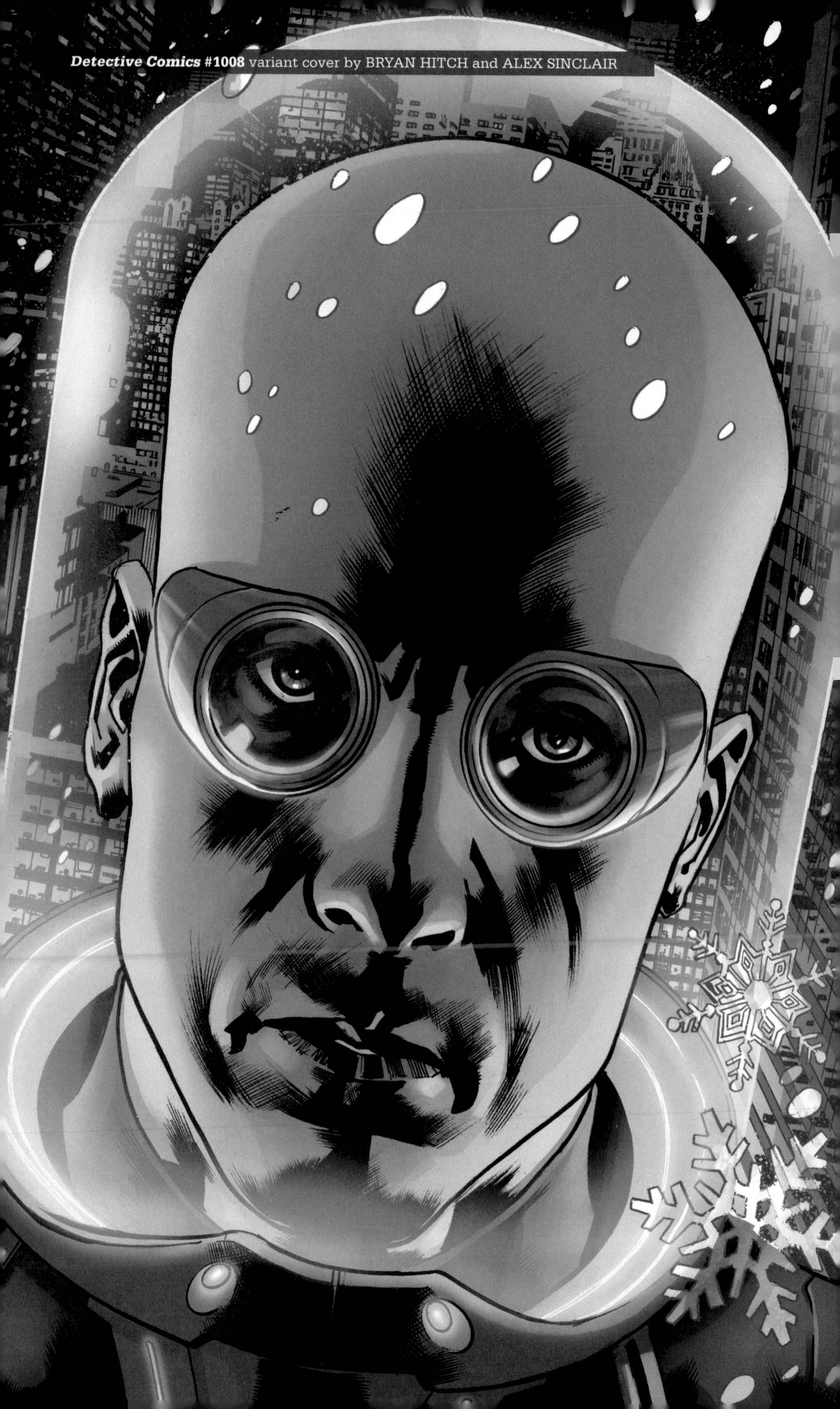

Detective Comics #1009 variant cover by BRYAN HITCH and ALEX SINCLAIR

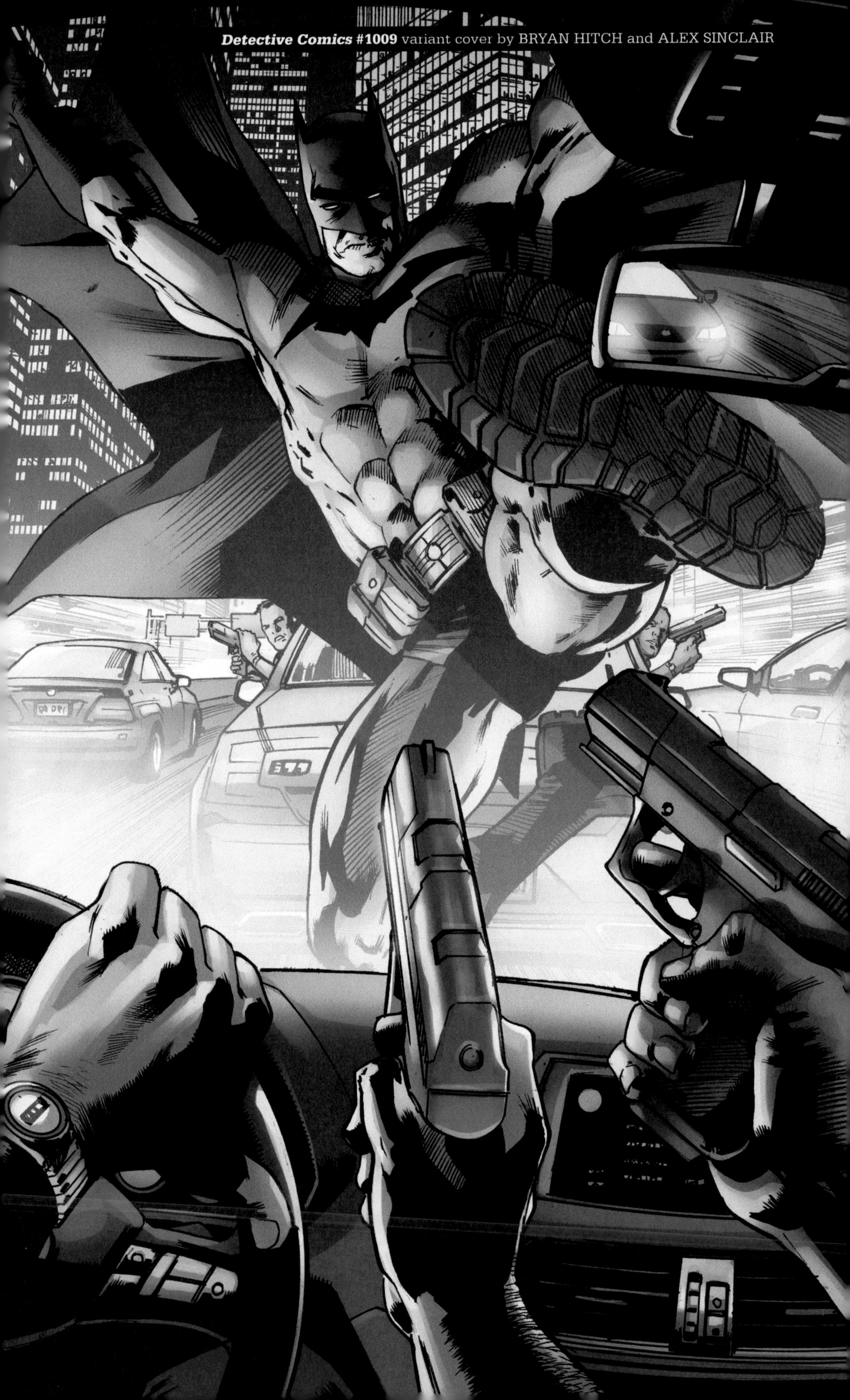

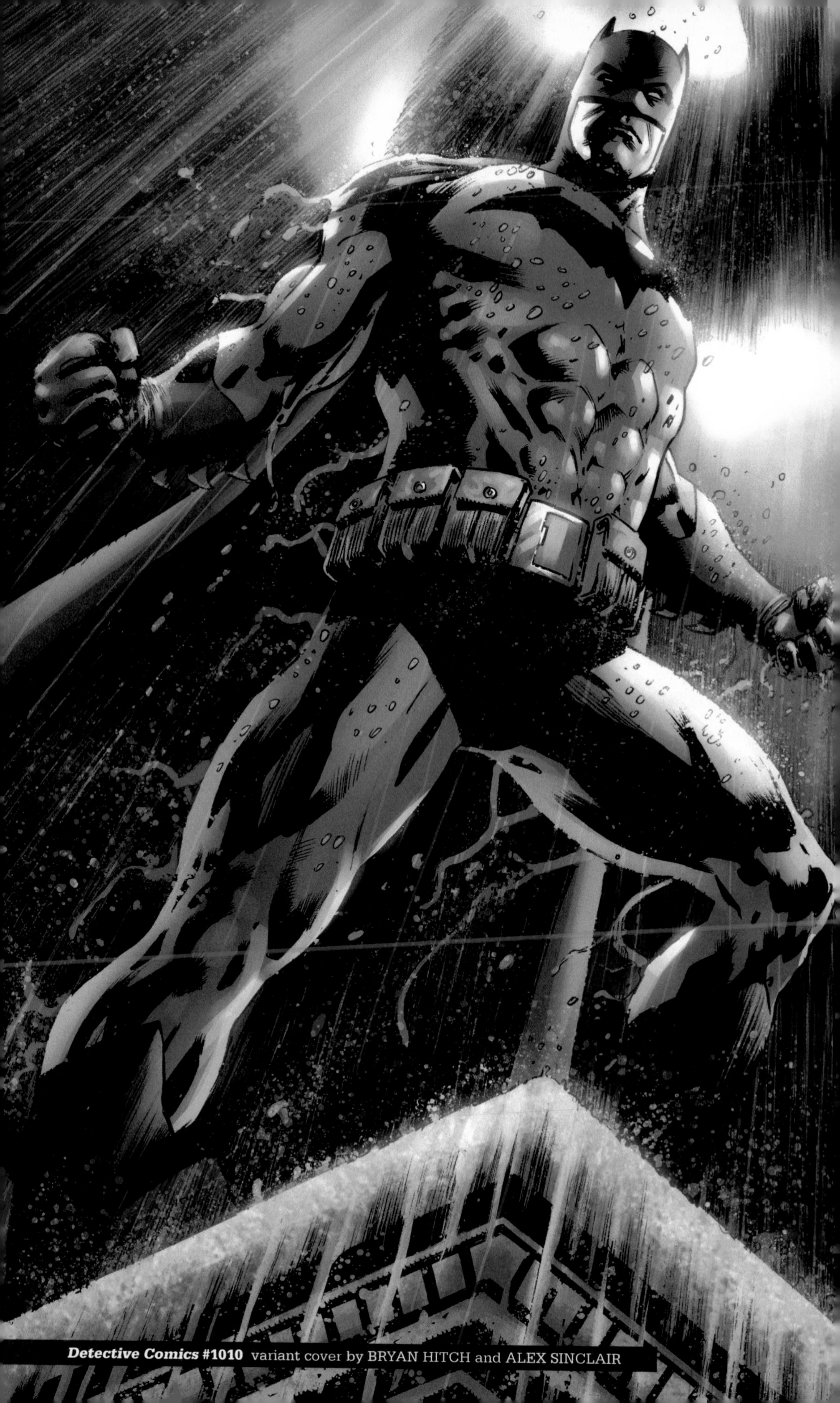

***Detective Comics* #1010** variant cover by BRYAN HITCH and ALEX SINCLAIR

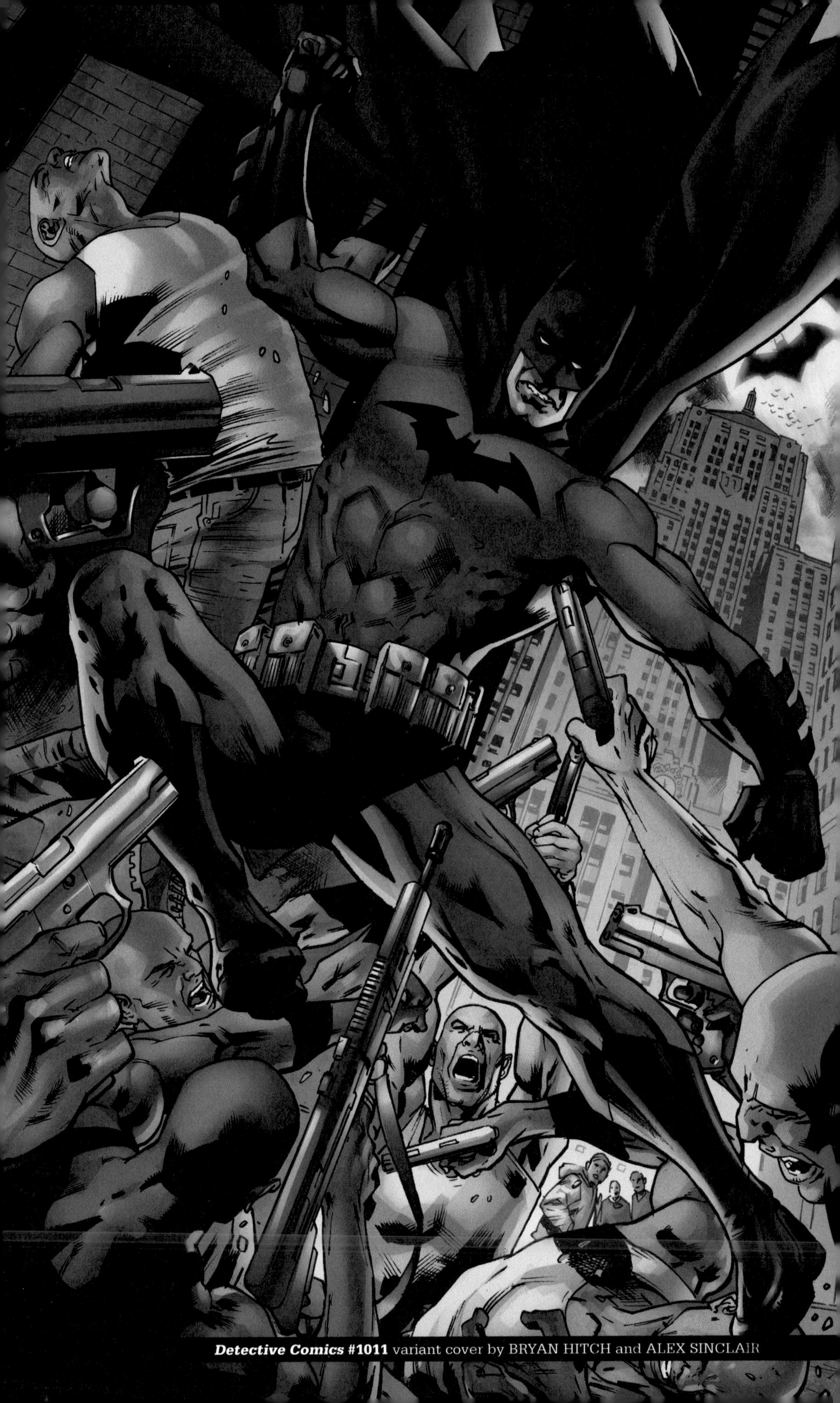

***Detective Comics* #1011** variant cover by BRYAN HITCH and ALEX SINCLAIR

BATMAN & ROBIN

VOL. 1: BORN TO KILL
PETER J. TOMASI
with PATRICK GLEASON

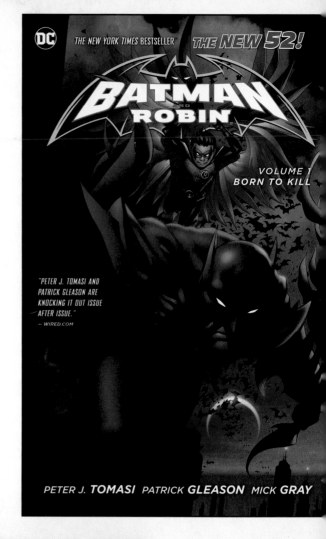

BATMAN AND ROBIN

THE NEW YORK TIMES BESTSELLER THE NEW 52!

VOLUME 1
BORN TO KILL

"PETER J. TOMASI AND PATRICK GLEASON ARE KNOCKING IT OUT ISSUE AFTER ISSUE."
— WIRED.COM

PETER J. **TOMASI**   PATRICK **GLEASON**   MICK **GRAY**

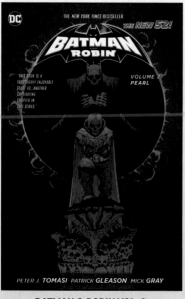

BATMAN & ROBIN VOL. 2: PEARL

BATMAN & ROBIN VOL. 3: DEATH OF THE FAMILY

READ THE ENTIRE EPI

BATMAN & ROBIN VOL
REQUIEM FOR DAMI

BATMAN & ROBIN VOL
THE BIG BU

BATMAN & ROBIN VOL
THE HUNT FOR RO

BATMAN & ROBIN VOL
ROBIN RIS